STUDENT STUDY GUIDE

to Accompany

Educational Psychology
Windows on Classrooms

Fourth Edition

Paul Eggen
University of North Florida

Don Kauchak
University of Utah

Merrill,
an imprint of Prentice Hall
Upper Saddle River, New Jersey   Columbus, Ohio

©1999 by Prentice-Hall, Inc.
Simon & Schuster/A Viacom Company
Upper Saddle River, New Jersey 07458

Printed in the United States of America

10 9 8 7 6 5 4 3 2 1

ISBN: 0-13-080092-9

TABLE OF CONTENTS

INTRODUCTION 1

ANALYZING CASE STUDIES: SUGGESTIONS AND GUIDELINES 3

CHAPTER ONE: Teaching in The Real World 9
   Chapter Outline 9
   Chapter Objectives 9
   Chapter Overview 10
   Feedback for Margin Questions 10
   Self-Help Quiz 13
   Self-Help Quiz Answers 14

CHAPTER TWO: The Development of Cognition and Language 15
   Chapter Outline 15
   Chapter Objectives 16
   Chapter Overview 16
   Feedback for Margin Questions 17
   Application Exercises 23
   Feedback for Application Exercises 26
   Self-Help Quiz 30
   Self-Help Quiz Answers 34

CHAPTER THREE: Personal, Social, and Emotional Development 36
   Chapter Outline 36
   Chapter Objectives 37
   Chapter Overview 37
   Feedback for Margin Questions 37
   Application Exercises 42
   Feedback for Application Exercises 44
   Self-Help Quiz 47
   Self-Help Quiz Answers 50

CHAPTER FOUR: Learner Differences 52
   Chapter Outline 52
   Chapter Objectives 53
   Chapter Overview 53
   Feedback for Margin Questions 54
   Application Exercises 60
   Feedback for Application Exercises 61
   Self-Help Quiz 64
   Self-Help Quiz Answers 68

CHAPTER FIVE: Learners with Exceptionalities 69
   Chapter Outline 69
   Chapter Objectives 70
   Chapter Overview 70
   Feedback for Margin Questions 71
   Application Exercises 75
   Feedback for Application Exercises 76
   Self-Help Quiz 78
   Self-Help Quiz Answers 82

CHAPTER SIX: Behaviorism and Social Cognitive Theory 83
   Chapter Outline 83
   Chapter Objectives 84
   Chapter Overview 84
   Feedback for Margin Questions 85
   Application Exercises 90
   Feedback for Application Exercises 93
   Self-Help Quiz 97
   Self-Help Quiz Answers 101

CHAPTER SEVEN: Cognitive Views of Learning 103
   Chapter Outline 103
   Chapter Objectives 104
   Chapter Overview 104
   Feedback for Margin Questions 105
   Application Exercises 111
   Feedback for Application Exercises 115
   Self-Help Quiz 120
   Self-Help Quiz Answers 124

CHAPTER EIGHT: Complex Cognitive Processes 126
   Chapter Outline 126
   Chapter Objectives 127
   Chapter Overview 127
   Feedback for Margin Questions 128
   Application Exercises 135
   Feedback for Application Exercises 138
   Self-Help Quiz 141
   Self-Help Quiz Answers 145

CHAPTER NINE: Cognition in the Content Areas 146
   Chapter Outline 146
   Chapter Objectives 147
   Chapter Overview 147
   Feedback for Margin Questions 148
   Application Exercises 152
   Feedback for Application Exercises 153
   Self-Help Quiz 156
   Self-Help Quiz Answers 159

CHAPTER TEN: Increasing Learner Motivation 161
   Chapter Outline 161
   Chapter Objectives 162
   Chapter Overview 162
   Feedback for Margin Questions 163
   Application Exercises 168
   Feedback for Application Exercises 170
   Self-Help Quiz 173
   Self-Help Quiz Answers 175

CHAPTER ELEVEN: Creating Productive Learning Environments 177
    Chapter Outline 177
    Chapter Objectives 178
    Chapter Overview 178
    Feedback for Margin Questions 179
    Application Exercises 186
    Feedback for Application Exercises 188
    Self-Help Quiz 191
    Self-Help Quiz Answers 195

CHAPTER TWELVE: Teacher-Centered Approaches to Instruction 196
    Chapter Outline 196
    Chapter Objectives 197
    Chapter Overview 197
    Feedback for Margin Questions 197
    Application Exercises 201
    Feedback for Application Exercises 203
    Self-Help Quiz 206
    Self-Help Quiz Answers 209

CHAPTER THIRTEEN: Learner-Centered Approaches to Instruction 211
    Chapter Outline 211
    Chapter Objectives 212
    Chapter Overview 212
    Feedback for Margin Questions 212
    Application Exercises 216
    Feedback for Application Exercises 216
    Self-Help Quiz 218
    Self-Help Quiz Answers 222

CHAPTER FOURTEEN: Assessing Classroom Learning 224
    Chapter Outline 224
    Chapter Objectives 225
    Chapter Overview 225
    Feedback for Margin Questions 226
    Application Exercises 231
    Feedback for Application Exercises 233
    Self-Help Quiz 236
    Self-Help Quiz Answers 240

APPENDIX: Standardized Testing 242
    Appendix Outline 242
    Appendix Overview 243
    Application Exercises 244
    Feedback for Application Exercises 245
    Self-Help Quiz 247
    Self-Help Quiz Answers 250

INTRODUCTION TO THE STUDENT STUDY GUIDE TO ACCOMPANY EGGEN AND KAUCHAK'S

EDUCATIONAL PSYCHOLOGY: WINDOWS ON CLASSROOMS

TO THE STUDENT

As with our revision of the text, we have prepared this guide to *Educational Psychology: Windows on Classrooms* (4th ed.) with you, the student, in mind. This review is intended to complement and reinforce the content in the text. If you use the guide in concert with your study of the text, it should help give you a more thorough and deeper understanding of the nature of learning, and how factors such as learner development and individual differences, motivation, classroom management, instruction, and assessment all affect student learning. Our goal is for this guide to contribute to your success as you study educational psychology--a critical foundation for understanding learning and teaching.

USING THE GUIDE

In writing the text and preparing this guide, we have attempted to be consistent with the implications for learning that appear in each chapter. Some examples are included as follows:

Using Case Studies

You will see, or have already seen, that each chapter begins and ends with a case study taken from classroom practice. Learning is improved when learners have the opportunity to study concrete examples of the topics they study. These cases are concrete examples of classroom practice. To help you learn as much as possible from these case studies, this Study Guide begins with a section called *Analyzing Case Studies: Suggestions and Guidelines* which offers suggestions for maximizing the amount you learn from the case studies.

Organization of the Study Guide

Following the section called *Analyzing Case Studies: Suggestions and Guidelines*, the Study Guide is organized according to the chapters of the text, and each chapter of the Guide is divided into six sections: 1) A detailed Outline of all the headings in the chapter, 2) Chapter Objectives, 3) An Overview that summarizes the chapter content, 4) feedback for all the Margin Questions that appear in the chapter, 5) Application Exercises that ask you to apply the content to new situations, together with feedback for each exercise, and 6) A Self-Help Quiz, followed by answers, that will allow you to assess your understanding of the topics.

Each section is summarized below.

CHAPTER OUTLINE

The Chapter Outline presents the organization of each chapter. All section headings are identified in the outline.

CHAPTER OBJECTIVES

The Chapter Objectives specify what you are expected to achieve as you study each chapter.

CHAPTER OVERVIEW

The Chapter Overview summarizes the content of each chapter. You can use the overview in different ways. You may want to read it before you begin your detailed study of the chapter in the text to provide you with a frame of reference, you may want to read it after completing your study to help you identify the most important elements of each chapter, or you may combine the two.

FEEDBACK FOR MARGIN QUESTIONS

As you will see, or perhaps have already seen, questions appear in the margins of each chapter of the text. When you study the content of Chapter 7, you will see that learning is more meaningful when learners are put in as *active* a role as possible when they study. These questions are designed to put you in an active role and help you apply the content of the section to new situations, relate the topic to topics you've studied in earlier chapters, or connect the topic to your everyday life. Feedback for these margin questions appears in this section of the Student Study Guide.

APPLICATION EXERCISES

The Application Exercises ask you to apply the content of each chapter to an authentic classroom situation. As with using the margin questions, the application exercises are designed to put you in an active role. Feedback immediately follows the exercises. We strongly encourage you to take a piece of paper, respond to the exercises in writing, and then compare your answers to the feedback. Your study will be much more effective if you follow this procedure than if you merely read the exercises and then read the feedback.

SELF-HELP QUIZ

Each chapter concludes with a quiz. You can use the quiz in different ways. You may choose to respond before you begin your study, to pretest your background with the chapter content, you may wait until you've completed your study, or you can combine the two. Answers to all the items are provided at the end of each quiz. As with other sections of the guide, the self-help quiz is designed to put you in an active role and give you feedback about your responses. We strongly recommend that you first answer all the questions on the quiz before looking at the feedback. To put yourself in an even more active role, you may choose to write an explanation for your choice before you look at the feedback.

Good luck in your study. We hope you find this Study Guide useful and meaningful.

ANALYZING CASE STUDIES: SUGGESTIONS AND GUIDELINES

As you read the text, you will see that each chapter begins with a case study (commonly called a "case"), and Chapters 2 through 14 also end with case studies. Cases are written accounts of actual classroom episodes. They include a description of the teachers' and students' behaviors, and dialogue that took place during the episode is presented as it occurred. In a sense, case studies read like short stories about classroom incidents. The fact that each incident is on paper allows us to study the teachers' and students' behaviors in detail. We can examine different parts as many times as we want, and we can study and discuss these parts in depth.

Though case studies are somewhat like short stories, they differ in two important respects. First, short stories are fictional, whereas case studies are based on real classroom experiences. Second, specific case studies have been selected because the teachers' and students' behaviors in them illustrate (or violate) the principles of learning and teaching that are presented in the text.

Because cases contain information that illustrate important ideas, they must be read with more care and concentration than would be needed to read a short story or novel. To facilitate this process, some simple techniques can be used to help you learn more from each case than you would learn if you only read them casually.

The purpose in preparing this part of the study guide is to offer you some suggestions that will make your examination of case studies more meaningful. As your ability to analyze cases improves, your understanding of the content in the text will increase, and hopefully, your ability to assess your own teaching will also increase.

Focusing on the beginning-of-chapter cases, the techniques can be outlined in the following four steps:

1) Skim the case study:

The purpose in the first step is to give you an overall feel for the episode. If, for example, the case illustrates a teacher trying to help his or her students learn some content, you will identify the topic and what--in general--the teacher did to help the students understand the topic. At this point in your reading, you are not expected to recognize some of the subtle or sophisticated actions of the teacher. Skimming the case study should take only a matter of minutes.

2) Read the case a second time, and make a written list of behaviors the teacher or students displayed that you believe are significant:

The second step is important to learning the most from cases. Remember, cases are presented for a purpose, and much--but not all--of the information in them illustrates noteworthy teacher or student behaviors. The process of making a decision about what is significant and what isn't is the critical part of your study. You won't know until you've read the chapter whether or not the items you've included are the most significant ones, but the decision-making process will make your study much more meaningful. As you gain experience in analyzing cases, you'll improve in your ability to predict the significance of a behavior. The items on the list can be tersely stated and written in outline form. Preparing the list should not be time consuming or laborsome.

3) Read the chapter, relating your list to the topics as you read. Add items to the list that you didn't originally include:

As you read, keep the list you've prepared at your side for easy reference, relating the items on the list to the section you're reading. Check off items on your list as you read, making notes and adding additional items that you realize are significant.

4) Examine unchecked items on the list:

Look again at your list and ask yourself why items you originally believed to be important turned out to be insignificant. They may be unimportant, or they may be significant but not in the context of the present chapter. Your analysis of these items will further increase your understanding of the chapter.

To illustrate these four steps, let's look at the case study that introduces Chapter 7, "Cognitive Views of Learning." Then let's apply the steps to the case.

David Shelton is preparing a unit on the solar system for his ninth-grade earth science class. In his filing cabinet he found a color transparency showing the sun throwing "globs" of gases off into space. He assembled a large model of the solar system illustrating the planets in their orbital planes and their relative distances from the sun. Finally, he prepared a large matrix, made from a roll of chart paper, which he taped onto the back wall of the room. (The matrix appears on page 240 of your text.)

David began his unit on Monday by saying, "We're getting ready to study the solar system for the next several days, so I've prepared some things to help us get started. Take a look at the chart I made," he said, pointing to the back of the room.

"This chart is going to help us learn about the solar system. . . but first, we need information to fill in the chart. . . . So, I want you to work in your groups to gather the information. Think about it for a moment and decide which planet you want. If more than one group wants a planet, you'll have to negotiate to see which group gets its first choice."

The students turned to their groups, talked briefly, and quickly made their choices, compromising in a few cases.

David listed the groups' choices on the board and then directed the students to books, computer software, and other resources in the room. The students spent the rest of Monday's class gathering their information and putting it on the chart using marking pens.

At the beginning of Tuesday's class, David displayed and briefly discussed the color transparency showing the sun throwing "globs" of gases off into space. He also referred them to the model of the solar system he had assembled and suspended from the ceiling after school on Monday, reminding them that it might serve as a frame of reference for their study. The students then spent the rest of Tuesday's class continuing to put information onto the chart.

On Wednesday David began, "Okay, let's review what we've found out so far. Then, I'm going to do a little demonstration, and I want you to think about how it relates to what you've been doing."

After completing his review, David tied a pair of athletic socks to a 3-foot piece of string, another pair to a 5-foot piece of string, and whirled the two around his head simultaneously to demonstrate that the planets revolve around the sun on the same plane and in the same direction.

After having the students make a number of observations about what they saw, he continued, "Now the task gets a little more challenging. Each group should identify a piece of information from the chart that might explain or provide evidence about how the solar system was formed . . . . Let me give you an example . . . . For instance, when we look at Pluto, we see that the plane of its orbit is different than the plane for all the other planets. What Tanya, Juan, and Randy, who are studying Pluto, must do is figure out why it's different," he said pointing to the orbital plane cell for Pluto on the chart, "and be able to explain to the rest of the class why you think that's the case. Use any of the information you have--the demonstration I just did, the transparency, the model we have hanging from the ceiling--and anything else.

"Let me give you one more example," he went on. "Here," referring to the diameter and gravity cells for Saturn, "Saturn is much bigger than the Earth, but its gravity is about the same as the Earth's. Now, why might that be the case? . . . Karen, Jack, and Karl will have to explain that to the rest of us. . . Okay, see what I mean? . . . If you get totally stuck, let me know, and I'll come around and help you. . . . Any questions. . . . Go ahead."

The room was again quickly filled with the buzz of voices as the students prepared for the discussion to follow. As they worked, David moved from group to group, offering periodic comments, suggestions, and compliments to groups that were working hard.

"Pluto wasn't part of the solar system to begin with," Juan commented to Randy and Tanya as they started their work.

"What do you mean?" Randy responded.

"I was watching *Nova* with my Mom, and they said that they think that Pluto was floating around and the Sun kinda grabbed it. . . . See, when Mr. Shelton did that thing with the socks, the socks stayed sorta level," he continued moving his hand back and forth to demonstrate a flat plane.

"What's that got to do with it?" Randy asked, still confused.

"Oh, I get it! Pluto isn't level with the rest of them," Tanya interrupted.

"Gee, I didn't even notice that," lamented Randy.

"Yeah, and look there," Tanya added, pointing to the chart. "See how little Pluto is? It's the littlest one, so it would be sorta easy to capture."

"And it's the last one," Randy added, beginning to warm to the task. "I better write some of this stuff down, or I'll never remember it."

David listened as the students in this group talked and then suggested, "I think you're doing a super job, but you might be forgetting something. Take another look at the transparency and see how it relates to what you're talking about. . . . Look at how the globs are coming off the sun, and look at the title of the transparency."

The students studied the transparency for a moment, and Juan finally said, "Look, all those globs are even too, you know, level, like the socks. . . . And it says, 'One Theory of the Formation of the Solar System.' So, that's how the planets were made."

"Now, what was that again about Pluto being the littlest?" Randy wondered. "What's that got to do with anything?"

"If it was really big and floating around out there, the sun's gravity might not be strong enough to grab it," Juan offered.

"But it's easier to grab if it's little," Tanya added.

The students continued their work for a few more minutes, and then David called the class together. "Now, let's see what we've got. Are you all ready? . . . Which group wants to go first?. . . "

"We will," Tanya offered after several seconds.

"Go ahead."

"We can explain why Pluto isn't on the same plane with the other planets," she continued, pleased with her group's accomplishments. "It wasn't part of the solar system when it was first made."

"Now, the rest of you should be asking for what. . .what else do you need to know?" David probed.   ". . ."

"You should be asking for evidence," David continued after hearing no response. "Each group needs to provide evidence that makes sense to the rest of us. . . . Go ahead, Tanya or Juan or Randy."

Juan and Randy motioned for Tanya to continue. "It's the littlest one and it's way out there," motioning to the end of the model.

"Does that support or contradict what the group said?" David queried.

". . . Supports," Lori volunteered.

"How?" David nodded, gesturing for her to continue.

". . . If it were captured from somewhere else, it makes sense that it would be the last one."

"Wait, Mr. Shelton, you're going too fast. I'm getting lost. What is this about supporting the theory?" Alfredo asked.

"That's a good question, Alfredo. Let's think about that one, everyone. What do you think?"

". . . If the rest of the solar system were already in place, and Pluto came by and was snagged by the sun's gravity, then it would be the farthest one out," Dena offered.

"I see that, but what if Pluto was snagged first? Then how could it be the farthest out?" Alfredo continued.

". . . Yes, but we found out that the planets weren't snagged; they spun off as molten stuff, . . . globs, so Pluto, if it was caught by the sun would be the last one," Dena returned.

"What do you think, Alfredo?" David gestured.

". . . Yeah, I see what she means. . . . I guess it makes sense."

"And, it isn't in line with the others," Juan added, motioning with his hand to indicate that its orbital plane was different from the others, "And its path is funny, too. Sometimes it's actually inside Neptune's."

"And what did we call the 'paths'?" David probed.

"Orbits," several of the students responded in unison.

"Okay. Excellent, everyone. See how this relates to what Dena said a minute ago? When I think of location and orbit, the first thing that pops in my mind is 'origin.' I relate the location and orbit to their origins," David continued, thinking out loud for the students.

David continued with the process of having groups present their information and explanations until he saw that the period was nearing an end. He then said, "Okay, everyone. We'll continue tomorrow. You've done an excellent job of gathering and relating items of information about the solar system. Now, to check on us, I have a short assignment. For tonight's homework I want you to write a paragraph summarizing how the Earth became a member of the solar system and compare that to how Pluto became a member. Use all the information we have and today's discussion to help you. This should take less than a page.

"Just a reminder in passing," he added as he pointed to the overhead, "This is just one theory of how the solar system was formed. There are others, but we're focusing on this one for now. Also remember," David emphasized, "the information must be in a paragraph. You cannot merely write down isolated sentences."

As students began their summaries, David circulated around the room, answering questions and offering suggestions.

Now let's apply the four steps to the case we've just read.

1) Skim the case study:

In reading the case, we see that we're in a 9th-grade earth science class where the students are studying the solar system. The lesson covers three days. On the first day, the students gather information about the solar system--the planets, their relative sizes and distances from the sun, the length of their days and years, average surface temperatures and gravity compared to earth.

On the second day, the teacher begins by displaying a transparency and a model of the solar system, and the students then turn back to putting information on the chart.

On the third day, the teacher leads a review, performs a demonstration, and then has the students study the chart to identify and explain information with respect to the solar system. The students again work in their groups. Finally, the groups present their information and a whole-class discussion follows.

2) Carefully read the case, and make a written list of things the teacher or students did that you believe are significant:

As we look at the case in detail we jot down items such as the following:

David takes a color transparency out of his file drawer.
David suspends a model of the solar system from the ceiling.
David tapes a large matrix on the back wall of the classroom.
The students gather information that is put in a matrix.
David whirls athletic socks around his head.
David asks students to relate the demonstration to the model and transparency as they prepare their explanations.
The groups present information.
David emphasizes that students search for and provide evidence.

David gives an assignment in which the students are to compare how the Earth and Pluto became members of the solar system.

3) Read the chapter, relating your list to the topics as you read:

In reading the chapter we see that it begins by telling us that our information processing systems are composed of three locations where information is stored--sensory memory, working memory, and long-term memory--and a number of cognitive processes that move information from one storage area to another. As we continue we see that the chapter describes the characteristics of each storage area, noting that sensory memory will hold a large amount of information for a very brief period of time, working memory will hold only a limited amount of information for a relatively short period of time, and long-term memory will hold information indefinitely if it is interrelated (in what are called networks and schemas).

In studying the characteristics of long-term memory we see that the chapter illustrates differences in the way Randy and Juan have stored information in their long-term memories; Juan's is more interrelated than is Randy's, and interrelated information is more meaningful to students than is information that exists in isolation. This suggests that the discussion between Juan, Tanya, and Randy, which illustrates differences in the way the three students think about what they're learning, is significant. Because of a better organized schema, the information is more meaningful to Juan than it is to Randy.

We then add "Juan says Pluto wasn't originally part of the solar system," "Randy is confused," "Tanya catches on," and "Randy decides to take notes," to our list and check them off.

As we continue our reading, we begin to study the cognitive processes that move the information from sensory memory to working memory (and ultimately to long-term memory). From our reading we see that getting the learner's attention is the first step, which is followed by perception--the process of attaching meaning to what we see, hear, feel, taste, or smell. David's transparency, model, and whirling socks were all attention getters, and David's materials were as concrete as he could make them, which helped the students accurately perceive the information that was presented.

As we move to the next section, we see that students' awareness of and ability to control their cognitive processes also increases learning. This helps us understand the significance of *Randy deciding to take notes*, and *Alfredo protesting that David is going too fast*. Taking notes helped Randy control his attention, and Alfredo was aware that he wasn't fully understanding what was being discussed. If we hadn't included these items on our original list, we would add them now.

/David takes a color transparency out of his file drawer.
/David suspends a model of the solar system from the ceiling.
/David tapes a large matrix on the back wall of the classroom.
/The students gather information that is put in a matrix.
/David whirls athletic socks around his head.
David asks students to relate the demonstration to the model and transparency as they prepare their explanations.
/The groups present information.
David emphasizes that students search for and provide evidence.
Alfredo protests that David is going too fast.
/David gives an assignment in which the students are to compare how the Earth and Pluto became members of the solar system.
/Juan says that Pluto wasn't originally a part of the solar system.
/Randy is confused.
/Tanya catches on.
/Randy decides to take notes.

As we read further, we see that learning is increased if new information is made meaningful by interrelating it and connecting it to information the students already know. Organizing information and requiring the learners to be active instead of allowing them to sit passively also increases learning.

David's chart is a way of helping students interrelate information by organizing it in a matrix, and asking the students to relate the demonstration to the model, reviewing the previous day's lesson, emphasizing that students understand why events are true, the discussion of whether or not Pluto was an original member of the solar system, and the assigned paragraphs further encourage the students to interrelate the information. Review also helps them connect new information to old, and the discussion and writing require the students to be active.

Finally, as we study Constructivism we see how important background knowledge and social interaction are in helping learners construct their understanding of the topics they study. We add these items to our list, so it now appears as follows:

/David takes a color transparency out of his file drawer.
/David suspends a model of the solar system from the ceiling.
//David tapes a large matrix on the back wall of the classroom.
//The students gather information that is put in a matrix.
/David whirls athletic socks around his head.
/David asks students to relate the demonstration to the model and transparency as they prepare their explanations.
//The groups present information.
David emphasizes that students search for and provide evidence.
/Alfredo protests that David is going too fast.
/David gives an assignment in which the students are to compare how the Earth and Pluto became members of the solar system.
/David consciously puts the students in groups to capitalize on social interaction.
//Juan says that Pluto wasn't originally a part of the solar system.
//Randy is confused.
//Tanya catches on.
//Randy decides to take notes.

4)   Examine unchecked items on the list.

In examining our list, we see that we have only one item remaining: "David emphasizes that students search for and provide evidence." The search for evidence is significant in developing critical-thinking skills (Chapter 8), and it is implied in the process of making information meaningful, even though it isn't referred to directly in the chapter.

As you see, the focus in this section has been on the beginning-of-chapter cases. Those at the end of each chapter have their own sets of directed questions, and you will also have the benefit of studying the chapter before you do your analysis. For this reason we have focused on the cases at the beginning of the chapters in this part of the Student Study Guide.

Good luck in your analysis of cases.

CHAPTER 1: TEACHING IN THE REAL WORLD

Chapter Outline

I. Educational psychology: Teaching in the real world
II. Beginning teachers and learning to teach
   A. Misconceptions about teaching and learning to teach
      1. Misconception: Teaching is a process of transmitting knowledge to learners
      2. Misconception: Majoring in an academic subject provides all the knowledge needed to teach the subject
      3. Misconception: To learn to teach, experience in classrooms is all that is necessary
   B. Goals for this book
III. Themes for this book
   A. Research on learning and teaching
      1. A knowledge base
      2. Role of theory in a body of knowledge
   B. Classroom application
   C. Teacher decision making
      1. Informed decision making
         a. Critical decision making: Impact of classroom context
         b. Practical decision making: The need for efficiency
         c. Artistic decision making: Creativity in teaching
      2. Reflection and decision making
   D. A focus on learners
      1. A focus on learners: Developing self regulation
      2. A focus on learners: Caring
      3. A focus on learners: Learner diversity
         a. Dimensions of diversity
         b. Strategies for dealing with diversity
         c. Adapting instruction to meet learners' needs
IV. Organization of this book
   A. Part I: The learner
   B. Part II: Learning
   C. Part III: Classroom processes
V. Using this book

Chapter Objectives

- Identify the implications that studying educational psychology has for classroom practice.

- Explain how research in educational psychology is applied to classroom practice.

- Describe the relationships between research and theory.

- Explain how professional decision making affects teaching.

- Explain how reflective teaching uses educational psychology to improve professional decision making.

Chapter Overview_____

This chapter introduces you to educational psychology, which analyzes learning and factors that influence it. As you examine the contents of your text, you will study, in addition to the nature of learning itself, learner development, individual differences, and motivation, together with the impact that teachers have on learning as a result of their instruction, management, and assessment.

Novices often have misconceptions about learning to teach, such as believing that teaching is a simple process of transmitting knowledge to students, underestimating the important role that learners themselves play in the process. They also tend to think that majoring in an academic area provides all the knowledge necessary to make them effective teachers, not realizing that knowledge of learning and learners, as well as knowledge of how to represent topics in ways that learners can understand--called *pedagogical content knowledge*--are also critical. Finally, many beginning teachers embrace an "apprenticeship" model, believing that experience in classrooms is all that is necessary to become an expert teacher. While classroom experience is necessary, alone it isn't adequate. Acquiring knowledge about learning and learners, the processes of instruction, and how learning and instruction interact is the reason we study educational psychology.

This text is organized around four themes: the importance of *research* in learning to teach, the need to be able to *apply* this research in classrooms, the crucial role of *decision making* in applying the content of educational psychology to complex classroom settings, and the importance of maintaining a *learner-centered perspective* as we think about our teaching.

As you study your text, you will grow in all of these areas. You will acquire a background of research, theory, and the "wisdom of practice." This background will be combined with experiences that will require your analysis, judgment and reflection. In the process you will be moved toward expertise in teaching--the most noble profession that exists.

Feedback for Margin Questions_____

1.1:   According to Calderhead and Robson (1991), these views are based on the individuals' own observations of role models when they were students.

1.2:   Most people's experiences with teaching have involved teachers as "transmitters of knowledge." They've had little experience in which teachers did otherwise. As with the answer to 1.1, knowledge transmission is what they've seen in their role models.

1.3:   As with 1.1 and 1.2, most of the experiences that majors and nonmajors have had in all content areas have involved simple presentations--usually in a lecture format--of ideas in the abstract. Few people have had the good fortune to have ideas illustrated and represented in other ways. As a result, they have few if any modeled experiences that they can use as a basis for their own efforts to create meaningful examples and representations.

1.4:   Classrooms involve a great deal of complex organization and interaction between teachers and students. Some of what makes a teacher successful is subtle and easy to miss. Novice observers tend to react to the most salient, concrete, perceptually obvious aspects of interaction, such as an incident where a student misbehaves, or a teacher is doing an eye-catching demonstration. More subtle factors, such as a teacher having well-established routines often go unnoticed.

1.5:   Knowledge of "how ideas can be represented so they're understandable" refers to pedagogical content knowledge.

1.6: The most common teaching method is probably lecture. It is the most common method in most classrooms, probably because it is the simplest and least demanding for the teacher (Cuban, 1984).

1.7: Intuitive research results are more common than non-intuitive results, which probably reflect a tendency in humans to expect the world to operate in sensible and predictable ways. The same is true in other professions as well. Many more research results in medicine, for example, are intuitive rather than non-intuitive.

1.8: Research, while somewhat controversial, indicates that an approach where the mechanics of grammar and spelling are taught outside the context of actual writing (i.e., taught in isolated sentences and exercises) is often ineffective. Research indicates that mechanics should be taught in the context of a student's own writing; in other words, grammar and punctuation should be learned within the context of meaningful attempts to communicate through writing.

1.9: If the research base in teaching were complete, controversies would be minimized. The research bases in other areas, while probably more advanced than the one in teaching, are far from complete. This is evidenced by the fact that controversies exist in these fields as well, and subsequent findings often conflict with earlier ones. For instance, conflicting studies have been reported about the effect of salt intake and hypertension, and the relationship between cholesterol intake and an individual's cholesterol level. Similar controversies exist in economics. For example, application of "supply side" economics is enormously controversial. It is blamed by many for the rapid increase in the national debt, whereas others view it as a means to national prosperity.

1.10: Keith's attempt to ignore Kelly's misbehavior would be one example of using reinforcement theory to explain and predict her behavior. He was inferring that his attention was reinforcing her antics, and he tacitly predicted that if he ignored her (withheld the reinforcer), the misbehavior would cease. Trying to "catch her being good" was also an effort to reinforce desired behavior.

1.11: The case studies are intended to illustrate the topics you'll study in the text. The case you've just read illustrates a problem to solve. Other cases will illustrate specific concepts and principles that make up the content of each chapter.

1.12: Her most obvious decision was whether or not to give the students materials if they didn't bring them. Other decisions included whether to allow them to sit passively if they had the necessary materials or whether to attempt to design a reward or punishment system to address the problem.

1.13: In the study that was cited, the students were in a small reading group, and they could predict when they would be asked to read. They could then prepare for their portion by looking ahead. In whole-group instruction, and particularly with older students, calling on students in predictable patterns often results in some of them "tuning out" when they know they won't be called on.

1.14: We might look for nonverbal behaviors, such squirming in their seats, looking at other students, looking down, and stumbling in an effort to answer. Much of our decision making when working with students is based on their nonverbal behaviors, so it is important to observe students and be sensitive to their behavior--particularly their nonverbal behavior.

1.15: The greatest benefits of one-to-one instruction are the abilities to determine exactly how much the learner understands and to direct instruction at precisely that level. Also, the personal attention involved in one-to-one instruction can be strongly motivating. While no form of group instruction can match the benefits of one-to-one, some strategies such as cooperative learning, peer tutoring, and the use of computers can approximate these benefits.

1.16:   Both teachers were faced with the problem of making abstract ideas meaningful to students. Both responded by using concrete examples to illustrate these abstract ideas. In Keith's case, Jan offered the example of finding the percentage of the banana that was edible, a concrete and practical problem. The music teacher used the different recordings to make the different aspects of Beethoven's "Eroica" more concrete.

1.17:   She commented to Keith, "I'll do parts of it differently next time. At times I think I jumped in too soon when they could have figured it out for themselves, and at other times I think I let them stumble around too long, and they wasted more time than necessary . . . " She wouldn't have made those decisions if she hadn't reflected on what she was doing.

1.18:   Reflection was demonstrated when she "fretted" over the fact that her students weren't learning an important idea, when she mentally tried and rejected different strategies and when she discussed the problem with other teachers.

Many people mistakenly believe that creativity and artistry just "happen," but this is not at all the case. Artistry in teaching is the result of a great deal of effort, thought and reflection. The saying, "Creativity is 10% inspiration and 90% perspiration" illustrates this point.

1.19:   Explanations, by their nature, come from a teacher's perspective and they're based on the teacher's understanding of the topic. They don't take the student's background, or lack of background, into account as well as would a more learner-focused approach.

1.20:   While answers to this question depend on the individual, some questions can give you an indication. For example: What grade do you expect to get in this class? How do you plan on achieving this goal? How will you study? How are your study plans related to your instructor's goals and grading system? How will you know if your learning efforts are successful? What will you do if they aren't? Answers to all these questions reflect self-regulation.

1.21:   In his conversation with Jan he demonstrated that he was concerned both about the students' understanding of math and their emotional reaction to it. He also took responsibility for their learning. A less caring teacher would have been more inclined to conclude that students lacked background, last year's teacher didn't prepare them well, they had bad attitudes, or some other factor that removed the responsibility from him.

1.22:   First, the problem was concrete and practical; all students could identify with it. Second, as she guided students she could gauge their understanding, and when they lacked understanding, she could help them. Simply "explaining" doesn't take learners' backgrounds into account.

1.23:   These three strategies relate most strongly to *a focus on learners*. An attitude of acceptance and caring, positive expectations, and valuing all learners are all learner-focused characteristics.

TRUE/FALSE QUESTIONS: Write T in the blank if the statement is true, and write F if the statement is false.

_____ 1. Professions, such as medicine, are based on theory, while education is developed primarily on the basis of classroom experience.

_____ 2. Research is of no value if the results of different studies are conflicting.

_____ 3. A body of knowledge is of little value unless it is complete.

_____ 4. Research results and theories are essentially unrelated to each other.

_____ 5. Education is virtually the only profession that has conflicting research results.

MULTIPLE-CHOICE QUESTIONS. Circle the best response in each case.

6. Of the following, the best description of a theory is:
   a. the information known about a particular field of study.
   b. the knowledge and facts that people in professions know.
   c. classroom applications of principles in the real world of teaching.
   d. combinations of related patterns.

7. Which of the following statements are true of theories?
   1. They are based on the results of patterns identified by research.
   2. They serve as a basis for predicting the outcome of future events.
   3. They serve as a basis for explaining events.
   4. Once developed, they are not modified.

a. 1,2,3,4   b. 1,2,3   c. 1,2,4   d. 2,3,4   e. 1,4

Use the following description for items 8-10.

Mrs. Adcox, was having a difficult time getting her students involved in her lessons. She would begin by telling them that the content they were studying was important, but the students were unresponsive.

She thought a lot about the problem, asking colleagues and looking for ideas. In reading an article in one of her professional journals one evening, she saw a report indicating that students are often curious when teachers begin their lessons with a question or problem that doesn't have an apparent solution. It sounded like it might help her in her frustration with her students, but she asked herself, "How am I going to do this in language arts? That's where the students are the most listless."

Then she hit on an idea. She began her next class by telling the students, "Look, kids, when we have one baby we spell it b a b y, but when we have more than one we spell it b a b i e s. On the other hand, we spell boy, b o y, but when we have more than one we spell it b o y s rather than b o i e s. Why do you suppose we have the difference?"

She then made it a point to call on her cultural minority students as much as she called on those who were not minorities. She was pleased to discover that all her students were more interested in what she was doing, so much so that whenever possible, she began her lessons with a problem or question.

8. Of the following, the above description best illustrates a:
   a. theory.
   b. body of knowledge.
   c. research result.
   d. case study.

9. Mrs. Adcox read her professional journal and learned about the effects of beginning lessons with a question or problem. She then figured out an original way that this information could be applied with her language arts students. This process best illustrates:

    a. critical decision making.
    b. artistic decision making.
    c. reflection and decision making.
    d. developing learner self-regulation.

10. In the episode we saw that Mrs. Adcox ". . . made it a point to call on her cultural minority students as much as she called on those who were not minorities." Of the following, this practice best illustrates:

    a. developing learner self-regulation.
    b. reflection and decision making.
    c. positive expectations for learner success.
    d. the development of a theory of teaching.

Self-Help Quiz Answers

1. f
2. f
3. f
4. f
5. f
6. d   Theories are defined as sets of related principles based on observations that in turn are used to explain additional observations. Principles are patterns. Some of the information in a field goes beyond theory (choice a), and some of the information that professionals "know" go beyond theories (choice b). Theories don't necessarily result in classroom applications (choice c).
7. b   Theories, are based on the results of patterns identified by research, they do serve as a basis for predicting the outcome of future events, and they serve as a basis for explaining events. They are, however, modified if they are unable to adequately explain observations.
8. d   The episode is a sample of students' and teachers' experiences in the teaching-learning process.
9. b   Being able to take a research article discussing the value of beginning lessons with a problem and figuring out an original way of applying the information in her classroom is an example of creativity. The ability to think in original and creative ways suggests artistic decision making.
10. c   Calling on students communicates that teachers expect students to be able to answer successfully. While learning to call on all students is probably based on reflection (choice b), and developing self-regulation is a goal (choice a), the practice, itself, best illustrates positive expectations for success.

CHAPTER 2: THE DEVELOPMENT OF COGNITION AND LANGUAGE

Chapter Outline_____

I.   Piaget's theory of intellectual development
   A.   Development: A definition
   B.   The drive for equilibrium
   C.   Organization and adaptation: The creation of schemes
      1.   Adapting schemes
   D.   Factors influencing development
      1.   Maturation
      2.   Experience with the physical world
      3.   Background experience: A source of diversity
         a.   Dealing with student diversity
      4.   Social experience
   E.   Stages of development
      1.   Sensorimotor stage (0 to 2 years)
      2.   Preoperational stage (2 to 7 years)
         a.   Egocentrism
         b.   Centration
         c.   Transformation
         d.   Reversibility
         e.   Systematic reasoning
         f.   Conservation
      3.   Concrete operational stage (7 to 11 years)
         a.   Seriation and classification
         b.   Teaching the concrete operational student
         c.   Concrete materials and language
      4.   Formal operational stage (Adolescent to adult)
         a.   Characteristics of formal thought
   F.   Piaget's theory: Classroom applications
      1.   Influence on instruction
      2.   Influence on curriculum development
   G.   Putting Piaget's theory into perspective
      1.   Research on Piaget's theory
      2.   Criticisms of Piaget's theory
II. A sociocultural view of development: The work of Lev Vygotsky
   A.   Language: A vehicle for development and a tool for thinking
   B.   Language, social interaction, and activity
   C.   Language: A tool for self-regulation and reflection
   D.   Vygotsky's work: Instructional applications
      1.   Zone of proximal development
      2.   Applying the zone of proximal development to teaching
         a.   Scaffolding: Interactive instructional support
         b.   Types of instructional scaffolding
III. Constructivism: A developmentally based view of teaching and learning
   A.   Piaget's and Vygotsky's views of knowledge construction
   B.   Applying constructivist ideas to teaching

IV. Language development
   A. Theories of language acquisition
      1. Behaviorist theories
      2. Social cognitive theory
      3. Psycholinguistic theory
      4. A constructivist view of language development
   B. Stages of language acquisition
      1. Early language: Building the foundation
      2. Fine-tuning language
      3. Advancing development
      4. Increasing language complexity

Chapter Objectives

- Explain how development is influenced by learning, experience, and maturation.

- Explain the role of language, activity, and social interaction in Vygotsky's theory of development.

- Describe the implications of constructivism for teaching.

- Explain how language development reflects constructivist views of learning.

Chapter Overview

As students progress through our schools, their development exerts a subtle but powerful influence on learning. Development refers to the orderly, durable changes in a learner resulting from learning, maturation, and experience. As our students develop they not only acquire new abilities but also come to view the world in different ways.

Jean Piaget, described cognitive development in terms of an individual's drive for equilibrium. He suggested that we organize our experiences into schemes or patterns, we use these schemes to interpret our environment. When new events can be interpreted in terms of existing schemes, they are *assimilated*; when new events don't fit into existing schemes, disequilibrium occurs and the schemes are modified and new schemes are created--a process he called *accommodation*. Through the reciprocal processes of assimilation and accommodation, development occurs.

Piaget found that the way children responded to the world and processed information could be described in patterns which he called stages. As they move through the stages their thinking progresses from processing information primarily through the senses to logically processing abstract information. Piaget's theory has had profound influences on the way we think about teaching and learning. Curriculum developers now emphasize the importance of experiences that proceed from concrete to abstract. Instruction is more learner-centered, with increased emphasis on hands-on experiences.

A second important view of development is based upon the work of Lev Vygotsky, a Russian psychologist. This *sociocultural view* of development emphasizes the central role that language, culture, and activity play in development. Teachers utilize Vygotsky's theory when they design learning activities within the learner's zone of proximal development, which represents a range of instructional tasks which students can accomplish with assistance. Teachers provide this assistance through instructional scaffolding that provides flexible help to students.

Constructivism, a view of learning suggesting that learners "construct" their own understanding of the way the world works, is a developmentally based view of learning and teaching; it emphasizes the critical role that learners play in creating their own understandings of the topics they study. Piaget's influence on constructivism can be seen in the emphasis on background knowledge and the critical role that direct experience plays in learning. Vygotsky's influence is reflected in constructivism's emphasis on social interaction and language.

Language development coincides with and complements other aspects of development. As students develop, their ability to talk about their world, and their ability to think about it also develops. Increased vocabulary and increasingly complex sentence structures reflect students' growing abilities to think about the world using language as a tool. Teachers can further this growth by encouraging students to use existing language patterns as the basis for future growth.

Feedback for Margin Questions

2.1: The maturation part of development involves her physical growth in size and strength and coordination. The experiential part involves her practice in basketball and in other sports. The learning part involves specific techniques she learns from her brother and others. The line between learning and experience is often blurred. Learning is the component of development that typically involves formal schooling with specified goals. Experience is an informal component, and a great deal of experience is acquired outside of formal schooling.

2.2: The drive for equilibrium, as individuals try to make sense of the world, is very strong. Hearing a familiar story confirms a sense of equilibrium. The child corrects any mistake the father makes, also to remain at equilibrium. If the same story sounded even slightly different, the child's equilibrium would be disrupted.

2.3: You should have a *development* scheme, which reflects your understanding of what development means, and you should have formed an *equilibrium* scheme which is your understanding of the concept of equilibrium. Keep in mind as you study the content of this chapter, however, that "schemes" don't merely represent concepts. They are also abilities, such as the ability to drive a car, as we saw in the text.

2.4: "Inadequate" means that our schemes don't allow us to cope with the world as effectively as we might. As a simple example, suppose a child has a "doggy" scheme that includes furry animals that walk on flat feet and say "grrr" in addition to furry animals that say "bow wow," wag their tails, and lick hands. This scheme is inadequate, since trying to pet bears can be dangerous. When schemes prove to be inadequate, accommodation occurs.

2.5: When she encounters a short-haired male or a long-haired female and classifies each into her original scheme, she is *assimilating*. Reconsidering her original classification system illustrates adaptation through the process of accommodation. She modifies her original men-have-short-hair-and-women-have-long-hair scheme, and creates a new scheme, which allows for the possibility that some men have long hair and some women have short hair. The process of modifying the original scheme and creating a new scheme illustrates accommodation.

2.6: When a child categorizes a whale as a fish, the whale is assimilated into a fish scheme; it illustrates the concept of assimilation. Changing the fish scheme so it doesn't include whales illustrates the process of accommodation.

2.7:   The principle, "All growth depends on existing schemes," helps us understand this research. Students who have developed schemes for successfully dealing with academic work can bring these to bear on future academic tasks. The converse is also true. Pre-existing schemes are most useful in areas such as math where learning is cumulative.

2.8:   The best remedy for this situation is to take the students outside at different times of the day and measure the direction and length of the shadows their own bodies cast. This is a form of direct experience, that will help them make the topic meaningful. (The process could be simulated in the classroom by using an artificial light source, such as a strong flashlight.)

2.9:   Many of Celena's students had inadequate schemes for ideas such as subway, skyscraper, mass transit, elevator, and escalator (just as the child in 2.4 had an inadequate scheme when she tried to pet a bear). To help them develop adequate schemes she provided experiences with her pictures, descriptions, and the children's examples, which helped them adapt by accommodating their inadequate schemes. They would then be prepared to assimilate new experiences into the more effective schemes.

2.10:   Each of these activities provides experience for the child. An increased emphasis on rich and varied experiences has also spawned some general social programs. Programs have also been designed to help children by providing an alternative source of foundational experiences. "Sesame Street" is an attempt to use television to meet this goal. Head Start and school programs such as Chapter I (formerly Title I) are formal, government-sponsored efforts to provide these enriched experiences in the context of the classroom.

2.11:   Students from the urban area would be less likely to have concrete experiences with farm animals, so she would try to provide more concrete experiences for the students than would the teacher from the rural area. Her students' schemes would be less developed than the schemes for the rural students. Since their schemes would be develped more fully, the rural students would be likely to assimilate more of the experiences she provides into already existing schemes. Accommodation would be required more likely of the urban students. For example, urban students would be less likely to realize that we drink milk from goats as well as cows, so the scheme for sources of milk would require adaptation through the process of accommodation.

2.12:   Play provides children with the opportunity to test their schemes against the schemes of others. This suggests that early childhood programs need to provide ample opportunities for "play."

2.13:   Movement up the ramp is continuous while movement up the stairs involves discrete movement (You're on one step or another; there's no in-between). Another example of continuous change is increase in height. An infinite number of possibilities exist. In contrast, the number of chocolate chips in a cookie is discrete. There are 4, or 5, or some other number with no in-between possibilities.

2.14:   Without object permanence the child is likely to quickly turn his attention to something else, since the object hasn't been recorded in his memory. When object permanence is acquired, the child records the information in his memory, so he is likely to crawl or walk over and look behind his mother's back, searching for the missing object.

2.15:   The practice is appropriate according to our understanding of cognitive development. Preoperational children are capable of learning concepts, the concepts are concrete and they can be easily illustrated with tangible examples.

2.16: Social interaction is probably most important for helping to reduce egocentrism. Through social interaction children test the adequacy of their schemes against the reactions of others. When they find the schemes are inadequate, gradually they learn to consider points of view different from their own.

2.17: Concrete experiences are important for children at this stage of development. (Concrete experiences are important for children at the concrete operational stage as well.) One possible strategy is guided "play" where the instructor encourages the child to count the coins, for example, then change the spacing, count the coins again, repeat the process, and compare the counts in each case.

2.18: The child centers on either the height or the length of the clay, she is unable to *mentally record* the process of flattening the clay (nontransformation), she is unable to *mentally trace* the process of going from the flattened piece of clay back to the ball (irreversibility), and she doesn't question her own thinking (egocentrism). The combination of these factors leads her to conclude that the amounts are different.

2.19: While the fourth-grader wouldn't articulate it this way, the logic might exist as:
The number of coins in the two rows is the same.
All you did was spread the second row apart.
Therefore, the number of coins in the two rows is still the same.
This type of thinking is a form of deductive reasoning. (The three statements illustrate the deductive syllogism.)

2.20: A variety of possibilities exist. The following is just one example. You might have a student walk rapidly and then slowly across the front of the room. Then, have the children describe how the student walked, and write the description on the board, such as,

Joanne walked rapidly across the floor the first time.

Joanne walked slowly across the floor the second time.

You could then ask the students what word in the sentence described how she walked, what part of speech "walked" represents, and link this information to the fact that adverbs describe verbs. You would then do something similar to help the students see that adverbs also modify adjectives and other adverbs.

2.21: She would need to help relate what they saw to the formula. While there isn't one series of questions that is necessarily more correct than another, some important questions would be as follows:
"How does the mass of the compressed cotton compare to the mass of the uncompressed cotton?" (It's the same.)
"How do we know?" (We haven't added or taken away any cotton.)
"How do the volumes compare?" (The volume compressed is less than the volume uncompressed.)
"How do we know?" (The compressed cotton takes up less space.)
"How does the cotton look when it's compressed compared to the way it looks uncompressed?" (It's more "squashed together" when it's compressed.) (At this point it would be appropriate to say that the cotton is more "dense." The more compressed it is, the more dense.)
"So, what does density mean?" (It is the amount of mass in a certain volume.)
"How might we write the amount of mass in a certain volume?" ($D = m/v$).
In an actual classroom, the sequence wouldn't be this fast or smooth. It does, however, illustrate how critical questioning and language are in linking concrete experiences to abstract ideas.

2.22: Addition and subtraction are operations that can be readily illustrated with concrete objects, such as beans, sticks, or cubes. In contrast, to understand percentage, such as taking 25% of 48, requires a mental link to "parts of 100," which is a form of abstract thinking. (The simple, and concrete, idea of percentage, such as shading 25 squares on a 100-square grid can easily be demonstrated, however.)

2.23: The need for experience implies that unless students have prerequisite experiences they will be ill-equipped for the abstract thinking that is commonly required in junior high, high school and work. This means that teachers *must provide the experiences*, as Karen Johnson did, if students are to develop deep understanding of the topics they study. Notice also, that Karen avoided the use of the abstract formula and numbers until the students had a thorough conceptual understanding of density. Research indicates that few individuals are formal operational outside their own areas of expertise, so even many university students will be concrete operational in most of their areas of study. This means that concrete experiences are important for university students as well.

2.24: They lack the prerequisite concrete, conceptual experiences that are needed before they're able to think in the abstract that is typical of formal thought. This means that teachers of junior-high students must make an effort to provide concrete experiences for them.

2.25: Since the size of the blocks is the most perceptually obvious aspect of the system, students *center* on size, ignoring the fact that the balance is level.

2.26: This illustrates the idea of language being a "cultural tool kit." In our culture, snow is a fairly simple idea. In the Eskimo culture, however, snow is a more complex concept, and they have more terms and more ways of describing it. Their language reflects the fact that snow is a more complex idea in their culture than it is in ours.

2.27: Based on the information in this section, we would conclude that "English only" programs would be less effective than programs that allow students to make a gradual transition to English. As we saw in the text, "When we learn language, we aren't just learning words, we also learn the ideas that are connected with those words." Spanish-speaking students, for example, have their understanding of the world attached to the language symbols of Spanish. They haven't yet attached ideas to the English language, so they don't have anything in their "cultural tool kit." It takes time to attach ideas to a new language. (As we'll see in Chapter 4, research confirms the superiority of transitional programs compared to English-only programs.)

2.28: Research indicates that private speech increases when tasks are difficult or children are confused. Your children's muttering may suggest that they're having a difficult time with the problems. Also, you might infer that the children who are muttering are working harder on the problems than those who aren't muttering, since research indicates that children who use private speech are more attentive and goal oriented than those who don't use it. You would be less likely to hear audible private speech from 6th graders, since it generally becomes internalized by the time children are about 9 years old (fourth grade).

2.29: You're in the zone. You can function effectively with help but can't yet work on your own. Presumably with some additional assistance you will soon move beyond the zone, which is where your friend already is.

2:30: The father assessed his daughter's abilities as he watched her try to take steps. This was a form of *dynamic assessment* since it occurred in the context of the activity (her attempts to walk). He adapted the learning task to his daughter's developmental level by requiring that she be able to walk with support rather than totally on her own. The support he provided was holding her hand (a form of scaffolding) as she attempted to walk. She was in the zone, since she was able to walk with her father's support.

2.31: Scaffolding is support learners receive that allows them to make progress *on their own*. If explaining allows learners to make progress on their own, it is a form of scaffolding. However, if a teacher explains a problem, but the learner hasn't improved in his problem solving ability, the explaining is ineffective and is not a form of scaffolding. A teacher doing a problem for a student is not a form of scaffolding unless the teacher models thinking as she does the problem. The key characteristic of scaffolding is that it helps learners make progress *on their own*.

2.32: Vygotsky's work, through developing shared understanding, providing scaffolding and guiding social interaction, suggests a more prominent role for teachers than does Piaget's.

2.33: Guided discovery would be an approach that would be consistent with constructivism. It suggests providing students with experiences and then "guiding" them as they develop (construct) their understanding of the ideas you're teaching.

Lecture as an approach would be inconsistent with constructivism. Lecture puts learners in a passive role and makes no provision for guiding the development of understanding or providing scaffolding.

2.34: Social cognitive theory provides the better explanation. The bilingual child hears both languages modeled and imitates them. Parents are unlikely to systematically reinforce both languages, which would be a behaviorist explanation for children learning both languages.

2.35: A behaviorist explanation would require that the child demonstrates a form of language and is then reinforced for demonstrating it. Behaviorism can offer no explanation for a child's ability to produce language they've never heard before.

Similarly, social cognitive theory suggests that learners imitate language they've heard from others. Again, they cannot explain children's ability to produce language they've never heard before.

2.36: The key elements of Vygotsky's view of language development, which is constructivist, are *active practice* and *the zone of proximal development*. Vygotsky would suggest that children literally learn to use language by actively practicing it as they interact with adults and peers. In contrast, behaviorism views learners as passive, responding to the environment in the form of reinforcers. Of behaviorism, social cognitive theory, and psycholinguistic theories, social cognitive theory is the most closely related to constructivism in that it suggests that learners imitate language they hear in others, which can be viewed as a form of practice. Constructivism makes no assumptions about innate abilities as does Chomsky's (psycholinguistic) view.

None of the other views provide a role in development that is implied with the concept of scaffolding. Scaffolding suggests that learners gradually learn to use more sophisticated language because of active practice and support. Again, since modeling is (or can be) a form of scaffolding, constructivism and social cognitive theory are the most closely related.

2.37:   A child calling all men "Daddy" would be an example of overgeneralization. Children typically learn to discriminate through simple experience, but providing feedback ("No, that's not Daddy. It's just another man.") can accelerate the process.

2.38:   Chomsky's position best explains why virtually all children learn a language. Environmental theories, such as social cognitive theory, constructivism, and even behaviorism, can all explain why some children have better language backgrounds than others.

Exercise 2.1

For Items 1-4, explain the individual's behavior by using the following concepts: *accommodation, adaptation, assimilation, development, equilibrium,* and *scheme.* The person you focus on is the one whose name is *italicized.* In each case, use as many of the concepts as necessary to form a full and complete explanation.

1. Mrs. Andre's class has completed a unit on the multiplication of fractions and is now working on division. *Tim,* when faced with the problem

    $2/3 \div 1/3 = $, gets 2/9 as an answer.

2. *Celena* commented to her friend Jane in the teachers' lounge one morning, "Susan really puzzles me. You never know how to take her. One day she's your best friend, and the next she barely squeaks out a hello."

3. *Kathy's* English class has been assigned to write a paper making a persuasive argument. "I was initially confused, but I think I know how to do it now," she commented to her dad, who was helping her with it. "It's like making and defending a position, except you have to include a suggestion or a plan of action."

4. "*Malivai's* spelling has improved dramatically since the beginning of the year," Mrs. Stone enthusiastically told Dan's mother in a conference in May. "At first he approached spelling as if every new word was completely new. Then he started seeing patterns in the words and his spelling performance took a jump."

5. Karin Dunlop is a ninth-grade English teacher. She knew that students take the PSAT (Preliminary Scholastic Aptitude Test) as tenth graders, and she wanted to prepare them as well as possible, so she did extensive work with antonyms and analogies. She gave her students the following words with brief definitions.
    relic--keepsake
    ordain--officially appoint
    acuteness--sharpness
    dawdle--waste time
    superfluous--more than needed
    She directed students to learn the words, and the next day she gave them an exercise involving antonyms for the words in the left column. Even through students vigorously claimed that they had studied the words carefully, the results were disappointing.

    Using Piaget's work as a basis, provide a specific explanation for why the students did so poorly, and then specifically suggest what Karin might have done differently to get better results.

6. James Washington has been working with his fifth graders on a unit involving air and air pressure. He has discussed air and air pressure in detail, and the children read about it in their books. In a demonstration, he adds a cup of water to an empty ditto fluid can, heats the can to drive out some of the air inside, caps the can, and watches while the atmospheric pressure crushes the cooling can. To speed up the cooling, however, he pours cold water on the can. To his dismay, students suggest that the water crushed the can.

    Based on the research results discussed in this section, explain specifically why students would conclude what they did.

Exercise 2.2

Classify the behavior of the person whose name is *italicized* in the following examples into one of Piaget's four stages of development. Then explain your classification based on information from the example.

1.   Conchita Martinez is discussing the causes of World War I in her junior-high American history class. "It started with the assassination of the archduke," Brad suggested. "But," *Karen* added, "there was also a rising spirit of nationalism all over Europe at the time."

2.   *Cher* knows that the word *horse* represents horses.

3.   *Tim* is 5 minutes late for class and jokingly says, "I have minus 5 minutes to get there."

4.   *Susan* didn't understand the fulcrum of a simple lever until the teacher used a meterstick to pry up a stack of books.

5.   *Luis* is playing somewhat roughly with the family cat, and his mother, concerned that he might be scratched, puts the cat around the corner. Luis's attention quickly turns to something else.

6.   *Ann's* teacher is working on numbers in base 6. She shows the students bundles of six sticks and individual sticks. After a series of examples, she displays two bundles of six sticks each and three more sticks and asks the class to write the number in base 6 that represents the 15 sticks. Ann correctly responds with the numeral 23. She can't do this without the bundles of sticks.

Exercise 2.3

Read the following example and answer Items 1-4, which follow.

Delores Robles is trying to help her sixth grade students understand how to write narrative stories. They have read several narrative stories as a whole class and recently have broken into groups to identify the setting, characters, and plot in short stories. In addition students have started writing their own stories, sharing them with each other and getting feedback.

Jason, Dana, Elena, and David seem to be having trouble understanding the need to develop characters in any depth. The rest of the students don't appear to need help, and Delores allows them to go to a corner in the back of the room to work on their stories. To help those who need it, she shows them drafts from a previous year's class in which the development of the characters becomes clearer and more explicit in each subsequent draft. After having seen the examples Jason and Dana are able to write their own, but Elena and David still struggle and seem to be making little progress. Delores decides to read their drafts tonight before deciding what to do about tomorrow's class.

1.   Identify two aspects of the lesson in which Delores used social interaction to promote learning.

2.   Were most of Delores' students in the zone of proximal development--yes or no? Carefully explain why you think they were or were not.

3.   How did Delores use scaffolding to help her students understand character development?

4.   Identify at least two instances where the concept of dynamic assessment appeared in the case.

Use the following short case study to answer Items 5-7.

Kevin and Linda are working on a science activity in Mrs. Lake's class. "Magnets pick up iron, and other metal stuff," Kevin says. "See," and he demonstrates how a paper clip is attracted to a magnet.

"Oh, neat," Linda responds. "So, what do we write down ? . . . Magnets . . . pick . . . up . . . metals," she writes carefully on her paper.

Mrs. Lake, who has been watching their progress, comments briefly, "Maybe try this," as she points to the aluminum foil on the desk where they're working.

"Hey, it doesn't work," Linda responds, as she tries the magnet and aluminum foil.

"Uh huh," Kevin, who didn't notice Mrs. Lake's suggestion, argues. "Does too. . . . See?" and he shows how a metal spoon is attracted to the magnet.

"Nope, . . . look," Linda retorts. "Look, it doesn't work on this (the aluminum foil), and she demonstrates for Kevin how the aluminum foil is not attracted to the magnet.

After several more minutes, Mrs. Lake calls for the students' attention. "What kinds of patterns did we find?" she asks.

The students volunteer their findings, the class discusses them in detail, and they summarize the results.

5.   Specifically identify the aspects of the activity that are consistent with implications for instruction that would be based on Piaget's theory.

6.   Specifically identify the aspects of the activity that are consistent with implications for instruction that would be based on Vygotsky's theory.

7.   What particular type of scaffolding did Mrs. Lake use with the children.

Exercise 2.4

Identify whether the following more emphasize Piaget's (cognitive constructivism) or more emphasize Vygotsky's (social constructivism) views of knowledge construction.

1.   A pre-school class has a sand table set up in which students can put sand into different shaped containers. Students are encouraged to experiment and measure with these containers.

2.   In a pre-school corner different costumes and outfits are available. Students are encouraged to put these on and pretend, creating mini skits with each other.

3.   A second-grade teacher places students into groups to create dioramas that depict ideas from their study of different Native American Indian tribes. As they work he encourages them to discuss the ideas behind the art.

4.   A fourth-grade teacher has developed a learning center on electricity. Students go to the center and pick up "Brain Teasers." These contain a box of batteries, wires and bulbs, and students are encouraged to experiment with them to find out how electricity works.

5.   A high school physical education teacher notices that some of her students are still having trouble learning how to score volleyball games. To help these students she pairs these students up with "experts" and has the pair score a videotaped game.

Exercise 2.5

In Items 1-3, identify the theory of language acquisition best illustrated by each.

1. "Me toy," says 2-year-old Tanya, holding out her hand.
    "Oh, Tanya wants the toy. Say, 'I want the toy.'"
    "Want toy," replies Tanya.
    "Good girl!"

2. An eager dad was playing with his daughter and working on her vocabulary. He had a small box of toy animals. As he held each one up, he asked, "What is it?"
    When the child responded correctly, he replied, "Good! . . . Now, here's another one. What is it?" When the response was incorrect, he'd say, "No, that's not a rhino. That's a hippo. You say it."

3. Mom was walking through the park with her 1 year old on her back. People looked at her a little strangely as she carried on the following monologue: "Look at the dog. What a funny-looking dog. Look at his legs. They're so short.
    "Oh, there's some water ahead. It looks like a pond. See the ducks swimming in the pond. The one with the green head is the daddy. Should we go feel the water?"
    The child listened with wide-eyed detachment.

Read the following sentences/phrases, and classify them as reflecting early (E) (0-2) or later stages (L) (beyond 2) in language development. Explain why in each case.

4. He was there.

5. Was he there?

6. The boy brought the toy because he thought he would be bored.

7. Me go.

8. The car that was skidding slid off the icy road.

Feedback for Application Exercises_____

Exercise 2.1

1. Andre has a "multiplying fractions" *scheme*. Rather than *adapting* by *accommodating* the scheme to allow the formation of a division of fractions scheme, he *assimilated* (incorrectly) the problem into his already existing scheme, which allowed him to remain at *equilibrium*.

2. Susan's unpredictable behavior disrupts Celena's *equilibrium*, which makes her uneasy and uncomfortable. Celena's "Susan *scheme*" does not allow her to understand or predict Susan's behavior.

3. Kathy is demonstrating *adaptation* through the process of *accommodation*. She has a "making and defending a position" *scheme*, and she now is accommodating the scheme to form a "persuasive argument" scheme. Her writing is *developing* as a result.

4. This example illustrates year-long *development*, and as a result, Malavai now has *schemes* that he didn't have earlier.

5. The words were presented only in the abstract, so the students merely memorized the brief definitions. As a result they performed poorly on the antonym exercise, which is a form of application. Karin needed to develop the words beginning with concrete experiences, much as Carol Barnhart had done earlier in the chapter.

6. While James has discussed air and air pressure with the students and has also had them read about it, there is no indication in the example that James has provided any concrete experiences for the children. As a result, they remain dominated by their perception, and perceptually they see water pouring on the can and the can collapsing. Given the students' limited experience, their conclusion is not surprising.

Exercise 2.2

1. Karen is demonstrating formal operational behavior. She is able to simultaneously consider two variables. Further, she appears to deal comfortably with abstract concepts, such as nationalism. It is important to note that merely because she is at least 12–13, and therefore chronologically fits the stage of formal operations, doesn't mean that her thinking is necessarily formal operational. Without prerequisite experience learners' thinking might be concrete operational at best.

2. Cher is displaying preoperational characteristics. Knowing that the word *horse* represents the category horses is a form of symbolic thought.

3. Tim is indicating formal operational thinking. He is applying an abstract concept (negative numbers) in an even more abstract way by referring to "negative time."

4. Susan is displaying concrete operational thinking. She could handle the concept of fulcrum when shown the concrete materials.

5. Luis is demonstrating sensorimotor behavior. The example suggests he hasn't acquired the concept of object permanence.

6. Ann's thinking was concrete operational. She was able to perform a logical operation when she had concrete materials to manipulate.

Exercise 2.3

1. In addition to the social interaction that occurred in whole group activities, she broke students into groups twice. The first time they identified setting, characters, and plot; the second time they shared their stories with each other.

2. After the initial experiences, most of Delores's students were beyond the zone of proximal development; they were able to write their stories on their own. Jason and Dana were in the zone--they were able to move along with their work after having seen some additional examples. Elena and David were below the zone. In spite of the extra support, they were still unable to make much progress in their work.

3. Delores used scaffolding by providing examples of characters at different stages of development. The examples could be thought of as *prompts* or *models* that were designed to support the students in their efforts to write their own stories.

4. Dynamic assessment occurs when teachers use realistic tasks to gauge student understanding. One instance occurred when Delores gave students the developing draft examples to analyze. The second occurred when Delores planned to read their drafts before deciding what to do next.

5. The children are involved in a direct experience with the physical world. Also, according to Kevin's scheme for magnetic materials, all metals are attracted to magnets. Linda demonstrated that his scheme wasn't adequate, when she showed that the aluminum foil was not attracted to the magnet. According to Piaget, social interaction provides an avenue for allowing learners to test their schemes against the schemes of others.

You might note that--other than providing the materials and creating the environment--Piaget's theory doesn't actually provide a role for the teacher in the process.

6. Three aspects of Vygotsky's view of development are demonstrated in the activity. First, the children were faced with the problem of finding out what kinds of materials are attracted to magnets. Second, the students were involved in a discussion of what was happening. According to Vygotsky, discussions of this type are critical for learning and development. Third, in contrast with Piaget, Vygotsky's theory provides an important role for the teacher. We saw in the activity that Mrs. Lake briefly intervened by suggesting that they try the aluminum foil. According to Vygotsky this role is critical in learners' development. In contrast, a strict application of Piaget's work would suggest that the students be allowed to "discover" on their own that the aluminum foil wasn't attracted to the magnet.

7. The particular form of scaffolding that Mrs. Lake provided was a simple *cue*; she merely suggested that they try the aluminum foil. She didn't, however, explain to the students that the aluminum foil is not attracted to the magnet; she let the students find this out on their own. Her brief intervention and the guidance she offered illustrated how scaffolding is different from traditional instruction.

Exercise 2.4

1. Cognitive constructivism. This typical Piagetian task is used to help students form conservation of volume.

2. Social constructivism. Note how the teacher encourages social interaction through the dialogues in the skits.

3. Social constructivism. The combination of group work and encouragement to discuss ideas promotes learning from a social constructivist perspective.

4. Cognitive constructivism. Cognitive constructivism suggests that teachers encourage students to tinker around with concrete manipulatives while they're learning. Note that no mention was made of social interaction.

5. Social constructivism. Working in pairs and discussing authentic, meaningful tasks are characteristics of teaching based on social constructivism.

Exercise 2.5

1. This parent was using social cognitive theory to teach language. She modeled the desired language ("Say, 'I want the toy',") and she reinforced Tanya for her reply. Behaviorism doesn't account for the importance of modeling.

2. This dad applied behavioral views of language acquisition to improve his daughter's vocabulary. When the child correctly identified an animal she was reinforced with praise. When the child was incorrect, she was corrected and provided with the correct answer.

3. Psycholinguists believe that children acquire language by being exposed to it in its varied forms. On page 58 of the text it says, "When children are exposed to language, this program [the language acquisition device] analyzes speech patterns for the rules of grammar . . . that govern a language." The results of this analysis can

explain why children have the ability to produce novel and unique sentences. Neither behaviorism nor social cognitive theory can explain this ability.

4. (E) This is an example of past irregular which usually occurs around the age of 2.

5. (E/L) The ability to ask questions (reordered sentences) usually occurs around age 3.

6. (L) This is a very complex sentence structure expressing cause and effect relationships. These usually appear around first grade.

7. (E) One and two utterances are the first stage of language acquisition.

8. (L) Embedded sentences (i.e., The car was skidding. The car slid off the road.) are usually found in pre-school and kindergarten children.

Self-Help Quiz_____

TRUE/FALSE QUESTIONS: Write T in the blank if the statement is true, and F if the statement is false.

_____ 1. Development and learning are coordinate concepts, both describing similar types of changes in a learner.

_____ 2. When a child modifies his idea of a football and a tennis ball so that both fit into his previously formed concept of "ball", this is an example of assimilation.

_____ 3. A major theme in Vygotsky's work is that children frequently use language to describe problem solving or goal-reaching steps to themselves, especially on difficult tasks.

_____ 4. Children pass through Piaget's stages of development in distinct steps, although some may skip a stage if they are intellectually mature.

_____ 5. Most junior high students typically have reached the stage of formal operations and are able to think and reason in the abstract.

MULTIPLE-CHOICE QUESTIONS: Circle the best response in each case.

6. A child is shown two sponges and identifies them as identical. One sponge is then cut up while the child watches so that it is now in twelve smaller pieces. When asked which has more sponge, the child says the amounts of sponge are the same. The concept best illustrated by the child's actions is:
- a. egocentrism.
- b. centration.
- c. transformation.
- d. conservation.

Mrs. Park has taught her students the process of subtracting one-digit from two-digit numbers without regrouping and is now teaching them subtraction with regrouping. Jimmy, a boy big for his age from an upper-income family, is having trouble with the process, however. When given the problems

64   32
-7 and -5   Jimmy gets 63 and 33 as results.

7. Of the following, the Piagetian concept most closely related to Jimmy's tendency is:
- a. accommodation.
- b. centration.
- c. reversibility.
- d. maturation.

8. Of the following the best explanation for why Jimmy got 63 and 33 as answers is:
- a. Jimmy is accommodating his subtraction without regrouping schema to the new problems.
- b. Jimmy's maturation isn't advanced enough to allow him to solve problems with regrouping.
- c. Jimmy is reversing the process from problems with regrouping to problems without regrouping.
- d. Jimmy remained at equilibrium by getting the results that he did.

9. You're teaching the concept of noun to your third-grade students. Using Piaget's theory as a basis for making your decision, the best example of the following to use in illustrating the concept would be:
- a. a soccer ball.
- b. a drawing of a house.
- c. a colored picture of an oak tree.
- d. a picture of a girl with the word "girl" written underneath it.

10. Mr. Kenna's chemistry students are having a difficult time understanding how a solid and a liquid can be at the same temperature when the material is the same (such as an ice cube turning to water). Mr. Kenna explains that it takes energy to change the "state" from solid to liquid without changing the temperature. This change in state is the result of changing the arrangement of the molecules from a solid to a liquid and it takes heat to do that. The kids still don't get it. Based on Piaget's work, which of the following is the best explanation for the students' difficulty?
   a. The students are not yet chronologically at the age of formal operations and this is a formal operational task.
   b. The students' maturation isn't to the point where they are ready to handle this topic.
   c. The students are among the 50% who don't reach the stage of formal operations.
   d. The students lack the concrete experiences needed to understand the ideas involved.

11. Of the following, the best solution to Mr. Kenna's problem according to Piaget would be to:
   a. describe the process of the change in molecular motion between a solid and a liquid in more detail, so they see the difference.
   b. show them a model illustrating the molecular motion of the substance in each state and the change in motion as it melts.
   c. melt a piece of ice in front of them and have them describe it as it melts.
   d. have them explain their ideas about melting (instead of describing the process for them).

12. Of the following four concepts the one conceptually least related to the other three in Piaget's theory is:
   a. accommodation.
   b. assimilation.
   c. schema.
   d. adaptation.

Jackie puts a pencil and ruler together because they are both straight.

13. The stage of development that this behavior best illustrates is:
   a. sensorimotor.
   b. preoperational.
   c. concrete operational.
   d. formal operational.

14. The characteristic Jackie is demonstrating is:
   a. identifying cause-effect relationships.
   b. grouping on the basis of a functional relationship.
   c. seriation of objects.
   d. grouping on the basis of a perceptual feature.

Use the following case study to help in answering Items 15-17.

Mrs. Wilson breaks her first graders into groups of three and gives each group 12 plastic cubes and a container the cubes will fit into (2 x 2 x 3). They identify the pieces as *cubes* and conclude that they're all the same size. She has them put the cubes into the container. They remove the cubes and she asks them how much space the cubes took up, and leads them to conclude "12 cubes." She asks them what they call the space, and when they're unable to say "Volume," she tells them they have a *volume* of "twelve cubes." To reinforce the idea, she then asks them what the *volumes* of their boxes are, and leads them to say "twelve cubes."

15. Based on this information and Piaget's work, which of the following is the best assessment of Mrs. Wilson's teaching of the concept *volume*?
   a. Her instruction was effective because the students had concrete illustrations for both *cube* and *volume*.
   b. Her instruction was effective because she reinforced the concept by having them say they had a volume of "twelve cubes."
   c. Her instruction was ineffective, because she should have used actual units (such as twelve cubic inches) instead of "twelve cubes."
   d. Her instruction was ineffective, because she shouldn't have *told* them they had an *volume* of twelve cubes.

16. Consider the students' understanding of *cube* compared to their understanding of *volume*. Which of the following is the most valid description of their understanding?
   a. Their understanding of *cube* and *volume* will be similar, since they saw concrete examples of each.
   b. Their understanding of *volume* will be more complete than their understanding of *cube*, since the lesson focused on volume.
   c. Their understanding of *volume* will be more complete than their understanding of *cube* since Mrs. Solomon reinforced the idea at the end.
   d. Their understanding of *cube* will be more complete than their understanding of *volume*, since *volume* requires concrete operations and *cube* doesn't.

17. The next day Mrs. Wilson has her students make a stack of blocks (2 x 2 x 3) and count the cubes, and she then has them make another one (1 x 2 x 6) by putting the blocks in two rows of 6, side by side. They again count the cubes. She then asks them if the two volumes are the same or if they are different. Based on Piaget's work, if the students' behaviors are typical for children their ages, which of the following is the most likely response?
   a. The students will conclude that the volumes are the same, since they can see 12 cubes in each case.
   b. The students will conclude that the volumes are the same since they actually counted the cubes.
   c. The students will conclude that the volumes are different, since their understanding of *volume* is likely to be incomplete.
   d. The students will conclude that the volumes are different, since they look different.

Use the following case study to answer Items 18 and 19.

The second-grade team at Crystal Lake Elementary school is trying to increase their second graders understanding of the need to pay attention.

Mr. Winthrop says to his students, "Now listen everyone. It is very important to pay attention, so that we can all learn more." He reminds the students about the need for attention every day.

Mrs. Grimley says to her students, "Attention is very important. Let's see what we mean by attention," and she had Mrs. Myers, a parent volunteer, talk to her while she kept her eyes focused on Mrs. Myers's face as Mrs. Myers talked. Mrs. Grimley then makes comments such as, "Jeanna is doing a very good job of paying attention," whenever she sees them demonstrating attentive behaviors.

Mr. Minchew has a rule that says, "Pay attention at all times when the teacher is talking." When students don't pay attention, he first reminds them, and after three infractions, they're isolated from the class.

Mrs. Patterson makes comments, such as, "David has been very attentive for this whole lesson. He has kept his eyes focused on the front of the room all the time while I've been talking. That's excellent," whenever she sees students who are particularly attentive.

18. Based on research, the teacher's approach likely to be *most* successful is:
    a. Mr. Winthrop.
    b. Mrs. Grimley.
    c. Mr. Minchew.
    d. Mrs. Patterson.

19. Based on research, the teacher's approach likely to be *least* successful is:
    a. Mr. Winthrop.
    b. Mrs. Grimley.
    c. Mr. Minchew.
    d. Mrs. Patterson.

Use the following information for Items 20-22.

Karen Skram, a third-grade teacher, is working with four of her students on solutions to word problems in math. She gives the students a problem, tells them to try it and watches their progress.

Tanya sits, stares at the problem, puts some numbers on the paper, but makes little progress. Karen sits with her, offers a suggestion, Tanya tries it, Karen offers another, Tanya tries again, and with a struggle Tanya gradually solves the problem.

Felice looks at the problem briefly, grumbles, "Mrs. Skram, I can't do this," writes a few things down on the paper after Karen responds, "Oh yes, I think you can. Give it a try," and murmurs that, "We must have to subtract, cuz they ask for how many more the girls had," and as Karen watches over her shoulder, Felice solves the problem.

Billy also grumbles that he can't solve the problem, Karen watches over his shoulder, she sees that he makes little progress, and she offers a suggestion. He tries it and soon solves the problem.

Leroy mumbles, "I don't see this problem," he stares at it for a few seconds, almost inaudibly mumbles again, "add these, . . . no, subtract, I think," as he scratches on his paper, and after a couple minutes he solves the problem.

20. Based on this information and Vygotsky's work, which of the following is the most valid conclusion?
    a. All the students are in the zone of proximal development.
    b. Tanya is in the zone of proximal development, but Felice, Billy, and Leroy are below the zone, since they said that they couldn't solve it.
    c. Tanya and Billy are in the zone, whereas Felice and Leroy are beyond the zone.
    d. All the students are beyond the zone, since they all ultimately were able to solve the problem.
    e. Felice, Billy, and Leroy are beyond the zone, but Tanya is below the zone, since she (Tanya) was only able to solve the problem with great difficulty.

21. The student(s) that demonstrated private speech was/were:
    a. Felice
    b. Felice and Leroy
    c. Felice and Billy
    d. Felice, Billy, and Leroy

22. The students that were provided *scaffolding* were:
    a. Tanya and Billy
    b. Felice and Leroy
    c. Tanya, Felice, and Leroy
    d. All the students were provided scaffolding, since Karen carefully monitored their progress.

23. Consider Piaget's and Vygotsky's views of knowledge construction. Of the following, the most valid conclusion is:
   a. Vygotsky emphasizes the role of social interaction in development, whereas social interaction is not important for Piaget.
   b. Vygotsky's view provides for the teacher a more prominent role in guiding learning than does Piaget's view.
   c. Piaget views learners as active, whereas Vygotsky views them as passive recipients of guidance through scaffolding.
   d. Language is critical in Vygotsky's view of development, whereas it is irrelevant in Piaget's view, since, according to Piaget, manipulation of concrete materials is the primary cause of development.

Self-Help Quiz Answers

1. f
2. t
3. t
4. f
5. f
6. d   Understanding that the "amount" stays the same regardless of the number of pieces is best described as conservation.
7. b   Jimmy is centering on the large and small numbers and is ignoring the fact that the small one is on top and the larger one is on the bottom. He subtracts the smaller from the larger regardless of their positions.
8. d   Subtracting the smaller from the larger number allowed Jimmy to remain at equilibrium.
9. a   The soccer ball is the most concrete example. Also, there would be no point in showing a picture of a girl when the class has several "real" girls in it.
10. d   When learners are unable to understand information, assuming they have the ability, lack of experience is usually the cause.
11. b   The model is the only one that actually *illustrates* the process. Melting the ice merely illustrates change of state and doesn't illustrate anything about the motion of the molecules.
12. c   Schema, assimilation and accommodation are types of adaptation.
13. b   Jackie is classifying on the basis of a perceptual feature, which is characteristic of preoperations.
14. d   Jackie is classifying on the basis of a perceptual feature.
15. a   The students had concrete illustrations of both the concept *cube* and the concept *volume*. Experiences with the physical world are important according to Piaget's theory. Piaget's theory doesn't call for using language to reinforce ideas (choice b), and Mrs. Wilson's instruction helped the students understand the *concept* volume regardless of whether or not she used conventional units (choice c). She merely supplied a *label* by saying the word "volume." They were able to understand the concept based on her instruction.
16. d   "Cube" is perceptual, i.e., learners can "see" the characteristics of cube. Understanding "the amount of space" something takes up goes beyond mere perception. (For example, a 5 year old will recognize a cube, whereas he or she is unlikely to have a clear concept of volume; in fact many children in elementary school have difficulty with the concept *volume*.)
17. d   The students are likely to base their understanding on their perceptions and conclude that the volumes are different.
18. b   Mrs. Grimley used a combination of modeling and positive reinforcement to help her students understand the need to pay attention.
19 c   Mr. Minchew didn't actually teach his students what paying attention means, and second-graders may not understand the concept of attention merely from stating it in a rule. Further, he used punishment when they were inattentive rather than reinforcing attentive behaviors.

20. c   Tanya and Billy were able to solve the problem with Karen's help. Felice and Leroy were able to solve it without Karen's assistance.

21. b   Felice murmurs, "We must have to subtract, cuz they ask for how many more the girls had," and Leroy mumbles, "I don't see this problem," he stares at it for a few seconds, almost inaudibly mumbles again, "add these, . . . no, subtract, I think." These are examples of private speech.

22. a   Karen made comments that helped Tanya and Billy solve the problems.

23. b   Vygotsky's view of development provides an important role for a teacher or more knowledgeable peer in promoting development.

CHAPTER 3: PERSONAL, SOCIAL, AND EMOTIONAL DEVELOPMENT

Chapter Outline

I. Erikson's theory of personal and social development
   A. Erikson's stages of psychosocial development
      1. Trust versus mistrust (Birth to 1 year)
      2. Autonomy versus shame and doubt (Ages 1 to 3)
      3. Initiative versus guilt (Ages 3 to 6)
         a. School and the development of initiative
      4. Industry versus inferiority (Ages 6 to 12)
      5. Identity versus confusion (Ages 12 to 18)
         a. Stages of identity development
         b. Helping adolescents grow
      6. Intimacy versus isolation (Young adulthood)
      7. Generativity versus stagnation (Middle adulthood)
      8. Integrity versus despair (Old age)
   B. Erikson's work: A further look

II. Self-concept: Integrative personal development
   A. Self-concept and self-esteem
   B. Sources of self-concept
   C. Self-concept and achievement
      1. Academic self-concept
         a. Subject-matter specificity
      2. Improving learner self-concept
      3. Self-concept: Instructional implications
   D. Ethnic pride: Promoting positive self-esteem and ethnic identity
      1. Self-esteem and ethnicity
      2. Ethnic pride and identity formation

III. Development of morality, social responsibility, and self-control
   A. Increased interest in moral education and development
   B. Piaget's description of moral development
   C. Kohlberg's theory of moral development
      1. Level I: Preconventional ethics
         a. Stage 1: Punishment-obedience
         b. Stage 2: Market exchange
      2. Level II: Conventional ethics
         a. Stage 3: Interpersonal harmony
         b. Stage 4: Law and order
      3. Level III: Postconventional ethics
         a. Stage 5: Social contract
         b. Stage 6: Universal principles
      4. Putting Kohlberg's theory into perspective
         a. Research on Kohlberg's work
         b. Criticisms of Kohlberg's work
         c. Gender differences: The morality of caring
   D. The moral education versus character education debate
   E. Moral development and classroom structure
      1. Promoting moral development through peer interaction
      2. Moral framework of schools

Chapter Objectives

- Explain the implications that Erikson's theory has for teaching.

- Explain the relationship between self-concept and academic achievement and what teachers can do to influence each.

- Describe similarities and differences between Piaget's and Kohlberg's theories of moral development.

- Identify different stages of moral reasoning and how they apply to classroom practice.

Chapter Overview

This chapter examines the process of development from three perspectives--personal, social, and emotional--and asks how schools can help children develop in healthy ways. These different dimensions of development interact to help determine both student growth and learning.

Eric Erikson focused on students' psychosocial development. Like Piaget, he believed that development occurs in stages and that these stages influence how the individual interprets and interacts with the world. Unlike Piaget, Erikson's theory focuses on social and emotional development and describes how people use psychosocial challenges, which he called crises, to grow and develop.

The three major stages that students face during the school years are *initiative versus guilt, industry versus inferiority* and *identity versus confusion*. Teachers influence psychosocial development directly through their interactions with students and indirectly through the academic tasks they ask students to perform.

An important area of psychosocial development is a child's self-concept. Successful experiences with instructional tasks help build a healthy academic self-concept, which in turn has a positive influence on later achievement.

A second area of development examined in this chapter describes the growth of moral and ethical reasoning. Piaget's work in this area suggests that moral development relates to a shift from external to internal control. Kohlberg also studied moral development and described it in terms of orderly stages or steps in response to the environment. As children progress through these stages, they first think of right and wrong based on the consequences for them, later move to considering others, rules, and order, and finally progress to viewing ethics as a matter of social contracts.

The most effective ways to teach morals is controversial, and the controversy is demonstrated by the moral education versus the character education positions.

Feedback for Margin Questions

3.1: As opposed to differences in motivation, Piaget's stages reflect differences in the way learners process information, such as perceptually in the case of preoperational learners and logically (with concrete materials) in the case of concrete operational learners.

3.2: Motivation is an important part of *both* theories of development. In Erikson's theory learners are motivated to resolve the psychosocial challenge at each stage of development. According to Piaget, we have a need for cognitive equilibrium--a need for the world to make sense. When an individual's equilibrium is disrupted, he or she is motivated to reestablish it.

3.3:   Effective kindergarten teachers structure their classrooms to allow maximum opportunities for exploration. There would be different centers or locations where students can manipulate objects, try on clothes and costumes and build things. In addition, initiative is encouraged by providing all students with responsibilities that share in the care of the room, such as feeding the fish, watering plants, emptying wastebaskets, and many others.

3.4:   Competition, with its emphasis on winners and losers, is especially unhealthy in the early school curriculum. Students who consistently "lose" in a competitive environment, will learn that taking initiative goes unrewarded, which in turn detracts from a positive resolution of the initiative/guilt crisis. Instead, the curriculum should emphasize mastery of basic skills for all, as well as cooperation and group cohesiveness.

3.5:   Work that is too easy doesn't provide necessary challenge, which detracts from the development of perseverance and industry. On the other hand, constantly being faced with work that is too difficult can leave students with a sense of helplessness. This sense can lead to feelings of inferiority, which also detract from a positive resolution of the industry/inferiority crisis.

3.6:   Report cards at the elementary level often have an effort component next to the grade. This component is designed to provide parents and students with feedback about industry. Also, a section on work habits is often included, which gives additional information about industry. References to social comparisons would be missing.

3.7:   The answer to this question varies with the type of students. Academically-oriented students will be strongly influenced by the formal curriculum; for others, friends and extra-curricular activities are more powerful. Families strongly influence all students.

3.8:   In general, small towns and communities, in which role expectations are clear and career paths are better defined, provide easier paths to identity resolution. Whether these clearly defined paths are better for the individual in the long run is not clear, and many arguments both ways have been made.

3.9:   American youth have the luxury of extended school, postponing clear career decisions into late adolescence and the early twenties. At the turn of the century most teenagers worked. Now over half go on to college and many delay choosing a career path until after four years of college.

         Young people from most other countries are directed into clearly defined career paths at an earlier age than are American students. This has advantages and disadvantages. Young people from other countries face less uncertainty than do American students, but they also are left with fewer choices.

3.10:   Schools are probably most successful at developing industry--at least for students who do well academically. To help develop initiative, teachers can recognize, encourage and reward students for going beyond basic requirements. Teachers can help students develop a sense of industry by ensuring an adequate level of success on challenging tasks. This is obviously demanding, but it is important to the development of industry. Teachers can help with identity development by relating the topics they teach to issues in the real world. Also, class discussions are effective methods for helping students develop views about themselves and their relationship to the world.

3.11:   Based on Erikson's work, we would conclude that he hasn't successfully resolved the initiative/guilt crisis. The quality of his work is adequate, and he seems well adjusted, so his problem doesn't appear to be with a sense of industry or identity. Erikson's work would suggest that he simply has a personality "glitch" with respect to initiative. It may never have a significant effect on his personal functioning unless he finds himself in a job in which initiative is needed and valued.

3.12:   Self concepts are people's perceptions about their physical, social, and academic competence. (Self-esteem is an emotional or affective reaction to the self. It is related but not identical to self-concept.) For example, a skilled athlete would have a positive physical self-concept; a person who relates well to others would develop a positive social self-concept; and a high achiever would develop a positive academic self-concept. Our contacts with the world are powerful forces in shaping these different self-concepts. Schools, family, and peers all play a role in the development of self-concept.

The way self concept is formed and its importance in schools is misunderstood and misrepresented. The following quote from Pintrich and Schunk (1996) illustrates this point.

> For example, on many TV talk shows or in many popular self-help books, high self-esteem is offered as the major panacea for all individual problems. The basic argument is that poor or low self-esteem is the root of all problems, whether they be child abuse, spouse abuse, substance abuse, weight or body image problems, marital infidelity, delinquency, personal unemployment, criminality, learning problems or just personal unhappiness and depression. Given this assumption, it then follows that increasing self-esteem will result in the remediation of these problems. . . . This logic leads people to believe that they will avoid these problems by rehearsing simple positive statements about the self (i.e., I'm a good person). Of course, any view this simplistic is absurd in the face of the complexity of these problems.
>
> The difficulty is that in U.S. schools today, many teachers do subscribe to this simplistic view. There are schools and classrooms that engage in self-esteem programs whereby children are asked to chant positive statements about themselves in order to enhance self-esteem (pp. 312-313).

Self esteem is much too complex to be enhanced by programs that simply have children chant, "I am a good person," over and over.

3.13:   While formal classroom activities can enhance both social and physical self-concepts to a certain extent, they are probably most strongly influenced by extra-curricular activities. This suggests that the total school program should include a rich menu of these activities. Further evidence for this point exists in studies of at-risk students. At-risk students tend to have low self-esteem, and they also tend to have a lower rate of participation in extracurricular activities than do their peers who are not at risk. (You will study at-risk students in detail in Chapter 4.)

3.14:   Any learning activity that provides students with feedback about their competence provides data that students use in the formation of self-concept. The teacher can influence these sources by stressing the relationship between effort and achievement, emphasizing and providing evidence of improvement, deemphasizing competition, by designing activities that provide success and moderate challenge, and by building classrooms where all students feel that they belong and are accepted.

3.15:   The strongest effect is the influence of achievement on improving self-concept. Efforts to improve achievement by first improving self-concept are largely unsuccessful. However, students with healthy self-concepts are sometimes more motivated than their peers with lower self-concepts, which means that they may work harder, and as a result achieve higher. The formation of self-concept is complex and results from both home and school factors. Schools can promote heathy self-concepts primarily by accepting and welcoming students and helping them achieve success on challenging tasks.

3.16:   Grades are an important influence on academic self-concept, especially for older children. They have less influence on social and physical self-concepts. Teachers can use grades constructively by having them reflect improvement and mastery of topics rather than performance compared to other students.

3.17:   A somewhat similar relationship exists between achievement and self-esteem. High-achieving learners tend to have higher self-esteem than do low-achieving learners. However, if a learner doesn't value achievement, the relationship between achievement and self-esteem is less strong. The relationship between achievement and self-concept is stronger than the relationship between achievement and self-esteem.

3:18:   Children used data from television, radio, movies and other forms of media along with their personal interactions in their neighborhoods in forming their ethnic evaluations. When certain ethnic groups are portrayed stereotypically and negatively, these evaluations suffer. As with the process of forming personal self-concepts, evaluations result from the child's interactions with the world.

3.19:   Positive ethnic role models can help students see that independence does not necessarily mean rejection of their family and culture. In addition, they can help teenagers understand how their membership in an ethnic group relates to positive social development and the choice of a career. Finally, they can help teenagers develop a healthy balance between their own personal needs and the need to belong to a group.

3.20:   The advantage in avoiding ethical issues is that controversy is avoided. However, moral and ethical issues are impossible to avoid in schools. For example, virtually all schools encourage fairness and respect for others. When they do, they're teaching values; they're taking a moral position. The more valid position is to acknowledge that schools cannot be value free and then deal with values openly and honestly. Highly charged and controversial issues should be acknowledged as such. For instance, if the issue of abortion came up in a class discussion, teachers can acknowledge that it is highly controversial, has both religious and political overtones, perhaps identify some of the points on each side of the issue, and leave it at that. Taking a position one way or another on an issue of that magnitude would be unwise (politically if for no other reason).

3.21:   In the stage of *external morality*, rules exist outside the individual and receive their legitimacy from their being enforced by others. An egocentric child would view the rules as the same for everyone and would not think of them varying by person or situation. An egocentric learner has difficulty with *autonomous morality*, because it requires an understanding of morality as a reciprocal process of treating others as we would want to be treated and a willingness to look at the world from others' points of view. Flexibility, modeling, and discussion of moral issues, when they arise, help students progress from one stage to the next.

3.22:   Some possibilities are dating ethics, dilemmas with friends and friendships, and honesty with parents. An increasingly prominent dilemma for schools is the issue of ability grouping. Advocates for high achievers argue that their learning is retarded when they are placed with low achievers, whereas advocates for low achievers argue that ability grouping is discriminatory, short-changing opportunities for these students. (You will examine the issue of ability grouping in detail in Chapter 4.) Cheating is another moral dilemma facing students in schools.

3.23:   Authoritarian classrooms, where teachers rigidly enforce adherence to rules encourage students to think about rules as absolute and dependent upon external authority for their legitimacy. Teachers can promote development to the next level by explaining the reasons for rules and emphasizing their impact on the rights and feeling of others.

3.24:   A driver reasoning at Stage 3 would be likely to say that everybody else is going 65, so it's okay for me to do the same. At Stage 4 a person would be more likely to say that the law says 55, so I'm slowing down. I don't care what everyone else is doing.

3.25: People at this stage would say that to live in this country we have agreed to pay taxes in order to maintain the greatest good for the greatest number of people; paying taxes is a social contract. People reasoning at this stage would say that not paying taxes violates this agreement.

3.26: Both theorists suggest that development proceeds in stages, that development is continuous and unique to individuals, that development is gradual and depends on experiences, and that once a level or stage is attained the individual rarely regresses to a lower stage. Both focus on individuals' reasoning.

3.27: Gilligan's work would suggest that a woman would be more likely than a man to interpret this incident from an interpersonal perspective. For example, a woman might reason that whispering is justified because they're helping Gary out, whereas a man might be more likely to reason that the assignment was given, and Gary, as with everyone else, should know it. According to Gilligan, the major difference between women and men involves the relative emphasis placed on caring and social problem solving (for women) versus abstract justice (for men).

3.28: Teachers reasoning at higher levels would be more likely to view classroom rules as social contracts designed to make classroom life fair for all. Involving students in the process helps students think about these rules, understand why they are necessary, and agree on principle to follow them.

3.29: The conventional level of moral reasoning would require concrete operations. According to Piaget, concrete operations includes overcoming preoperational egocentricity, which allows learners to consider the perspectives of others. The postconventional level would require formal operations. Since postconventional reasoning is based on principles, which are abstract ideas, the ability to reason in the abstract would be required before postconventional reasoning is possible.

3.30: While specific statements will vary, a possibility might include the following:

First, it is impossible to avoid dealing with some moral issues, such as cheating and appropriate treatment of others. Second, this position is similar to one which argues that schools should focus on academics and avoid other aspects of students' lives (such as psychosocial). This position ignores the child as a whole person and fails to promote development in these other important areas.

Application Exercises

Exercise 3.1

In Items 1 through 6, classify the person whose name is *italicized* into one of Erikson's eight stages of psychosocial development.

1. *Carmella* washes her hair every day. Her mother says she is going to wash it out of her head. "But, Mom," Carmella protests, "I'll look so gross if I don't wash it."

2. *Deon* is small for his age, and schoolwork isn't quite his "thing." He loves sports, though, and puts a lot of his energy into competition. He's the fastest runner in his grade. He pitches for his Little League team, even though he's a year younger than most of the other kids, and he set a team record by striking out 10 batters in one five-inning game.

3. "Guess what happened today?" Kathy's dad asked her mother as she walked in the door from work. He laughed. "*Kathy* scratched some stuff on some papers--she called them pictures--and glued them to the wall of her bedroom. It ruined the wallpaper."
   "Did you get after her?"
   "I thought about it, but then she said, 'Look at the pictures I made for you, Daddy.' That did it. I told her that the pictures were nice. We'll talk to her later and push the dresser in front of the marks."

4. *Mr. Thomas* raves to his wife about the present national administration's apparent lack of concern about the environment. "Those S.O.B.s are trying to ruin the parks," he yells. "If there isn't a policy change, there will be nothing left for our kids or anyone else's kids to see and enjoy when they grow up."

5. "Are you getting serious about Joyce?" *Tom* was asked. "I could be, but I'm not going to allow myself to," he answered. "I've been through two relationships that didn't work out, and I've hurt two people. I'm beginning to wonder about my ability to feel strongly about someone else. I was fascinated with Sheri's great looks, and it was nice having Jan chase me like that, but now I don't know what to think."

6. "Guess what I found under *Mike's* mattress," his mother said somewhat uneasily to her friend as they were jogging. "*Playboy* magazine opened to the centerfold."
   Her friend laughed. "Not to worry. He's a boy. He isn't even sure himself what he's feeling. Relax. He's normal," she said with an unconcerned wave of her hand.

7. *Emmitt* is an eighth-grader who can't seem to "get going." He never volunteers answers in class and does only the minimum required on homework assignments and projects. However, the work he turns in is always acceptable, and he has been an above-average student throughout his schooling. In other ways, he seems to be a typical, "normal" youngster for his age.
   Analyze the boy's behavior using Erikson's theory as a frame of reference. Then suggest what you might do to help change his behavior.

Exercise 3.2

Classify the following statements as indicating one of the following--*general self-concept, academic self-concept, social self-concept, physical self-concept,* or *subject-specific self-concept.* The example may indicate a positive self-concept or it may indicate a somewhat negative self-concept.

1. I hate it when I look in the mirror. I'm fat and my face has zits.

2. I guess I'm basically an OK person. I try my best, and it seems to work.

3. School is fine. I would like to have more friends though.

4. I do pretty well in school; I'm not the smartest kid there, but I'm not the dumbest either.

5. If I could only pass chemistry. I hate that subject and I just don't get it.

6. I wish I would start growing. I hate always being the shortest kid in the class.

7. I like school. I have to study, but when I do, I can do pretty well.

Exercise 3.3

Look at the following examples and classify each as illustrating either *external morality* or *autonomous morality*. Then classify the same statements as demonstrating *preconventional reasoning, conventional reasoning*, or *postconventional reasoning*.

Students found that a Coke machine could be "tricked" by hitting two selections at the same time to get a free drink. Three students responded as follows:

1. "I don't think it's right. What about the guy who runs this business? It's like stealing from him."

2. "I'm not taking one. We talked about this stuff in class, and we agreed that we should only take what we've earned."

3. "I'd take one, but what if somebody saw us and reported us to the office?"

Middle school students are standing around the playground talking about a new student who has a speech impairment. Some of the students have been making fun of his speech. The following are some student comments:

4. "Hey, quit that. How would you feel if that was you?"

5. "If Mrs. Janek finds out, they're gonna be in big trouble. She wants us to be nice to each other."

6. "What about Mrs. Janek's rule that she keeps reminding us about? She's always saying, 'Treat each other with respect'."

Exercise 3.4

For the following items, consider each of the stated reasons for not using drugs. Classify each description into one of Kohlberg's first five stages.

1. If I'm caught using drugs, my reputation will be ruined.

2. If everyone used drugs, our society would disintegrate.

3. It's expensive, and I don't get that much out of it.

4. If I get caught, I could go to jail.

5. If my parents found out I used drugs, they would be crushed.

6. My dad drinks, and alcohol is a drug, so who are they to tell me not to use them.

7. If my parents knew I used drugs, I'd be grounded.

8. Freedom to choose is critical, and drug use results in the loss of that freedom.

Feedback for Application Exercises

Exercise 3.1

1. Carmella is in the identity-confusion stage. Her concern for her appearance and what others think of her is typical of this stage.

2. Deon is in the industry-inferiority stage. While he isn't a strong student, he is developing a sense of accomplishment and competence through his success in sports, and through them should positively resolve the crisis.

3. Kathy is in the initiative-guilt stage of development. She is past doing things on her own and has taken the initiative to make the pictures for her father. Her parents supportive attitude in the face of a potentially aggravating experience should help her positively resolve the crisis.

4. Mr. Thomas is in the generativity-stagnation stage. His concern for the next generation is an indicator of a positive resolution of the stage.

5. Tom is in the intimacy-isolation stage. His superficial relationships and his inability to feel strongly about someone indicates that he is having difficulty with the crisis, which at this point is not being positively resolved.

6. Mike is in the identity-confusion stage. He is experiencing the normal feelings of an adolescent boy beginning his search for identity as he moves toward manhood.

7. The case study indicates that Emmitt has a problem with initiative indicating that he didn't fully resolve the initiative-guilt crisis, which in turn left him with this problem. On the other hand, he appears to be resolving the identity-confusion crisis acceptably as indicated by him being a typical "normal" youngster for his age. The best the teacher can do is to provide him with opportunities to take initiative and then strongly reward any activities that result. Also, make it a point to encourage initiative in all his work and then be careful not to penalize him in any way for taking it.

Exercise 3.2

1. This example refers to physical self-concept. Students in the middle, junior high, and high schools are often preoccupied with their looks.

2. This is a case of general self-concept. This statement suggests general satisfaction with who she is.

3. This example refers to social self-concept. Wanting friends suggests concerns in this area.

4. This example illustrates academic self-concept. Concerns about school work in general reflects academic self-concept.

5. This example refers to subject-specific self-concept. The individual has a poor self-concept with respect to chemistry.

6. This is an instance illustrating physical self-concept. This is a common concern of late-developing adolescent boys.

7. This refers to academic self-concept. Studying and doing well suggest an academic orientation.

Exercise 3.3

1. Piaget would describe this as illustrating *autonomous morality*. Autonomous morality views justice as a reciprocal process of treating others as they would want to be treated.

Kohlberg would describe this as *conventional ethics*. The student is expressing views based on concern for the owner of the Coke machine.

2. *Autonomous morality*. The student is demonstrating a rational idea of fairness and is relying on himself to make the decision.

Postconventional ethics. The statement, "We talked about this stuff in class, and we agreed that we should only take what we've earned," suggests that the student views 'taking only what we've earned' as a social contract.

3. *External morality*. External morality views rules as fixed and enforced by others.

Preconventional ethics. Concerns about being reported to the office reflects thinking that emphasizes consequences to the individual.

4. Piaget would describe this as illustrating *autonomous morality*. Autonomous morality sees justice as a reciprocal process of treating others as they would want to be treated.

Kohlberg would describe this as *conventional ethics*. The student is expressing views based on concern for the feelings of the student being taunted.

5. *External morality*. External morality views rules as fixed and enforced by others.

Preconventional ethics. Concerns about being reported to Mrs. Janek reflects thinking that emphasizes consequences to the individual.

6. *External morality*. External morality focuses on rules.

Conventional ethics. Conventional ethics is based upon concern for others and adherence to rules.

Exercise 3.4

1. *Stage 3*. The focus is on the individual's reputation, or the opinion of others. Although there is an element of the self involved, since it is his or her reputation, the primary focus is on others, making it Conventional Ethics.

2. *Stage 4*. The concern is for the general orderliness of society.

3. *Stage 2*. The focus here is on the self. The individual is not getting in return what the cost requires. No concern for others or principled ethics is indicated in the example.

4. *Stage 1*. The concern is strictly related to punishment.

5. *Stage 3*. The person's concern is for the feelings of family.

6. *Stage 3*. This example isn't as obvious as the others, but the individual is basing the decision on the ethical example of others. There is no evidence of fear of punishment, and no exchange, as in Stage 2, is implied.

7. *Stage 1*. Grounding is a form of punishment.

8. *Stage 5*. A principle is being stated. It could be argued that the statement exists in the form of a general principle, and is therefore more appropriately Stage 6, but as indicated in the text of the chapter, the description of Stage 6 isn't completely clear. Further, in Kohlberg's early work, he suggested that Stage 6 was a "universal" principle. It could be argued that all principles are grounded in specific cultures, such as the *preeminence of the individual* which is grounded in western culture.

TRUE/FALSE QUESTIONS: Write T in the blank if the statement is true, and F if the statement is false.

_____ 1.   Teachers can help children overcome severe obstacles later in life by challenging them and giving them opportunities in which they can succeed in the elementary grades.

_____ 2.   The industry versus inferiority stage of psychosocial development is characterized by exploration of personal, social, sexual, and occupational identity and a preoccupation with peer approval.

_____ 3.   According to Kohlberg, an effective way to teach moral behavior is to explain ethical laws and principles.

_____ 4.   One criticism of Kohlberg's work on moral development is that moral behavior cannot be predicted from his descriptions.

_____ 5.   Self-concept tends to be a general characteristic. If people "feel good about themselves" in one area, they tend to feel good about themselves in most other areas as well.

MULTIPLE-CHOICE QUESTIONS: Circle the best response in each case.

6. Erikson's work is based on which of the following ideas?
   a.   People from different cultures have different basic needs.
   b.   A person must resolve the crisis at each stage of psychosocial development in order to move to the next stage of psychosocial development.
   c.   Movement from one stage of psychosocial development to another is characterized by a change in individuals' motivations.
   d.   A crisis is a point in a person's psychosocial development that is characterized by a loss of personal identity.

7. The psychosocial stage of development characterized by the tendency to seek cognitive growth and to explore all areas of life is best described as:
   a.   autonomy versus shame and doubt.
   b.   initiative versus guilt.
   c.   industry versus inferiority.
   d.   identity versus confusion.

8. Which of the following best describes people who fail to successfully resolve the psychosocial challenge of identity/confusion?
   a.   Adolescents who feel competent to overcome questions about who they are.
   b.   Teenagers who are doomed to a period of distress and uncertainty.
   c.   Individuals who retain behavioral traits characteristic of adolescence later in life.
   d.   People who have a basic sense of trust, can function on their own, and can take initiative.

Ron, 24, is in a conversation with his fiance, Kathy. "What are you doing?" Kathy queries.
   "I want to give the boss a call to see what he thinks of this."
   "It bothers me when you do that all the time," Kathy responds. "You're so capable. Why do you want him looking over your shoulder all the time? It hurts me to see you operate like this."
   "Don't worry about it, Kat. I know what kind of a guy I am and how I operate best. And, it seems to be working. My last raise was a good one."

9. Based on Erikson's work and the information in the case study, which of the following would Kathy conclude Ron has *least* well resolved?
   a. Trust vs. distrust
   b. Autonomy vs. shame and doubt
   c. Industry vs. inferiority
   d. Identity vs. confusion

10. Based on the information in the case study, which crisis has Ron best resolved?
   a. Trust vs. distrust
   b. Autonomy vs. shame and doubt
   c. Industry vs. inferiority
   d. Identity vs. confusion

11. Mrs. Hanson is a teacher making an effort to apply Erikson's theory to classroom practice. Whenever the opportunity arises in a social studies lesson to discuss prominent figures and their accomplishments, she discusses them thoroughly in an effort to present them as models for the students. Based on this information, which of the following would be the best prediction of Mrs. Hanson's students' ages?
   a. 6
   b. 10
   c. 13
   d. 21

12. Cliff is very self accepting. He acknowledges his assets and limitations. He takes people at face value and in a reflective mood says, "Well, I've done pretty well. Anyway, I did my best, and that's all anyone can ask." Of the following, Cliff best fits which stage according to Erikson's theory?
   a. Identity vs. confusion
   b. Intimacy vs. isolation
   c. Generativity vs. stagnation
   d. Integrity vs. despair

13. If an individual decides not to do something because his father and his mother will be disappointed in him, he would best be described as reasoning at the:
   a. interpersonal harmony stage.
   b. law and order stage.
   c. social contract stage.
   d. universal principles stage.

14. One way to teach ethics and morals is for teachers to:
   a. give students opportunities to discuss moral dilemmas with each other which provides opportunities to hear other points of view.
   b. emphasize topics that involve values encouraged by the school and avoid those that don't.
   c. state explicit guidelines for school behavior and strictly enforce them.
   d. reinforce positive behaviors and punish negative ones.

15. We've heard of the moral ethic "Don't bite the hand that feeds you." This notion best fits which one of Kohlberg's Stages?
   a. 1
   b. 2
   c. 3
   d. 4

16. Joey tends to be a bit of a bully on the playground, shoving the smaller boys down and making them cry. You take him aside and say, "Joey, how do you think the other kids feel when you treat them like this?" with other related statements. Amazingly, this seems to help, and Joey's behavior has improved. In the absence of any other information, based on this anecdote, we would judge Joey's age to be no younger than which of the following?

    a.   4
    b.   8
    c.   13
    d.   16

In the following case study identify the stage of moral reasoning best illustrated by each of the numbered paragraphs.

    A group of people were sitting at a party discussing tax time with the same concerns people have at that time of the year.

    "I'm taking a trip this summer," Nick declared with a wry grin. "I plan to see my brother. He's a teacher too. We are really going to talk teaching. In fact my kids are going to talk teaching.

    "My trip is going to cost only 65% of what it would have," he finished with a sly look.

(17)   "You talk tough now," Judy replied seriously. "You won't be cute when you get audited."

(18)   "Well, my brother and I are very close emotionally, my folks are getting older, they'll be there, and they really want to see the kids," Nick responded.

(19)   "Shoot, I'd do it in a second," John added. "Besides, everyone does it, and no one would react to your little indiscretion."

(20)   "On the other hand," Frances responded pensively. "Nick is technically breaking the law."

    "Ahh, you're a lawyer," Betty responded with a tongue-in-cheek sneer.

(21)   "True," Frances responded, though not defensively. "Change the law and I'll go along with it. When we live in this country, we agree to pay our fair share of taxes. In effect, it amounts to an agreement to pay our fair share to make the system work."

    "It's a bad law," Sharon responded emotionally.

(22)   "Well, we can't just go around doing as we please," Tony added cautiously. "I mean what would the world be like if everyone thought like Sharon does. It would be chaos."

    "I'm sorry I brought it up," Nick said with a placating grin.

Four teachers were having coffee one day after school, and as their conversation went on, they began talking about the negative self-concepts of some of their disadvantaged students, particularly with respect to academic work. They then began to discuss the different ways that the students' academic self-concepts could be improved. As they were talking, Mrs. Ivanisevich commented, "I try to give my students some independence, and I let them help me decide on the learning activities that we're going to conduct."

    Mr. Lilyquist added, "I try to provide an environment where the students know I care for and trust them."

    Mr. Henderson continued, "I try to attack the problem formally. I have a series of activities in which we discuss how important it is to feel good about ourselves. The activities help the students to see that they're all worthwhile people and valuable to the world."

    Mrs. Gomez countered, "I think the primary thing is that the students accomplish something, so I try to be sure that they're successful on the learning activities we do. Then they feel good about what they've accomplished."

23. Based on research and these descriptions, the teacher *most* likely to be successful is:

    a.   Mrs. Ivanisevich.
    b.   Mr. Lilyquist.
    c.   Mr. Henderson.
    d.   Mrs. Gomez.

24. Based on research and these descriptions, the teacher *least* likely to be successful is:
   a. Mrs. Ivanisevich.
   b. Mr. Lilyquist.
   c. Mr. Henderson.
   d. Mrs. Gomez.

25. Jason, a capable student, loves animals and wants to work for the government in an environmental protection program. His parents, fearing that he wouldn't make much money in a career of that sort, pressure Jason into considering engineering. Jason acquiesces and enrolls in an engineering program at his state university.
   Of the following, Jason's decision best illustrates:
   a. Identity diffusion.
   b. Identity foreclosure.
   c. Identity moratorium.
   d. Identity achievement.

Self-Help Quiz Answers

1.	t	
2.	f	
3.	f	
4.	t	
5.	f	
6.	c	Each of Erikson's stages presents a psychosocial challenge to individuals, and individuals are motivated to meet the challenge, or in other words, resolve the crisis.
7.	b	During this stage children explore their environments looking for new challenges.
8.	c	Adolescence is a normal period of questioning and doubt; when this persists, it suggests a crisis hasn't been resolved.
9.	b	Kathy would suggest that Ron has not developed into an autonomous individual.
10.	d	Ron's comment, "I know what kind of a guy I am . . ." suggests that he has a clear sense of his identity. Admittedly, he commented that he got a good raise (choice c), but this is very indirect evidence of industry, and we have little other evidence about his sense of industry.
11.	c	Role models can provide powerful assistance in helping adolescents resolve the identity versus confusion crisis.
12.	d	People characterized as having integrity look back on their lives with few regrets.
13.	a	People at the interpersonal harmony stage are concerned with living up to the expectations of others.
14.	a	Discussion of dilemmas provides opportunities for students to compare their views with the views of others.
15.	b	At the market exchange stage people are concerned about reciprocity for their actions.
16.	c	Responding to concerns for others' feelings indicates that Joey is at the interpersonal harmony stage. This stage is part of conventional ethics, which is characteristic of 10-20 year olds.
17.		Concern about being audited is a form of being caught which suggests the *punishment obedience* stage.
18.		Living up to the expectations of parents suggests *interpersonal harmony*.
19.		Being caught up in majority opinion or behaving in a certain way because "everybody does it" is characteristic of *interpersonal harmony*.
20.		Emphasis on obeying laws and rules for their own sake is characteristic of a *law and order* orientation.
21.		Frances's comment, "In effect, it amounts to an agreement to pay our fair share to make the system work," describes a *social contract*.

22.   Tony's concern about chaos suggests a moral view describing the need for an orderly society, which is characteristic of the *law and order* stage.

23. d   Research suggests that ensuring success on meaningful tasks is the most effective way to influence self-concept.

24. c   Activities focusing on self-concept (or self-esteem) in the absence of genuine accomplishment are unlikely to be successful.

25. b   Identity foreclosure occurs when students adopt the ready-made decisions of others.

CHAPTER 4: LEARNER DIFFERENCES

Chapter Outline_____

I. Intelligence
   A. Intelligence: What does it mean?
   B. Measuring intelligence
   C. Intelligence: One trait or many?
      1. Guilford's structure of intellect
      2. Gardner's theory of multiple intelligence
         a. Gardner's theory: Educational applications
      3. Sternberg's triarchic theory of intelligence
         a. Processing components
         b. Contextual components: Intelligence and the environment
         c. Experiential components: Modifying intelligence through experience
         d. Educational implications of Sternberg's work
   D. Intelligence: Nature versus nurture
   E. Ability grouping
      1. Types of ability grouping
      2. Ability grouping: Research results
      3. Negative effects of grouping: Possible explanations
      4. Grouping: Implications for teachers
II. Socioeconomic status (SES)
   A. Influence of SES on learning
      1. Socioeconomic status, physical needs and experience
      2. Interaction patterns in the home
      3. Attitudes and values
   B. SES: Some cautions
III. Culture
   A. Ethnicity
   B. Culture and schooling
      1. Attitudes and values
      2. Cultural differences in adult-child interactions
      3. Classroom organization: Working with and against students' cultures
      4. School communication patterns: Cultural matches and mismatches
      5. Cultural matches with school learning
      6. Culture and learning: Deficit or difference?
   C. Culturally responsive teaching
      1. Accepting and valuing differences
      2. Accommodating different learning styles
      3. Building on students' cultural backgrounds
   D. Culture and language: English dialects
      1. English dialects: Research findings
      2. Dialects in the classroom: Implications for teachers
   E. Culture and language: English as a second language
      1. Types of bilingual programs
         a. Maintenance bilingual programs
         b. Transitional bilingual programs
         c. English as a second language (ESL) programs
      2. Evaluating bilingual programs

      3.   Teaching bilingual students
          a.   Awareness
          b.   Facilitating language and concept development

IV. Gender
    A.   Different Treatment of boys and girls
       1.   Societal and family influences
       2.   Different treatment in schools
          a.   Experiences in science and math
          a.   Gender stereotyping influences career decisions
    B.   Gender differences: Implications for teachers

V.   At-risk students
    A.   At-risk students: A definition
    B.   At-risk students: Promoting resilience
       1.   Effective schools for at-risk students
       2.   Effective teachers for at-risk students
       3.   Effective instruction for at-risk students: Structure and support
       4.   Effective instruction for at-risk students: The need for challenge

Chapter Objectives

- Explain how different views of intelligence influence your teaching.

- Define socioeconomic status and explain how it may affect school performance.

- Explain the role that culture and language play in school success.

- Describe the influence of gender on different aspects of school success.

- Describe ways that schools and classrooms can be adapted to meet the needs of at-risk students.

Chapter Overview

The students we teach differ in a number of important ways, each of which affects both their ability to learn and their ability to grow up happy and healthy. These individual differences also influence our effectiveness as teachers and impact the teaching strategies that we employ.

One of the most powerful of these differences lies in the area of general ability or intelligence, defined as *the ability to solve problems, reason abstractly* and *acquire knowledge*. A second is socioeconomic status (SES), which is a measure of a family's relative position in the community, determined by a combination of income, occupation and education level. Culture, or the combination of attitudes, values and beliefs, and ways of acting of different groups influences learning in a similar way. Ethnicity, an important part of culture, refers to a student's ancestry or national reference group. Members of an ethnic group share a common history, language, value system and set of customs and traditions. Gender differences also impact the effectiveness of our instruction. Though research suggests that boys and girls are quite similar in aptitude, it also reveals differences in how they are treated in school as well as the type of careers they pursue. Teachers can do much to minimize these differences by communicating high expectations for all students, by interacting with students equally, and by encouraging females to explore careers in math and science, areas often believed to be male domains.

At-risk students are in danger of failing to complete their education with the skills necessary to survive in a technological society. Resilient youth develop coping strategies that increase their likelihood of success in challenging environments. Parents and teachers promote resilience through nurturance and caring that help develop student self-esteem and feeling of self control.

Feedback for Margin Questions_____

4.1:   All learners come to school with existing schemes, based on their experiences. Building on students' cultural backgrounds takes advantage of and enhances their existing schemes in two ways. If existing schemes are capable of doing so, new information is assimilated into them. If they are not capable of assimilating new information, the schemes are adapted through the process of accommodation. In either case, the students' existing cultural backgrounds (their existing schemes) serve as the beginning point for development and learning.

4.2:   While the answer to this question is more opinion than fact, with the rapid changes that are occurring in our modern world, the capacity to *acquire knowledge*, or the *ability to learn*, is probably most important, because it influences our ability to adapt. While all three are very important, the ability to think and reason in the abstract is probably least important for most people, since thinking in the abstract is required less often than the ability to adapt or to solve problems. In a primitive nomadic culture, problem solving ability was probably most important, since these cultures were often faced with serious problems--many of them life threatening.

4.3:   Experience strongly influences the capacity to acquire knowledge, because it provides background to which new information can be related. For example, people study the topic *cognitive development* in educational psychology. Those who have experience with the topic will find it more meaningful than those who don't because they will have schemes for the terms *cognitive* and *development*. As a result of the topic being more meaningful, they will have the capacity to acquire more knowledge than a person who lacks the experience.

4.4:   Guilford viewed intelligence as having multiple traits.

4.5:   In fact, an intelligence test based on Guilford's model would have a large number of subtests--as many as 120--and each of these would be reported separately to students. This huge number would make intelligence testing and reporting very cumbersome.

4.6:   The typical school curriculum focuses most strongly on linguistic and logical-mathematical intelligence. Students who are involved in music get a chance to develop their musical intelligence and athletes have the opportunity to develop bodily-kinesthetic intelligence. Extracurricular activities in general help learners develop their interpersonal intelligence.

         More of the intelligences are dealt with at the elementary level and these are reflected in the report cards. One exception is spatial intelligence. Two that might need explaining are inter- and intrapersonal intelligence. These are reflected in items such as, "Works well with others," and "Demonstrates self control." Secondary schools are narrower in their emphasis, focusing primarily on linguistic and logical-mathematical intelligence.

4.7:   The metacomponent would probably act first and ask questions such as, "What do I know about cars?" and "Where can I find more information about them?" The knowledge acquisition component would regulate the intake of information and organize it in a meaningful way. The performance component would involve the actual data gathering and driving from dealer to dealer.

4.8:   Most would argue that schools emphasize students adapting to the school and curriculum, i.e., there is one "program" and students are expected to fit in. If possible, schools should place more emphasis on changing the environment to fit students' needs. This would better prepare students to be life-long learners. The least desirable goal is selecting out of the environment, but even this can be worthwhile if students learn from it. Examples might be changing a major or transferring to another school.

4.9:   Sternberg's theory stresses that intelligence is modified through experience. Similarly, Piaget's theory suggests that development strongly depends on experience. Both theories relate new to existing knowledge as patterns are created. An implication of both theories is that students should be placed into situations that give them the opportunities to relate new information to what they already know.

4.10:   Sternberg's processing components are most similar to Spearman's "g". The other two components attempt to explain how intelligence relates to the environment and how intelligence is modified by experience.

4.11:   The environments would need to include a great many more and better experiences than now exist for students, such as 1) trips to museums, factories, art galleries, zoos, and other places that advantaged learners often experience in family activities; 2) the opportunity to work with manipulatives; 3) the chance for students to conduct their own experiments; and 4) the amount of language experience children have, such as reading to children, talking with them, and giving them analogies to solve. In addition, students would need to be put into problem solving situations where they were required to solve real world problems. These attempts are based upon more recent views of intelligence, such as Sternberg's theory, which emphasize the role of experience, rather than more traditional ones.

4.12:   Guilford and Gardner would probably prefer within-class ability grouping. First, they would oppose between-class ability grouping because it typically groups students on the basis of verbal and math ability, which is a much narrower view of ability than Guilford and Gardner would prefer. Second, within-class ability grouping allows the teacher to observe all the characteristics of all the students, which would allow her to change the makeup of the groups when she felt it was appropriate.

4.13:   The primary reason for the lack of within-class grouping at the secondary level is the existence of tracks or between-class groups. Other possible factors include teachers' lack of training and large class sizes.

4.14:   Students finding themselves in low groups often view themselves in a negative light. One student described his experience in going from a heterogeneously grouped elementary school to a tracked junior high in this way:

> When you first go to junior-high school you do feel something inside--it's like an ego. You have been from elementary to junior high, you feel great inside. . . . You get this shirt that says Brown Junior High . . . and you are proud of that shirt. But then you go up there and the teacher says--"Well, so and so, you're in the basic section, you can't go with the other kids." The devil with the whole thing--you lose--something in you--like it goes out of you (Schafer & Olexa, 1971, pp. 62-63).

4.15:   Based on research that has examined ability grouping, the best advice would be to avoid ability grouping in science; the possible benefits to the high group do not outweigh the negative factors for the low group. Further, the content of elementary science is not so cumulative or hierarchical that ability grouping would be required. The advice would remain the same for the sixth grade.

4.16:   The children of poverty often come to school with some of their deficiency needs unmet, which leaves them less equipped to move on to growth needs.

4.17:   Cultural experiences and money in the bank can be compared in at least two ways. First, positive experiences and money both tend to accumulate. Second, experience makes new learning easier; in a sense, it behaves like interest on money. Cultural experiences and money in the bank differ, however, in that experiences are used as a basis for "constructing" understanding as we discussed in Chapter 2. There is no analogous process with money in the bank, which basically sits there passively.

4.18:   This finding can be explained from both a cognitive and an affective perspective. From a cognitive point of view, parents who have higher levels of education often provide better early language experiences for their children; they talk and read to their children more, and they use an enriched vocabulary. In addition they are more likely to provide stimulating early experiences, such as travel. From an affective or attitudinal perspective, parents who have succeeded in school will tend to have positive attitudes towards schools and will value learning. These attitudes and values are transmitted to their children. Walberg (1991) calls the combination of these factors the "curriculum of the home."

4.19:   Constructivists suggest that cultural experiences in the form of background knowledge strongly influence the new concepts we construct. As we will see when we study constructivism in Chapter 7, one of its characteristics is, "New learning depends on current understanding."

Culture is central to Vygotsky's theory of development; he describes development as a process of cultural transmission. Piaget, in contrast, views culture as a secondary factor, influencing the kinds of experiences we encounter.

4.20:   One indicator is the variety of foods we eat. Italian, Mexican, Chinese and Japanese restaurants are common in most American cities. Many middle to larger ones also have German, Greek, Indian, Korean, Vietnamese and several other ethnic restaurants. In the past, most ethnic groups in the United States originated in Europe and Africa; now they come from all over the world.

4.21:   Other examples of voluntary minorities include European immigrants at the turn of the century and Cuban immigrants who came to the United States after Castro took power in Cuba. An additional example of an involuntary minority might be the Chinese coolies who were brought here to work on the transcontinental railroads and who were forced by discrimination to live in "China Towns." Mexican Americans in the U.S. Southwest sometimes fall in between these two categories. Some were forced to become U.S. citizens by the annexation of large parts of the Southwest; others voluntarily came here seeking a new and better life.

4.22:   Minority role models are important to minority youth because they are living, positive examples that it is possible to succeed in mainstream America without losing an individual's cultural heritage. The idea of America as a "melting pot" has become antiquated. Immigrant groups have retained a certain amount of their native culture and have "accommodated without assimilating." The concept *accommodation without assimilation* and America as a *melting pot* are not consistent. The idea of melting pot has always been more a myth than a fact.

4.23:   One suggestion would be to teach *time* just as you would teach any other concept. This would include examples of how the concept is used differently in different cultures. In the process, characteristics of classroom time would be emphasized, such as being in school when school begins, noting that these characteristics are part of the school culture in which we work. In a different culture, such as the home culture of several of the students, time could and would be treated differently. While noting that the use of time is not more or less important in one culture compared to the another, the culture of the school requires adherence to the characteristics of time dominant in that school culture. This is a form of accommodation without assimilation.

   A second adjustment would be in modifying the level of classroom activity; minimize quiet activities in which the students sit passively, instead design learning activities that would allow all students to use their energies in productive ways.

4.24:   For many Native Americans competition is a foolish characteristic of white American society. For example, they would not be inclined to compete for turns to respond in class, instead withdrawing and remaining quiet. Withdrawal from participation would be an example of *cultural inversion*, since competing and participating are characteristic of white students.

4.25:   From this study we might infer that Chinese and Japanese parents place a higher value on schooling than do American parents. This conclusion obviously doesn't hold true for *all* members of these groups. This reminds us that we should exercise caution in inferring characteristics to different ethnic and cultural groups.

4.26:   Ogbu's concept of *cultural inversion* suggests that for some minorities school effort and achievement is a white American characteristic and to try hard at school is inappropriate for them because these are characteristic of white Americans. Lack of effort then results in falling farther and farther behind.

4.27:   From a cognitive perspective, learning about students' cultures gives us insight into the background experiences of our students, allowing us to use examples and relate ideas in ways that are meaningful to them. From an affective perspective, learning about students' cultures helps us understand our students' motivations and interests, which allow us to adjust our strategies to be more consistent with those motivations and interests.

4.28:   Behaviorism would explain the development of dialects by saying that children are reinforced by their parents and peers for speaking as they do. Social cognitive theory would suggest that dialects are learned by observing the speech patterns of models and imitating them.

4.29:   One disadvantage of the rejection-and-correction approach is that it pits the school and home cultures against each other, since this approach makes using the dialect unacceptable in school, whereas it remains acceptable at home. This is confusing for the child, since what is acceptable in one environment is "wrong" in another. The advantage of the rejection-and-correction approach is that it focuses on "Standard English" and attempts to provide positive and negative examples. The advantage of the complete acceptance approach is that it builds on the child's existing language base and minimizes home-school differences. The disadvantage is that it might not provide models who speak standard English, which can be a disadvantage for the learner in later schooling or in the workplace.

4.30:   Maintenance programs attempt to maintain equilibrium by continuing the child's first language. A bilingual teacher can help students assimilate aspects of the new language by helping learners identify similarities in the two languages. Differences in vocabulary, sounds, and sentence structure will be accommodated as the result of modifying existing schemes and forming new schemes.

4.31:   Maintenance and transitional programs are similar in that they both attempt to teach English. The primary difference is that maintenance programs attempt to retain the first language while transitional programs' main focus is on learning English. As world economies become more global, bilingualism will be increasingly valued, so maintenance programs would be preferable.

4.32:   An ESL program based on behaviorist principles would break instruction into discrete skills, acceptable performance of which would be reinforced. A program based on social cognitive theory would be based on various forms of modeling, which students would be encouraged to imitate.

4.33:   Successful bilingual programs offer instruction within the zone of proximal development, providing for acquisition of the new language. Unsuccessful programs offer instruction that is outside the zone, not allowing students to benefit from the teaching.

4.34:   The fact that Mattell thought that these phrases were unoffensive suggests one or both of two things: 1) for many groups in our country gender bias is not as offensive as in others, or 2) certain behaviors, or indicators, such as the phrase "Math class is tough," is not viewed as a form of gender bias. Gender equity experts argue that a great deal of gender bias is unconscious, and awareness that the bias exists in the first place is an important first step. When we teach, we will encounter broad ranges of views on proper gender roles and on gender issues, which will require sensitivity and awareness in our teaching.

4.35:   An extreme nature position would attribute all gender differences to genetic influences; an extreme nurture position would credit these differences to learning and experience alone. Interactionists would acknowledge the influence of both.

4.36:   The decline in gender-related differences is probably due to changes in our society as a whole, as well as increased awareness of gender stereotyping and the emphasis being placed on gender equity in the schools. With the emphasis being placed on gender equity, it would be sensible to predict a further reduction in the differences.

4.37:   As boys move into the junior-high years, they begin to mature physically. This maturation, coupled with a society that values initiative and competitiveness in boys, could account for the increases in male-initiated contacts.

4.38:   Teachers are products of the cultures in which they grew up, and they may be unable to distance themselves from the values and beliefs that permeate those cultures. For example, historically in our culture, aggressiveness has been valued in males and passivity and submissiveness has been valued in females. Seeing aggressive males and passive females would unconsciously be viewed as "normal." Also, classrooms are busy and complex, and teachers often act spontaneously and "automatically" rather than stopping to think about and reflect on what they are doing.

4.39:   Adolescence is a time when young girls are struggling to figure out "who they are" as young women. In the absence of female role models in science and math, young girls may conclude that these areas are not ones in which females can or should excel.

4.40:   Gender-related differences in math and science are probably wider with low SES students than they are with high SES students, because low SES students come from environments where more traditional roles for men and women are likely to be maintained and valued. This suggests that teachers of low SES students should make an extra effort to combat these tendencies, such as portraying women in nontraditional occupations like engineering.

4.41: At-risk children may come from homes where formal schooling isn't valued to the same degree that it is in families whose children are not at-risk. In addition, at-risk students often come to school with backgrounds that lack some of the experiences and "cultural capital" that increase the likelihood of school success. Figure 4.8 and Table 4.5 suggest modifications that can help increase success for these students.

4.42: In the early to middle part of the 20th century, schooling was seen as a luxury--not a necessity for people who would be working on farms and in factories. In the technological society of today, literacy, higher-order thinking, and problem solving are necessary for economic survival. Given the increasing emphasis on technology, at-risk students will probably be a bigger problem in the future.

4.43: Two of Gardner's intelligences stand out. One is interpersonal intelligence, or the ability to work with other people. The other is intra-personal intelligence, the ability to know and understand ourselves. In the chapter we saw that, "Resilient children have well-developed 'self-systems' including high self-esteem, and feelings that they are in control of their destinies. They are good at setting personal goals, and they have positive expectations for success and good interpersonal skills." These characteristics indicate high intra- and interpersonal intelligences.

4.44: Effective schools are places that communicate positive expectations for success and that create environments where learning can occur. This is especially important for students who may not have a consistent history of past school success.

4.45: Some of the common characteristics include high expectations and instructional support that focuses on student success. In addition, high-impact teachers add a human component; they show students they care by taking an individual interest in students' lives.

4.46: Greater structure and support, more frequent feedback, higher success rates, all focus on at-risk students' needs to experience success in schools. High expectations ensures that the success they experience will be on meaningful and worthwhile tasks. Success on trivial tasks does not lead to satisfaction and a sense of accomplishment. Success on challenging and worthwhile tasks can significantly increase learner motivation.

4.47: Answers to this question will vary. However, research indicates that the lack of challenge detracts from motivation and particularly from satisfaction with what has been learned. People usually feel dissatisfied, because no sense of accomplishment exists, and a sense of accomplishment is required for motivation and satisfaction with learning.

Application Exercises

Exercise 4.1

Tony was feeling both excited and a little nervous. He had just been moved to a new math group, and he knew that it would now be harder. At the same time, he felt good because Ms. Lemar had told him that he was doing so well that he needed an additional challenge. But, fourth-grade math!

He hoped everything would be all right. He went to Mrs. Anderson's second-grade class for reading, and he stayed in homeroom for the afternoon. "I think I'll be okay," he decided.

Ms. Lemar interrupted his thinking. "Okay, everybody, look up here. . . . We have two new members here today, and we want to welcome them. Celia, we're glad you're here. You too, Tony and Kareem. Welcome to our class. We're glad you're all with us.

Now, each of you in this class is a good math student. You can all do the work. I'm going to expect a lot from you during the next 9 weeks, and I'm sure you'll do super. Let me know if you have any problems. . . . Now, let's see where we were before vacation."

Think about the practice of ability grouping, and using ability grouping as the context, identify at least four *positive* characteristics or practices illustrated here.

Exercise 4.2

You are a teacher with a class of 24 students, 17 of whom fit Ogbu's description of involuntary minorities. Describe specifically what you might do in your teaching to help overcome the concept of *cultural inversion* in your class.

Exercise 4.3

Classify each of the following as maintenance, transitional, or ESL bilingual programs.

1. Pablo Suarez spends his day in a self-contained fifth-grade classroom. In that class he learns primarily in English. When he has a problem or doesn't understand something he can raise his hand and an aide will come over and talk to him in Spanish, explaining the content or directions he doesn't understand.

2. Jacinta Escobar is a first-grade student at Woodrow Wilson Elementary School. When she arrives in the morning her teacher greets her in Spanish. Jacinta is learning to read and write in both Spanish and English, and many of the songs the class sings are in Spanish.

3. Abdul Hakeem has recently moved to New York from his old home in the Middle East. He is in the seventh grade and attends most of the regular classes like the other students. Though his speaking skills in English are limited, he can read enough to get by in most classes. During fourth period every day he goes to a special class that focuses on English vocabulary and oral communication skills.

4. You are a fourth-grade teacher with 8 non-native English-speaking students in your class of 26. You're beginning a unit on *adjectives* and *adverbs* with your students in language arts. Based on the information in this section, describe *specifically* how you would teach the topic, taking into account the special needs of your non-native English speakers and capitalizing on the information in this section.

Exercise 4.4

Consider the situation in which Marti Banes (on page 131 of your text) found herself on the first day of her advanced-placement chemistry class.

1. What is the best explanation for the low number of girls in her class?

2. What short- and long-term strategies might she pursue to correct this problem?

Exercise 4.5

Look again at the example of Mrs. Higby's lesson (on pages 140-141 of your text) with her students. Identify in it the first six characteristics of effective instruction for at-risk students (found in Table 4.5 on page 141 of your text). Cite specific information from the case study to illustrate the characteristics. What could Mrs. Higby have done to address the last two characteristics?

Feedback for Application Exercises

Exercise 4.1

Some positive practices identified in the episode include:

1. *Flexible grouping*. Tony was in one math group and was moved to a higher achieving group in the middle of the year.

2. *Different groupings for different subjects*. Students are often successful in different subjects and having alternate grouping arrangements for different content volumes allows teachers to match instruction to student needs.

3. *Heterogeneous homeroom grouping*. This was only implied in the episode, but the fact that Tony stayed in his homeroom in the afternoon suggested that subjects like science, social studies, art and health were taught in groups with mixed abilities. This minimizes some of the negative affective consequences of grouping.

4. *Positive expectations*. Regardless of what group students are in they should be made to feel that they can and will succeed. Mrs. Lemar did a nice job of communicating this at the beginning of her math class.

Exercise 4.2

First, one of the most important things you can do is try to establish a climate where all students feel accepted and valued. One way to accomplish this is to carefully practice equitable treatment of your students. This means *call on all the students in your class approximately equally, prompt each one when they're unable to answer, give each similar feedback, and use the same body language with each.*

Second, use a constructivist approach to your instruction. Provide high quality examples and representations of the topics you study. For example, Karen Johnson and Jenny Newhall, in Chapter 2, and Diane Smith, at the end of this chapter, used high-quality examples to teach density, the properties of air, and comparative and superlative adjectives, respectively. Diane also did an excellent job of using open-ended questions to help her students be successful. Each of the teachers used a very effective approach for students who would be called involuntary minorities.

Third, keep all grades and other performance records private, and tell the students to avoid sharing their grades with anyone else in the class. This is designed to take the pressure off the students who want to perform well, but feel peer pressure to avoid doing so. (Many will probably share their grades anyway, but telling them not to gives the student who would rather avoid sharing his or her grades a "way out.")

Finally, you may even tell them to not raise their hands in class, (again to keep some students from "standing out" in front of their peers). Then be sure to call on all students equally, and be certain that you give them enough support to be certain that each is able to answer.

Exercise 4.3

1. Pablo attends a transitional program. In transitional programs the first language (Spanish) is used until English proficiency is reached. Then it is used as an aid or supplement to English to help students when they have problems with English instruction.

2. Jacinta's class is a maintenance program, designed to develop expertise in both Spanish and English.

3. Abdul's fourth period class is a pull-out ESL program designed to supplement his regular instruction.

4. The most effective strategy is to build on the students' experiences. One way to begin would be to label several objects in the room in both Spanish and English as Tina Wharton did in the example on page 128 of your text. Then describe the objects, writing the descriptions on the board, and discussing the descriptions in detail. In the discussion, point out that each of these describing words are adjectives. Then, follow a similar procedure with adverbs. Have the students describe the action of something, such as the way you walk across the floor. Again, write the description on the board and discuss is thoroughly, pointing out that the description of the action is an adverb in each case.

Exercise 4.4

1. Research indicates that female students take fewer elective and fewer advanced science classes. Probably the strongest explanation is cultural; female students don't perceive science as an appropriate field for them to major in nor do they view science-related careers as positively as do male students.

2. In the short term she should do everything she can to make the females in her class comfortable, modeling her interest in science and communicating positive expectations for them in the class. Long-term solutions might include recruiting in lower-level classes, working with other science teachers to make sure the science curriculum is gender friendly and actively talking with parents and counselors about careers in science.

Exercise 4.5

1. *Greater Structure and Support*: Students had assignments written on the board when they entered the room and expectations during the lesson were clearly laid out.

2. *Active Teaching*: The teacher was actively involved in explaining and modeling the new content.

3. *Instruction Emphasizing Student Engagement*: <u>All</u> the students in the class actively practiced <u>all</u> the problems.

4. *More Frequent Feedback*: Students received feedback after each problem as well as after they completed their seatwork.

5. *Higher Success Rates*: The teacher ensured that group success rates were high (90%) before proceeding to individual practice. Even then she spent additional time with students still having problems.

6. *High expectations*: She communicated high expectations by including all students in the lesson and by ensuring that all students were learning. She might have augmented this by explicitly stating that she expected all students to learn.

She could have emphasized learning strategies more by think-alouds during her modeling, and by asking successful students to share their strategies. She could have also used think-alouds to increase student motivation and self-regulation. For example, when first encountering a problem, she might say, "Hmm. Let's see now. What does the problem ask and what does it tell me?"

TRUE/FALSE QUESTIONS: Write T in the blank if the statement is true, and write F if the statement is false.

_____ 1. Lack of experience is a major factor contributing to poor performance on intelligence tests.
_____ 2. Gardner's theory of multiple intelligences adds dimensions to intelligence that help explain how a person selects effective problem solving strategies.
_____ 3. Homogeneous ability grouping has had little effect on the expectations of teachers and the motivation of low ability students.
_____ 4. Lower SES parents place greater emphasis on conformity and obedience than do their middle and upper SES counterparts.
_____ 5. Title I programs in the elementary schools have been found to be generally well taught, congruent with regular school instructional goals, and efficient in use of time.

MULTIPLE-CHOICE QUESTIONS: Circle the best response for each case.

6. Experts most commonly define intelligence as:
   a. the ability to achieve in school and get along with others.
   b. the ability to learn, reason in the abstract, and solve problems.
   c. the ability to adapt to unique environments.
   d. the ability to think clearly and make decisions after adequate deliberation.

7. Which of the following most accurately describes intelligence according to Sternberg?
   a. Intelligence is made up of fluid and crystallized abilities uninfluenced by school and culture.
   b. Schools should use more time and resources to address divergent thinking, the search for relationships and memorization of important content.
   c. Schools should treat intelligence not as a single trait, but a complex series of interacting components.
   d. Nature is more important than nurture in shaping intelligence.

8. According to Gardner's theory of multiple intelligences:
   a. the curriculum should be broadened to include emphases on alternate subjects and topics.
   b. schools should renew their focus on basic skills.
   c. teachers should use teaching strategies linked to students' learning styles.
   d. female students should be taught to think like male students and vice versa.

9. Individual teachers can accommodate different reading abilities in a classroom by dividing students into subgroups for teaching reading. This is best described as:
   a. between-class ability grouping.
   b. within-class ability grouping.
   c. the Joplin Plan.
   d. heterogeneous grouping.

10. According to research, which of the following tends to be the most common problem associated with ability grouping?
   a. Teachers tend to have inappropriately high expectations for students in low groups.
   b. Students in low groups tend to be stigmatized by both teachers and peers.
   c. Students are frequently moved from one ability group to another, which disrupts the continuity of their schooling.
   d. Low groups are often given work that is too difficult.

11. Which of the following statements best describe the way low SES parents tend to interact with their children? Circle the letter. Low SES parents tend to:
    1. explain ideas to their children.
    2. give vague directions.
    3. be encouraging and cooperative.
    4. use simple language.
    5. identify causes of events.

a. 1,3,4   b. 1,2,3   c. 2,3,4   d. 2,4   e. 1,5

12. Cultural conflict most often occurs when:
    a. schools embrace a philosophy of acceptance towards cultural diversity.
    b. there is a disparity between school and home language or language patterns.
    c. competition is used as a motivational tool.
    d. children from different cultures mix in one school.

13. According to research, of the following, which is most likely to be a problem in programs for at-risk students?
    a. Expectations for students are inappropriately high.
    b. Emphasis on higher-level thinking is lacking.
    c. Teacher warmth and enthusiasm tends to be excessive and artificial.
    d. Too much emphasis is placed on assessment and feedback.

14. According to research examining gender issues, which of the following statements best explain the difference in achievement scores in math between boys and girls in middle, junior high, and high schools?
    a. Societal expectations influence boys' and girls' behaviors with respect to math.
    b. Math is more innately appealing to boys, so they tend to be more motivated to study math than are girls.
    c. Boys are more naturally talented in math because of their better visual and spatial abilities.
    d. The physical differences between boys and girls at the junior high and high school level are more apparent.

Use the following case study to answer Items 15-19.

Gabriella is a fourth-grader at Oakridge Elementary School--a suburban school populated mostly by children whose parents are teachers, middle-management personnel from insurance companies and other businesses, and naval officers who are stationed at a nearby naval air station. Gabriella, whose native language is Spanish, lives with her divorced mother--a minimum-wage housekeeper who left school after the 10th grade. Gabriella has a limited background. In a discussion of American westward expansion, for example, she asked what a bridle was, as Mrs. Petschonek talked about the gear the cowboys used. Also, she had never heard of the country Hungary, confusing it with being hungry. However, Gabriella learns new ideas in class more quickly than many of her classmates, and she periodically asks questions atypical of fourth-graders, such as, "Why are there so many movies about cowboys if there weren't really that many of them?"

15. Based on the information in the case study, which of the following is the best prediction?
    a. Gabriella will get a lower score than will her typical peers on some sections of typical intelligence tests.
    b. Gabriella will score about the same as typical fourth-graders on most sections of typical intelligence tests.
    c. Gabriella will score higher than typical fourth-graders on most sections of typical intelligence tests.
    d. We can't make any predictions about Gabriella's performance on intelligence tests based on the information in the case study.

16. Based on the information in the case study and researchers' conceptions of intelligence, which of the following is the best description?
    a. Gabriella is less intelligent than most of her peers.
    b. Gabriella's intelligence is about comparable to that of her peers.
    c. Gabriella is more intelligent than most of her peers.
    d. We don't have any evidence one way or the other about Gabriella's intelligence based on the information in the case study.

17. Based on the information in the case study, of the following, which is the best conclusion we can make about Gabriella's socioeconomic status?
    a. It is lower than that of her peers.
    b. It is about the same as that of her peers.
    c. It is higher than that of her peers.
    d. We don't have enough information from the case study to make a conclusion about Gabriella's socioeconomic status.

18. Based on the information in the case study and research on school dropouts, if Gabriella fits patterns typical for students with her background and socioeconomic status, which of the following is the best prediction?
    a. She is much less likely to drop out of school than is a typical classmate.
    b. She is slightly less likely to drop out than is a typical classmate.
    c. The likelihood of Gabriella dropping out is about the same as that of a typical classmate.
    d. Gabriella is about twice as likely to drop out as is a typical classmate.

19. When Gabriella came to Oakridge at the beginning of the year, she was placed in a low-ability reading group. Based on research examining ability grouping, which of the following is the most likely outcome?
    a. Gabriella will be moved to a higher ability group before the end of the year.
    b. Gabriella will remain in the low group until the end of the year but will be placed in a higher ability group the following year.
    c. Gabriella will remain in a low-ability group for the remainder of the year and will be placed in a low ability group again the following year.
    d. We can't predict what is likely to happen based on research examining ability-group placements.

Use the following information for Items 20-23.

Verna Maxwell teaches in an inner-city school near some government-funded housing projects. In her class of 27 fifth-graders, she has 14 students who are cultural minorities. Among them are Henry, a Native American, Kim, a Cambodian refugee, Lu, a second-generation Chinese American, and Rom, who has recently moved to the United States from India. Twenty of her 27 students are boys.

20. Based on Ogbu's work, which of the four is most likely to experience *cultural inversion*?
    a. Henry
    b. Kim
    c. Lu
    d. Rom

66

21. According to research examining effective teaching for cultural minorities, in working with her minority students in question and answer activities, which of the following is the best advice we can give Verna?
   a. Call on the minority students only when they volunteer, because teachers often don't understand students' preferred learning styles.
   b. Call on students such as Henry and Lu, because they are Americans, but don't direct questions to Kim and Rom, because they may not be comfortable in an American classroom.
   c. Use typical questioning patterns with Henry and Lu, but ask Kim and Rom open-ended questions.
   d. Treat all the students, including the cultural minorities, as equally as possible in both the type and number of questions asked.

22. Which of the following statements most accurately describes Verna's class?
   a. The majority of her class will probably have the characteristics of at-risk students, since many are cultural minorities and come from low-income families.
   b. The majority of her class will probably have the characteristics of at-risk students since most of them are boys.
   c. The majority of her class will not be at-risk since most of them do not experience *cultural inversion*.
   d. We don't have enough information in the case study to make a conclusion about the at-risk characteristics of Verna's students.

23. According to research, which of the following would be the most effective assessment practice in Verna's class?
   a. Increase the number of assessments to provide the opportunity for frequent feedback to students.
   b. Decrease the number of assessments, since frequent assessments discriminate against cultural minorities.
   c. Give the students more independent work to accommodate their different learning styles.
   d. Decrease the emphasis on higher-order thinking, since many of her students probably lack background experiences.

Use the following case study to answer Items 24-25.

Mrs. Parker has 14 girls and 15 boys in her fifth-grade class. She says, "The Battle of Gettysburg is believed to be the turning point of the Civil War. In what state is Gettysburg?" Then she asks, "What do you suppose would have happened if the South had won the battle instead of the North?"

24. If Mrs. Parker's questioning is typical of the *types* of questions directed to boys and girls, which of the following is most likely?
   a. She will direct both her questions to girls.
   b. She will direct both her questions to boys.
   c. She will direct the first question to a girl and the second question to a boy.
   d. She will direct the first question to a boy and the second question to a girl.
   e. There will be no pattern in her questioning behavior.

25. If Mrs. Parker's questioning is typical of the *number* of questions addressed to boys and girls, which of the following is most likely?
   a. She will direct more questions to boys.
   b. She will direct more questions to girls.
   c. She will direct about the same number of questions to boys as to girls.

1.   t
2.   f
3.   f
4.   t
5.   f
6.   b   Experts generally agree on these three components of intelligence.
7.   c   Sternberg thinks of intelligence as having several components that can be influenced by instruction.
8.   a   Gardner's theory suggests many different kinds of intelligence that need to be addressed in the schools.
9.   b   Within-class ability grouping addresses differences in ability by grouping within the same classroom.
10.   b   Lowered teacher expectations and negative reactions from peers are both problems with ability grouping.
11.   d   Low SES parents tend to use simplified language and not give clear directions to their children.
12.   b   Language differences are a major source of cultural discontinuities in the schools today.
13.   b   Too much emphasis is placed on "basic skills" resulting in a "dumbing down" of the curriculum.
14.   a   Societal forces explain gender differences in math and science better than any genetic reason.
15.   a   Intelligence tests don't measure "pure" aptitude; instead they are heavily influenced by experience.
16.   c   Given her poor experiential background, the fact that she learns quickly and asks precocious questions suggests higher intelligence.
17.   a   Both her mother's occupation and level of education suggest lower SES than her peers.
18.   d   The combination of background factors suggests she is considerably more likely to drop out of school than her peers.
19.   c   Research on ability grouping suggests that these placements tend to be stable over time.
20.   a   Cultural inversion, or the tendency to reject majority values and behaviors, is most likely to occur in involuntary minorities such as Native Americans.
21.   d   Equal treatment and equitable distribution of questions are two of the best ways to communicate positive expectations.
22.   a   The combination of being a cultural minority and coming from low SES students places many of her students at risk.
23.   a   Frequent feedback is one of the characteristics of effective instruction for at-risk students.
24.   c   Teachers are more likely to address high-level questions to boys and low-level questions to girls.
25.   a   Research shows that boys are called on more frequently than girls.

CHAPTER 5: LEARNERS WITH EXCEPTIONALITIES

Chapter Outline

I. Students with learning problems
   A. Mental retardation
      1. Levels of mental retardation
      2. Programs for students with mental retardation
   B. Learning disabilities
      1. Characteristics of students with learning disabilities
      2. Attention deficit/hyperactivity disorder
      3. Identifying and working with students who have learning disabilities
         a. Using classroom-based information for identification
         b. Adaptive instruction
   C. Behavior disorders
      1. Prevalence of behavior disorders
      2. Kinds of behavior disorders
      3. Teaching students with behavior disorders
         a. Behavior management strategies
         b. Self-management skills
         c. Teacher flexibility and sensitivity

II. Communication, visual, and hearing disabilities
   A. Communication disorders
      1. Language disorders
      2. Helping students with communication disorders
   B. Visual disabilities
      1. Working with students who have visual disabilities
   C. Hearing impairments
      1. Working with students who have hearing impairments

III. Students who are gifted and talented
   A. Creativity: What is it?
      1. Measuring creativity
   B. Identifying students who are gifted and talented
   C. Programs for the gifted: More and faster or deeper and different?

IV. Changes in the way teachers help students with exceptionalities
   A. Federal laws redefine special education
   B. The evolution towards inclusion

V. A legal framework for working with students who have exceptionalities
   A. Due process through parental involvement
   B. Protection against discrimination in testing
   C. Least restrictive environment (LRE)
   D. Individualized education program (IEP)
      1. Functions of the IEP
      2. Curriculum-based measurement

VI. The teacher's role in inclusive classrooms
   A. Identifying students with exceptionalities
      1. Prereferral strategies: Gathering data for instructional problem solving
   B. Effective teaching for inclusive classrooms
         a. Adapting instruction
         b. A successful homework program
         c. Adapting reading materials

       2.   Strategy training: Learning how to learn
       3.   Collaborative consultation: Help for the classroom teacher
  C.   Strategies for social integration and growth
       1.   Helping regular students understand and accept students with exceptionalities
       2.   Helping students with exceptionalities behave acceptably
       3.   Using strategies that encourage social interaction and cooperation
           a.   Peer tutoring
           b.   Cooperative learning

Chapter Objectives

- Explain the role of classroom teachers in working with students with exceptionalities.

- Explain how different exceptionalities--mental retardation, learning disabilities, communication disorders, visual and hearing impairments--affect student learning.

- Describe different methods of identifying and teaching students who are gifted and talented.

- Explain how instructional strategies can be adapted to meet the needs of students with exceptionalities.

Chapter Overview

Learners with exceptionalities are those who require special help to reach their full potential. Students with exceptionalities fall at both ends of the ability continuum, including students who are mildly retarded and others who are gifted and talented. Most of the exceptional students in regular classrooms have mild learning problems. These include students who are intellectually handicapped, students with learning disabilities, students with attention deficit/hyperactivity disorder (AD/HD), and students who are behaviorally disordered.

Teachers will also encounter students with communication, speech, and language disorders, as well as visual and hearing impairments. Students who are gifted and talented are exceptional because they also need special help to reach their full potential.

The way that students with exceptionalities are helped in our schools changed when Public Law 94-142, the Individuals with Disabilities in Education Act (IDEA), was passed. It provides for: 1) due process through parental involvement; 2) protection against discrimination in testing; and 3) an individualized education program (IEP). *Inclusion*, advocates a total, systematic and coordinated web of support services; it has changed the classroom teacher's role in working with these students.

Effective teaching practices for students with exceptionalities provide extra support so that students can experience high rates of success. Pre-referral assessment strategies emphasize classroom-based data gathering for instructional problem solving. Support for classroom teachers often occurs in the regular classroom through the use of pre-referral teacher assistance teams, site-based teams or collaboration consultation teams. These teams often bring special educators into the classroom to help the regular teacher adapt instruction. Other strategies for working with students with exceptionalities in the regular classroom include cognitive strategy instruction and strategies to accomplish social integration and growth.

Feedback for Margin Questions_____

5.1:   The term *mentally retarded* has a negative connotation that can adversely influence people's perceptions and expectations. The term *intellectual handicap* more clearly describes the condition and helps us remember that the handicap doesn't necessarily involve physical or social problems.

5.2:   While the answer to this question is not cut-and-dried, adaptive behavior is probably most closely related to problem solving; adaptive behavior involves the capacity to cope under changing situations. Adaptive behavior is probably least related to abstract thinking and reasoning because most aspects of adaption involve concrete, real-world situations.

5.3:   Strategy training is most closely related to the capacity to acquire knowledge because it focuses on improving the ways students learn. Strategy training also focuses on problem solving to a certain extent, i.e., attempts have been made to teach students general problem solving strategies.

5.4:   Learning disabilities and mental retardation are similar in that both are disabilities that interfere with learning. In addition, both can result from a variety of causes, and they are related to some type of central nervous system dysfunction. They are different in that learning disabilities usually involve students with average intelligence or above and are often limited to a specific area such as math or reading, whereas intellectual handicaps involve a broad range of intellectual functioning.

5.5:   A "nature" explanation would suggest that males are genetically inclined to have this problem. An environmental explanation would contend that schools are not effectively designed for the characteristics of boys. An interactionist position would say that boys <u>are</u> programmed to be more active and prone to attention problems but that schools do an inadequate job adapting to and working with these children.

5.6:   The discrepancy model is based on the assumption that intelligence is average or above, an assumption not made with intellectually handicapped students.

5.7:   Most of these adaptations could be used in a regular classroom. The teacher's role would be to suggest alternatives to students, help them learn each strategy through explanation and modeling, and provide a supportive environment for all students.

5.8:   Some explanations for the disproportionate number of boys and cultural minorities referred for special help could include the following: One genetically-based explanation suggests that boys are born more active; another is that boys are born with more learning problems. An environmentally-based explanation asserts that boys are raised to be more active and aggressive. A third explanation focuses on a gender mismatch with schools; since most teachers are female they create "female-oriented" classrooms that don't meet the needs of male students.

5.9:   Both involve persistent, serious disabilities. Both disabilities also involve inappropriate behaviors that interfere with school performance. The nature of the disabilities is different for the two--learning disabilities are cognitive, whereas behavioral disorders involve inappropriate or unacceptable classroom behavior. Learning disabilities often appear as learning problems whereas behavioral disorders usually result in management problems.

5.10:   Extinction would probably be least effective. Teachers can't ignore fighting on the playground. The most effective would be actively teaching replacement behaviors and positive reinforcement for those behaviors. Each of the strategies except extinction should be reasonably effective.

5.11: Although ultimately teachers must judge for themselves, the general answer is no. Different treatment can send the wrong message, both to the student with a speech disorder and to classmates. The overall goal in working with these students should be to help them adjust to classroom life, and life in general. Specific questions should be addressed to a speech therapist.

5.12: Both Piaget and Vygotsky would support these adaptations. Piaget would stress the use of concrete materials to help build abstract concepts; Vygotsky would emphasize the use of language and interaction in addition to the concrete materials.

5.13: As with visual impairments, teachers need to be sensitive to the special needs of these students. Placement is a factor; students should be seated where they have the best chance of hearing or reading a teacher's lips. If a person who can communicate in sign language is not provided, the teacher should try to turn directly toward the student when speaking, to speak clearly and slowly, and to repeat students' answers. Extra use of the chalkboard or overhead will also be helpful.

5.14: In general, the definition of gifted and talented has been broadened and refined to better meet the needs of more students. The thrust has been a broadening of the category to fit students with different areas of giftedness. There has been a parallel thrust in working with students having learning or behavioral problems. Also, in all aspects of exceptionality, there is decreased reliance on IQ tests and more emphasis on performance in life-like environments.

5.15: Fluency is the ability to produce many solutions to a problem; a teacher might encourage fluency by brainstorming ways to think about pollution at the beginning of a discussion. Flexibility involves attacking a problem from new and unique perspectives; a teacher might encourage flexibility also through brainstorming or by using other sources for new ideas like examining pollution from a social science perspective. Originality consists of generating original solutions by using analogical reasoning (i.e., something is like something else) and by postponing the premature judging of ideas. For example, the teacher might ask students to compare pollution to crime or a transportation/distribution problem.

5.16: Both creativity and problem-solving depend heavily on knowledge of specific content. Chapter 8 shows how knowledge of content is important for transfer of learning and for effective use of study strategies.

5.17: Teacher nomination probably has the greatest probability of including all three criteria, because teachers are in a unique position to observe motivation and creativity in the classroom. This would be the most effective method if teachers had the ability to recognize creativity in students. Teachers often need special training to recognize creativity for what it is, however, since sometimes it is perceived as an annoyance in typical classrooms. Achievement and intelligence tests are probably least suited to capturing all three criteria because of the narrow range of abilities tapped by these instruments.

5.18: Curriculum compacting is most applicable in content areas that are fixed and somewhat linear, such as math and certain aspects of reading. In art, music, social studies, some aspects of science, and other areas that lack this structure, curriculum compacting would be less applicable.

5.19: Both enrichment and acceleration attempt to adapt instruction to provide an environment in which gifted and talented students can best reach their full potential. This is similar to the goals of a least restrictive environment.

5.20: The larger circle would be LRE. Other LREs in addition to mainstreaming include a pull-out resource room and all-day special education classes situated within a regular school. This latter arrangement would allow students with exceptionalities to use the school's facilities and participate in the school's activities.

5.21: Two advantages for inclusion include: 1) the regular classroom provides an environment for mainstreamed students that is better socially and academically than one in which the mainstreamed student is isolated, and 2) inclusion provides opportunities for regular students to learn about and interact with students having exceptionalities. A potential problem with inclusion is that the student diversity in the classroom increases, which places more demands on the teacher.

5.22: The Individuals with Disabilities in Education Act (IDEA) is the law that requires due process through parental involvement. IDEA also requires that his parents had legal access to his school records, an independent evaluation if they weren't satisfied with the existing one and access to an interpreter if they didn't speak English.

5.23: Even though he speaks understandable English, his native language is Spanish, and the law requires that a placement test be given in a student's native language. Therefore, under the law he cannot be given a placement test written in English.

5.24: Research indicates that integration into the regular classroom benefits students with exceptionalities in each of the following areas: 1) Academic performance improves because of a higher quality instructional menu and interaction with other students; 2) self-concept can improve as a result of academic growth and interaction with other students on an approximately "equal footing;" 3) peer acceptance can be increased if the teacher models acceptance and encourages acceptance from the regular students.

5.25: The least restrictive environments (e.g., regular classroom in which the IEP is implemented with no additional assistance) will serve the most students while the more restrictive environments, such as separate school facilities serve the fewest students. This implies that you likely will have some students with exceptionalities in your class.

5.26: The construction of an IEP must involve parents. Their involvement is one aspect of due process. The parents' signature at the bottom of the IEP in Figure 5.5, for example, indicates that they were involved. The specific information in the IEP provides for the least restrictive environment. For example, the IEP in Figure 5.5 indicates that Joe S. makes frequent computational errors in working familiar problems. The objectives in his IEP are intended to help him overcome this problem.

5.27: While a variety of curriculum-based measurements for finding main ideas could exist, one example, might be presenting the student with several paragraphs and asking the learner to identify the main idea in each. Another would be to present several paragraphs with choices of three or four main ideas associated with each. The student would be asked to identify the best description of the main idea from the list of choices. Using both forms of assessment would give teachers a reasonably accurate measure of the students' ability to find main ideas.

5.28: Tests, quizzes, and work samples give concrete indicators of a student's classroom performance. Curriculum-based measurement provides the same kind of specific information about student performance.

5.29: Most of these strategies are minor instructional modifications aimed at cognitive achievement. These include efficient use of time and effective feedback. Warm academic climate increases motivation, and success and effective classroom management increases both achievement and motivation. Students with exceptionalities need positive expectations for learning, a warm and orderly learning environment, and minor modifications in sound instructional practice.

5.30: "More of *degree* than *kind*" means that teachers don't need to abandon their effective teaching practices in favor of qualitatively different strategies. In the Rosenberg study, students were given regular homework with adaptations. For example, homework was an extension of successfully completed seatwork, parents orally administered a nightly quiz, and parents confirmed the completion of the homework and quiz with their signature.

5.31: One of the most effective ways to teach cognitive strategies is through think-aloud modeling. For example, a teacher might verbalize her thinking as she models a strategy for attacking a list of words, or she might ask students who have mastered this strategy to verbally describe what they're thinking as they attack a list. Each provides a model for the other students to imitate.

5.32: The most positive benefit of mainstreaming may occur in regular students learning to understand and accept students having exceptionalities. In order for this benefit to occur, however, the teacher must consciously work to change the attitudes and beliefs of regular students.

5.33: First, in both areas the skills should be specifically identified, explained and modeled by the teacher or other students. Second, students should practice the skill and be given feedback by the teacher.

Application Exercises

Exercise 5.1

Examine the following list of descriptors and decide whether they apply to all three types of learning problems (G = General) or whether they are more characteristic of a specific learning problem (MR = Mental Retardation; LD = Learning Disability; BD = Behavior Disorder).

_____ 1. Problems functioning in regular classrooms.
_____ 2. Below-average performance on intelligence tests.
_____ 3. Learning problems often involving language.
_____ 4. Management problems often interfering with learning.
_____ 5. Discrepancies between two measures of achievement.
_____ 6. Students sometimes withdrawn and extremely shy.
_____ 7. Failure and frustration often interfering with learning.

Exercise 5.2

Read the following classroom episode, and identify the different functions that the classroom teacher performs in working with students having exceptionalities.

Toni Morrison had been working with her class of second-graders for a week trying to get them into reading and math groups that matched their abilities. Marisse, a transfer student, was hard to place. She seemed to understand the material but lost attention during different parts of lessons. When Toni worked with her one-on-one, she did fine, but Toni often noticed her staring out the window.

One day as Toni watched the class work in small groups, she noticed that Marisse held her head to one side when she talked to the other side. Toni wondered . . . She spoke to the principal, who recommended that Marisse be referred to the school psychologist for possible testing.

Two weeks later, the school psychologist came by to discuss her findings. Marisse had a hearing problem in one ear that would require a hearing aid as well as special help from Toni.

In a few days, Marisse came to school with her hearing aid. She obviously felt funny about it and wasn't sure if this was a good idea. Toni moved her to the front of the room so she could hear better, made sure to give directions while standing in front of Marisse's desk, and double-checked after an assignment was given to ensure that the directions were clear to her.

After a couple of days, Toni took Marisse aside to talk about her new hearing aid. Marisse could hear better, but she still felt a little strange with it. Some of the kids looked at her curiously, and that made her uneasy. Toni had an inspiration: Why not discuss the hearing aid in class and let the others try it? This was a risky strategy, but Marisse reluctantly agreed to it.

It worked. During show-and-tell, Marisse explained about her new hearing aid and gave the class a chance to try it out themselves. The strange and different became understandable, and Marisse's hearing aid became a normal part of the classroom.

1. Explain how least restrictive environment was illustrated in the case.

2. Define adaptive fit and explain how it was illustrated in the case.

3. What did the school do to meet the legal requirements of IDEA?

4. What specifically did Toni do to facilitate social integration and growth?

Exercise 5.3

Read the following description of a team developing an IEP.

> Pablo Martinez had been falling further and further behind in math and reading. Mrs. Henderson, his second-grade teacher, felt it was time to act. She talked with the special education teacher, who called a meeting with Pablo's parents. At the meeting, the special education teacher explained why they were there and what they hoped to accomplish. English as a second language was explored as one possible source of Pablo's problem. Mrs. Henderson shared Pablo's reading and math scores with them as well as his standardized achievement scores from the previous year. Everyone concurred that Pablo was having troubles, and his parents agreed to have the school psychologist test him for possible placement in a special program. Fortunately, the school psychologist was bilingual and was able to administer his tests in Spanish.
>
> At the next meeting, the results of the tests were shared with the parents. They showed that Pablo had normal intelligence but that he performed poorly on the verbal parts of the scale. Everyone agreed that Pablo should remain in the regular classroom but that he would benefit from a resource program that was taught in his native language. In addition, the group developed a number of specific learning goals for Pablo, some of which would be met in Mrs. Henderson's classroom, some in resource, and some in both. The group was especially concerned about links between the two rooms and ways to reinforce learning activities at home.

Using information from the episode, describe how each of the following provisions of IDEA was met:

1. Due process

2. Protection against discrimination in testing

3. Least restrictive environment

4. Individualized education plan

Feedback for Application Exercises

Exercise 5.1

1. (G) Problems functioning in regular classrooms is characteristic of all three types of learning problems. These problems are typical of most students with exceptionalities and often require special, supplementary help for these students.

2. (MR) Below-average performance on intelligence tests is a distinguishing characteristic of mental retardation.

3. (LD) Learning problems often involving language is common for students with learning disabilities.

4. (LD,BD) Management problems often interfering with learning tend to exist for students with exceptionalities in general to a greater extent than for those not having exceptionalities. However, it is most characteristic of students with learning disabilities and behavior disorders.)

5. (LD) Discrepancies between two measures of achievement often indicate a learning disability and this discrepancy is commonly used to identify the disability.

6. (BD) Being withdrawn and extremely shy is most characteristic of students with an internalized behavior disorder (although it could be found in all students with exceptionalities).

7. (G) Failure and frustration that often interfere with learning is characteristic of all three types of learning problems.

Exercise 5.2

1. By retaining Marisse in the regular classroom and adapting that classroom to fit Marisse's learning needs, Toni tried to create a least restrictive learning environment.

2. Adaptive fit is the degree to which a student is able to cope with the requirements of a school setting and the extent to which the school accommodates the student's special needs. Toni attempted to insure adaptive fit by moving her to the front of the room, giving directions in front of her desk and double-checking to make sure directions were clear.

3. The legal requirements of IDEA include:
   - due process through parental involvement
   - protection against discrimination in testing
   - a least restrictive environment
   - individualized education programs.

The case study illustrated all of these except discrimination in testing which was not directly addressed.

4. To facilitate social integration Toni had Marisse explain and share her hearing aid. A major classroom obstacle to social acceptance is lack of understanding or ignorance on the part of other students.

Exercise 5.3

1. *Due Process*: Pablo's parents were consulted from the beginning and their approval for testing was obtained. If they hadn't given their approval, the process would have stopped there. In addition, their input was further solicited in the development of the IEP, and the decision to keep him in the regular classroom but require resource help. If they had not approved of these decisions, they had the right to an external independent review of the process.

2. *Protection Against Discrimination in Testing*: This is an especially critical component of IDEA because of the growing number of non-English speaking students in our schools. Because of this problem, and in response to a court case (Diana v. State of Education, 1970), one state, California, agreed to test all children whose primary language was not English in both their primary language and English (Salvia & Ysseldyke, 1991). Because of the close interrelationship between language and intelligence testing, this provision is probably essential to accurate testing.

3. *Least Restrictive Environment*: The general thrust of this provision is to keep children, as much as educationally possible, in the regular classroom. Research suggests that mainstreaming students like Pablo in the regular classroom has both academic and social advantages.

4. *Individualized Education Plan*: The individualized education plan specified goals for both the regular and resource classrooms. In addition, it outlined ways to coordinate efforts within the school and between the school and home.

TRUE/FALSE QUESTIONS: Write T in the blank if the statement is true, and write F if the statement is false.

_____ 1. One of the classroom teacher's main responsibilities is to help students with exceptionalities overcome negative attitudes of others towards them.

_____ 2. To maintain consistency in identification of children with exceptionalities, results of IQ and achievement tests should be given more weight than less objective information like classroom performance and adaptive behavior.

_____ 3. Students with mild handicaps can usually learn well enough to remain in the regular classroom without special help if they are accepted by their peers.

_____ 4. A student with a learning disability is typically below "normal" intelligence.

_____ 5. Research on mainstreaming reveals that knowledge and strategies that teachers use effectively with regular students need to be *qualitatively* changed in order to reach special education students.

MULTIPLE-CHOICE QUESTIONS: Circle the best response in each case.

6. The component of PL 94-142 that guarantees parent involvement in the classification and placement of their children, as well as access to their children's school records is called:
    a. due process.
    b. protection against discrimination in testing.
    c. provision for the least restrictive environment.
    d. mainstreaming.

7. Which of the following is the most accurate description of *inclusion* as it is conceptualized by experts?
    a. Placing students with exceptionalities in regular classrooms full time with the support of special education experts.
    b. Placing students with exceptionalities in regular classrooms whenever possible with the support of special education experts.
    c. Placing students with exceptionalities in regular classrooms for all their academic work *except* basic skill areas, such as reading and math.
    d. Providing instruction by special education specialists for students when they are pulled out of mainstream classes, but not providing special education support for teachers when students with exceptionalities are mainstreamed in regular classrooms.

8. Of the following, the best description of the purpose of curriculum-based measurement is:
    a. measure intelligence of the special education student in comparison to the rest of the regular class.
    b. assess achievement of the special education student in comparison to the rest of the regular class.
    c. identify specific areas that are encountered in the regular classroom in which the special education student needs help.
    d. identify long-term curriculum goals for the special education student.

9. Which of the following choices is the most accurate description of students with learning problems?
    a. These students can be mentally retarded, learning disabled, or behaviorally disordered.
    b. These students make up about 20% of the total school population.
    c. These students usually have other physical handicaps such as sight or hearing impairments.
    d. These students usually have average to above average IQs.

10. Of the following, the best description of the reason children with learning disabilities can be difficult to identify is:
   a. they have many of the same characteristics of the educable mentally retarded.
   b. they are easily confused with developmentally slow children or students with behavior problems.
   c. discrepancies between IQ and achievement tests do not show up when testing the learning disabled.
   d. high levels of creativity often compensate for problems in other areas.

11. Of the following, the most difficult kind of behavioral disorder to identify typically is:
   a. the student displaying hyperactivity.
   b. the child who is defiant and hostile.
   c. the child who does not respond to regular rules and consequences.
   d. the shy, timid, depressed child.

12. When teachers and other students overreact to a physical handicap by doing everything for the student, an unhealthy dependence upon others can result. This is best described as:
   a. negative self-concept.
   b. learned helplessness.
   c. a behavioral disorder.
   d. a communication disorder.

13. Which of the following is a symptom of a language disorder?
   a. Tuning out when information is presented on the chalkboard
   b. Poorly articulating words, especially consonants
   c. Using few words or very short sentences
   d. Stuttering

14. Which of the following is **NOT** considered a trait of a student who is gifted and talented?
   a. Highly organized and focused on details
   b. Unconventional and nonconforming
   c. Likes to work alone
   d. Talented in one specific area

15. Which of the following is **NOT** true of accelerated programs for the gifted and talented?
   a. They challenge students by increasing the pace.
   b. They broaden student interests by introducing them to other topics.
   c. They result in improved achievement in accelerated areas.
   d. They sometimes work by allowing students to skip grades or test out of classes.

16. The development of "meta" skills such as meta-attention and metacommunication are a part of:
   a. strategy training.
   b. effective feedback.
   c. cooperative learning.
   d. an accelerated curriculum.

Use the following case study to answer Items 17-21.

Jerry Griffin, a 5th-grade teacher, in observing Samone Duvalier, one of his students--originally from Haiti--thinks that Samone may have a specific learning disability. Samone, a native French-speaking child who speaks competent English, is given the WISC-III, an individually administered intelligence test (in English) by certified special education officials. He scores very low on the vocabulary section of the test compared to the other sections, and he is diagnosed as having a specific learning disability. Jerry and exceptional student specialists from the school prepare and implement an IEP. Part of the IEP calls for Samone being placed in a resource reading program for one hour a day. (He is mainstreamed the rest of the day.) Mrs. Duvalier, Samone's mother, after meeting with the school officials, objects to the placement, and asks for Samone's school records and test results. The school offers the name of a person who could do an independent evaluation of Samone but will not release their own test results, only saying that Samone's score was very low in the vocabulary section.

17. According to PL 94-142, the school's refusal to release the records was:
    a.   against the law, because of the provision guaranteeing parental involvement.
    b.   against the law, because of the provision guaranteeing minority protection, since Samone is a cultural minority.
    c.   within the law since Samone was found to have a disability. It would have been against the law if no disability was found.
    d.   within the law since Samone was mainstreamed for most of the school day (only in a resource program for an hour a day.)

18. The school officials violated a specific provision of PL 94-142 in their handling of Samone's case. Of the following, the best description of the violation is:
    a.   placing Samone in a resource reading program.
    b.   officials offering the name of an independent evaluator.
    c.   mainstreaming Samone for most of the day.
    d.   giving Samone the test in English.

19. Consider the school officials' use of the WISC-III as a basis for making their assessment of Samone. Based on PL 94-142, which of the following is the most accurate statement?
    a.   Officials' use of the test was within the law, since the WISC-III is validated and widely used.
    b.   Officials' use of the WISC-III was *not* within the law since it is an intelligence test.
    c.   Officials' use of the WISC-III was within the law, but should have been supplemented with another measure before Samone was placed in the resource program.
    d.   The use of the WISC-III was within the law, since the test was given by certified personnel.

20. Consider the school officials' offering of an independent evaluator to diagnose Samone's possible exceptionality. Based on PL 94-142, which of the following is the most accurate statement?
    a.   The offer was within the law.
    b.   The offer is prohibited by the law.
    c.   The law doesn't speak to the offer of an independent evaluation.

21. Consider the development and implementation of Samone's IEP. Based on PL 94-142, which of the following is the most accurate statement?
    a. The development and implementation of the IEP was done according to the law.
    b. The development of the IEP was against the law, since Mr. Griffin--a regular teacher rather than a certified special education expert--was involved in the process.
    c. The development and implementation of the IEP was against the law, since it called for Samone being removed from the regular classroom for part of the day.
    d. The development and implementation of the IEP was against the law, since Samone's mother didn't sign it.

22. Alfredo, an Hispanic student, and Ken, a white student in Mrs. Evans fourth-grade class both do consistently above-average work. Alfredo's homework periodically reflects a lack of care, but he has a good imagination, and often makes comments in class discussions of problems and issues that indicates insight atypical for a fourth-grader. He is periodically a bit disruptive, although he wouldn't be classified as a serious management problem.

Ken, in contrast, is every teacher's ideal. He follows directions, his work is extremely neat, and he is never a management problem. Ken and Alfredo scored similarly on achievement tests in the third grade.

Based on this information, if Mrs. Evans's class is consistent with patterns identified by research, which of the following is most likely?
    a. Ken is more likely to be identified as gifted than is Alfredo.
    b. Alfredo is more likely to be identified as gifted than is Ken.
    c. Ken and Alfredo are equally likely to be identified as gifted.
    d. Neither Ken nor Alfredo are likely to be identified as gifted, since we have no evidence that either has taken an intelligence test.

23. Which of the following are classified as students with exceptionalities?
    1. Students who have an intellectual handicap.
    2. Students who have learning disabilities.
    3. Students who have behavioral disorders (emotional handicaps).
    4. Students who are gifted and talented.
    5. Students who have hearing and visual impairments.

a. 1,2,3,4,5   b. 1,2,3,5   c. 1,2,5   d. 2,3,5   e. 1,2

24. Donna and John are two students in your second grade class. If they are consistent with patterns identified by research, which of the following is the most accurate statement?
    a. Donna and John are about *equally* likely to be diagnosed as having AD/HD (attention deficit hyperactivity disorder).
    b. Donna is *slightly* more likely than John to be diagnosed as having AD/HD.
    c. Donna is *much* (three to nine times) more likely than John to be diagnosed as having AD/HD.
    d. John is *slightly* more likely than Donna to be diagnosed as having AD/HD.
    e. John is *much* (three to nine times) more likely than Donna to be diagnosed as having AD/HD.

25. Which of the following statements most accurately describes effective teaching for students with exceptionalities?
   a.   Students with exceptionalities should be taught using methodology that is qualitatively different from the methodology used with regular students.
   b.   Students with exceptionalities should be taught primarily in an individualized format with heavy emphasis placed on drill and practice with basic skills.
   c.   Students with exceptionalities should be placed in special facilities that are geared to their individual needs.
   d.   The effective methods used for teaching students with exceptionalities are the same methods that are effective with regular students.

Self-Help Quiz Answers_____

1. t
2. f
3. f
4. f
5. f
6. a   Due process guarantees parents' involvement at critical points in the placement process.
7. b   Inclusion emphasizes the concept of adaptive fit--making sure instructional adjustments meet the needs of students.
8. c   Curriculum-based measurement is designed to ensure that adaptations fit the needs of students in the classroom.
9. a   Mild learning handicaps can include students who are mentally retarded, learning disabled or behaviorally disordered.
10. b   Many of the characteristics of a learning disability, such as shortened attention span and distractibility, are also symptoms of children who are developmentally slow.
11. d   Internalized behavior disorders often are undetected because the child does not act out or stand out in the classroom.
12. b   Learned helplessness is a negative by-product of well-intentioned overhelping.
13. c   Language or expressive disorders involve problems with understanding or using language to express ideas.
14. a   Gifted and talented students are often quite bright and creative but they are often disinterested in details.
15. b   Acceleration programs emphasize depth versus breadth.
16. a   Strategy training attempts to develop students' awareness of their own mental processes.
17. a   Parents are guaranteed access to all tests and test results by IDEA.
18. d   Students for whom English is not their first language should be tested in their native language.
19. c   Sole use of only one test, such as an intelligence test, is forbidden by the provisions of IDEA.
20. a   An independent evaluation is guaranteed by IDEA.
21. d   Not only should Samone's parents sign the IEP, they should have been involved in its design.
22. a   Teachers often mistake neatness and conformity for being gifted and talented.
23. a   All of these are considered students with exceptionalities.
24. e   Boys are much more likely to be diagnosed as AD/HD than girls.
25. d   Basically the same methods and strategies that work in the regular classroom are also effective with students with exceptionalities.

CHAPTER 6: BEHAVIORISM AND SOCIAL COGNITIVE THEORY

Chapter Outline

I. Behaviorist views of learning
   A. Contiguity
   B. Classical conditioning
      1. Classical conditioning in the classroom
      2. Generalization and discrimination
      3. Extinction
   C. Operant conditioning
      1. Reinforcement
         a. Positive reinforcement
         b. The Premack Principle
         c. Negative reinforcement
      2. Punishment
         a. Presentation punishment
         b. Removal punishment
         c. Using punishers: Research results
      3. Operant conditioning: Applications
         a. Generalization and discrimination
         b. Generalization and discrimination: The role of feedback
         c. Praise
         d. Shaping
         e. Reinforcement schedules
         f. Potency and satiation
         g. Extinction
         h. Cues: Antecedents to behavior
         i. Implications of behaviorism for instruction
   D. Putting behaviorism into perspective
II. Comparing behaviorism and cognitive learning theory
III. Social cognitive theory
   A. Differences between behaviorism and social cognitive theory
      1. Views of learning
      2. Interactions among behavior, the environment, and personal factors
      3. Interpretations of reinforcement and punishment
         a. Non-occurrence of expected consequences
   B. Modeling
      1. Cognitive modeling
   C. Vicarious learning
   D. Effects of modeling on behavior
      1. Learning new behaviors
      2. Facilitating existing behaviors
      3. Changing inhibitions
      4. Arousing emotions
   E. Learning from models: The processes involved
      1. Attention
      2. Retention
      3. Reproduction
      4. Motivation

      F.   Effectiveness of models
          1.   Perceived similarity
          2.   Perceived competence
          3.   Perceived status
      G.   Self-regulation
          1.   Goal setting
          2.   Self-observation
          3.   Self-assessment
          4.   Self-reinforcement
      H.   Putting social cognitive theory into perspective
III.   Dealing with diversity: Behaviorism and social cognitive theory
      A.   Classical conditioning: Learning to like and dislike school
      B.   Motivating hesitant learners
          1.   Roberto: A study in contrasts

Chapter Objectives

- Identify examples of classical conditioning in classroom situations.

- Explain cases of student behavior using concepts such as *reinforcement, punishment, generalization, discrimination, satiation*, and *extinction*.

- Explain the influence of different reinforcement schedules on student behavior.

- Identify examples of modeling and vicarious learning in classroom situations.

- Describe how self-regulation influences student learning.

Chapter Overview

The first section of your text focused on the learner and learner characteristics. We now turn to the first of four chapters devoted to the learning process itself. As you study your text and work your way through this study guide, keep the following question in mind: "How does the information I'm studying explain the way people learn and how they behave?" This question can serve as a reference point or "hook" to which the ideas you study can be attached.

Behaviorism is a view of learning that focuses on the relationships between observable behavior and experience. It doesn't consider internal processes, such as insight or perception, nor does it consider needs such as self-esteem or belonging to social groups. Three different types of learning--contiguity, classical conditioning, and operant conditioning all fit under the general theory of behaviorism.

Social cognitive theory describes the effects of watching others on our thoughts and behavior. Social cognitive theory differs from behaviorism in its emphasis on internal mental processes, in its recognition that learners not only are influenced by but also influence their environment, and in the central role that learner expectations play in motivating behavior. The tendency to imitate behaviors we see in others is called modeling. Models who are perceived as competent and similar to the observer are more effective than their opposite counterparts.

Vicarious conditioning is the process of observing the consequences of another person's behavior and adjusting our behavior accordingly. For instance, when a student is openly praised for diligent work, other students' diligence is likely to increase; the first student is positively reinforced, the student serves as a model for the others, and the others are vicariously reinforced.

6.1:   Any behaviors that are instinctive or reflexive would not be called learning. For example, infants instinctively suckle, and we all blink reflexively if something comes near our eyes.

6.2:   The two components of the question-answer sequence--Magna Carta and 1215--have not been presented together often enough to form an association, so the question (stimulus) didn't elicit the response.

6.3:   The unconditioned stimulus was Tim's failure on the test, to which he responded with a feeling of devastation, which was the unconditioned response. Subsequent tests became associated with his initial failure, so they became conditioned stimuli, to which Tim responded with nervousness as a conditioned response.

6.4:   For a child, school is initially a neutral stimulus. By becoming associated with anxiety-producing situations (unconditioned stimuli) in school, school itself becomes a conditioned stimulus. Because the school is now a conditioned stimulus (that is associated with the original anxiety-producing situations) it then produces the conditioned response--anxiety and illness.

In the case of parents being reluctant to attend school functions, if they felt alienated when they were students, schools remain associated with whatever caused them to feel alienated in the first place. Their child's school is a conditioned stimulus that elicits a negative emotion, such as uneasiness about going to school.

6.5:   The author has had, in the past, unpleasant, perhaps painful experiences in a dentist's office. The dentist's office (and perhaps the dentist) became associated with the unpleasant experience, making it a conditioned stimulus. Other dentists' offices are stimuli related to the conditioned stimulus (the original dentist's office), so they elicit similar unpleasant feelings (generalization). Medical doctors' offices are stimuli somewhat related to the original stimulus. However, the author discriminates between them and the dentists' offices, so they don't elicit the same unpleasant feelings.

6.6:   From a classically conditioned perspective, being bitten is an unconditioned stimulus, and the pain is an unconditioned response. Other dogs become associated with being bitten, so they become conditioned stimuli, producing fear as conditioned responses. The fear is an involuntary emotion.

From an operantly conditioned perspective, being bitten is a consequence. As a result, the child is less likely to approach dogs in the future (The child in fact runs away.) Running away is a voluntary behavior that occurs as a result of the consequence.

6.7:   From a behaviorist point of view, we would know that praise is not a positive reinforcer if the behavior being praised *doesn't* increase. (Praise might not work if it embarrassed the person being praised, or in some other way made the person feel awkward.)

6.8:   This situation illustrates positive reinforcement. Judy's behavior is increasing as the result of being given something--your admonishment.

6.9:   Darren's behavior illustrates negative reinforcement. His misbehavior is increasing (his behavior is worse the second day than it is the first day). The negative reinforcer is apparently being removed from class.

6.10:   If the behaviors they are intended to decrease actually do decrease, picking up trash is a punisher. If the behaviors increase, picking up trash is a reinforcer.

6.11: Through classical conditioning, neutral stimuli such as schools, classrooms and teachers can become associated with the pain and possible humiliation that can result from corporal punishment. These formerly neutral stimuli then become conditioned stimuli that elicit negative emotions (conditioned responses) similar to the negative emotions resulting from the corporal punishment. The net result is that students could develop negative emotional reactions to school.

6.12: Detention is designed to act as a punisher. Being allowed to talk or finish homework during detention might be reinforcing for the student. If this is the case, the detention no longer works as a punisher.

6.13: The desirable behaviors are identified, and when these behaviors are observed, they're reinforced.

6.14: First, generalization and discrimination are involuntary in classical conditioning situations, whereas they're voluntary in operant conditioning situations. Second, generalization in classical conditioning cases occurs when a stimulus similar to a conditioned stimulus elicits the conditioned response, and discrimination occurs when the stimulus related to the conditioned stimulus does not elicit the conditioned response. Generalization in operant conditioning situations occurs when the learner is reinforced for giving the same response to similar but not identical stimuli, such as calling a series of shapes triangles, even though they vary in size, color and orientation, and discrimination occurs when the learner is reinforced for giving a different response to different stimuli, such as calling one set of shapes "squares" and another set "rectangles."

6.15: The teacher should give Bryan *immediate* feedback that is *specific* and *provides corrective information*, such as saying something like, "Not quite. Sped describes the action in the sentence. That makes it a verb. Now, what word describes how it sped?"

An even more effective approach would be to prompt and guide Bryan to the correct answer with a series of questions. This is also immediate and specific and it allows him to provide his own corrective information.

6.16: The harsh feedback could produce instinctive fearful emotional responses. Attempting to answer questions could become associated with the harsh feedback, so attempting to answer would also produce fearful responses. As a result, learners would be less likely to try and respond, which in itself is reduced motivation. Also, not trying to respond would result in less learning.

6.17: Assessing the validity of teachers' praise and interpreting teachers' perceptions requires abstract thinking and perspective-taking, so--based on Piaget's work--we wouldn't expect these abilities from young children. Also, young children are unlikely to consider a teacher's motives, since their thinking tends to be egocentric. Small children are developing their sense of accomplishment, according to Erikson, and simply delight in any indicator of their good work. Older children are searching for identity, so they are more likely to be sensitive to reflections on their ability. A student might think, "That was an easy question. Why would she praise me for that answer? She must think I'm not too smart." We examine these issues again in Chapter 10 when we discuss student motivation.

6.18: Shaping involves the rewarding of approximations of the desired behavior. To get Felicia started on the assignment the teacher might encourage her to try the first problem and reinforce her first for simply making an effort. Then provide her with some assistance and reinforce her for making some progress on the assignment. On later assignments, Felicia would have to do more to be reinforced, and eventually she would have to complete the assignment. (It is important to note that shaping won't work unless Felicia makes progress. This means that the teacher must provide as much assistance as necessary to be sure that Felicia is improving.)

6.19: Playing the slot machine is an example of a variable ratio schedule of reinforcement. Receiving coins depends on behaviors (the number of times the handle is pulled), and when the player will receive coins is unpredictable.

6.20: Since the beeper going off depends on time, it is an interval schedule, and since it is unpredictable, it is a variable interval schedule.

6.21: The testing situation where pop quizzes are given might become associated with other testing situations that have induced anxiety, so the testing situation (involving pop quizzes) becomes a conditioned stimulus, with the anxiety being the conditioned response.

6.22: Satiation occurs more quickly with a continuous reinforcement schedule. This suggests that if continuous reinforcement is being used, a teacher should try to switch to an intermittent system as soon as possible. The beeper system illustrated in 6.20 would be one example; not all of students' on-task behaviors are reinforced--only those that occur at the time the beeper "beeps."

6.23: Initially writing is a neutral stimulus. If it's used as a punisher, the process (of writing) can become associated with other punishers that have caused negative emotions. Writing then becomes a conditioned stimulus that produces negative emotions (conditioned responses) similar to those caused by other punishers.

6.24: In both classical and operant conditioning, extinction involves the reduction (and ultimately the disappearance) of a behavior. In classical conditioning situations, the conditioned response disappears if the conditioned stimulus occurs repeatedly in the absence of the unconditioned stimulus. In operant conditioning cases, the behavior disappears if it isn't reinforced.

6.25: Satiation, extinction, and punishment all involve the reduction or elimination of a behavior. Satiation results from overreinforcement, extinction (in an operant sense) from lack of reinforcement, and punishment from either being presented with something (typically aversive for people) or having something (typically desirable) taken away.

6.26: The specific cues Mrs. Wendt used were her prompting questions: "What did John do?" "How did he jerk it?" and "So what is the adverb?" Her original question, "What is the adverb in the sentence?" was intended to elicit a response, but at that point Wendy was unable to answer. Prompting questions, such as the ones Mrs. Wendt used are very powerful in promoting student involvement and learning.

6.27: The teacher's goal is for students to use the cases appropriately. For example, the nominative case "I" would be used as the subject of a sentence, and the objective case "me" would be used as the object of a preposition. When students do so, they are generalizing. They discriminate when they recognize the need for the nominative case compared to the objective case.

6.28: Another internal process is *perception,* which is the way people interpret objects and events. For instance, one person might perceive an individual as shy, whereas another perceives the individual as aloof. A second process is *attention.* We attend to some stimuli but not others. Additional processes include *rehearsal,* which is the process of repeating information over and over in order to remember it, *organization,* which is forming connections between items of information, and *elaboration,* which is extending understanding.

6.29: According to behaviorism, people would organize the items on the list if they had had experience with those or similar items, and had been reinforced for organizing them.

6.30: Learning by watching others is a social experience. The examples are cognitive, because the individuals in each case wouldn't be able to replicate the behaviors they observed if those behaviors hadn't been recorded in their memories. Memory is a cognitive concept.

6.31: Greg's belief--"I seem to have a feel for French"--(a personal factor) influenced his behavior (working conscientiously on his homework). His behavior in turn influenced the environment (his hard work resulted in the teacher complimenting him; the compliment is an environmental factor). While we don't have direct evidence from the example, the environment is probably impacting his belief (The teacher's compliments probably are further increasing his beliefs about his ability to succeed in French), which again impact his behavior (as a result of his beliefs, his effort further increases).

6.32: *Expectation* is a cognitive process, since it is something that occurs within the learner. Since it is cognitive, we wouldn't expect to encounter it in our study of behaviorism.

6.33: Social cognitive theorists would suggest that the compliments impacted Greg's expectations. The teacher's compliments increased Greg's belief about his ability to succeed (he expected to succeed), and his increased effort was the result of the belief and expectation, not the direct result of positive reinforcement.

6.34: Social cognitive theory would suggest that the student is more likely to break the rule in the future. According to social cognitive theory, the nonoccurrence of an expected punisher can act as a reinforcer.

6:35: This is a false statement. People tend to imitate behaviors they observe in others regardless of whether or not the model is reinforced. Seeing the model reinforced enhances the impact on the observer through the process of vicarious conditioning.

6.36: This is a form of symbolic modeling, since the students are seeing a film or videotape of the speech rather than watching it directly.

6.37: Susan demonstrated cognitive modeling when she explained how she attacked problems that were different from the ones she was familiar with. She said, "See, this one is a little different," and then "The first thing I look for is how it is different from the others. Then, I attack it. . . . See, on this one I think we need to find c in terms of b, and then we have it down to two equations. . . . Now it's simpler."

6.38: A social cognitive theorist would say that observing someone being reinforced for a behavior would cause an observer to expect to be reinforced for the same behavior, just as being reinforced for demonstrating the behavior would cause the person to form similar expectations. The expectation of being reinforced results in an increased likelihood of displaying the behavior. Likewise, seeing a person being punished for displaying a behavior would cause the observer to expect to be punished for a similar behavior. The expectation of being punished would reduce the likelihood of displaying the behavior.

6.39: Social cognitive theory would suggest that the teacher should publicly reprimand Shelley for throwing the pencil, explaining why the behavior is inappropriate and how it might be harmful. (This would serve as a vicarious punisher for the other students.) Other factors teachers should consider are possible emotional reactions to public reprimands, the impact on classroom climate, Shelley's personal characteristics, and the history of her behavior.

6.40:   This is a form of direct modeling which produces a "facilitating existing behaviors" effect on the learners. The students already know how to "persist," so they are not acquiring a new behavior, and persistence is socially desirable. The teacher is "cuing" their persistence.

6.41:   A think-aloud would attract an observers attention and would demonstrate a desired behavior. The observer would retain the behavior in memory and could then (hopefully) reproduce the behavior in another setting.

6.42:   The pause serves as a cue, alerting all the students that they could be called on.

6.43:   The group that watched the children solved the most problems, and the group that saw no models solved the fewest problems (Schunk & Hanson, 1985). Research also indicates that when students are uncertain about the appropriateness of a behavior or have doubts about their capabilities, they are more likely to imitate a peer than an older child or adult (Schunk, 1987). This makes sense. Students uncertain about how to behave at a school dance, for example, are more likely to imitate the behavior of the other students than the behavior of the teacher chaperons.

   Perceived similarity is the most likely reason. Peers are perceived as more nearly similar than are older children or adults.

6.44:   The effect of a model's status on a person's behavior does not illustrate the concept of reinforcement potency, but the effect of status on behavior and the concept of reinforcement potency are indirectly related. Reinforcement is considered a direct cause of learning for behaviorists, and potent reinforcers are powerful in their ability to cause learning. A high-status model has a greater effect on observers than does a low-status model, but instead of directly causing learning, the effect motivates observers to imitate the model.

6.45:   Research indicates that the most effective goals are ones that are short-term, specific, and moderately challenging. You could, for example, set as a goal answering in writing all of the margin questions in the text. As a second goal, you could take each of the practice quizzes in the Student Study Guide, and as a third goal answering the application exercises also in the Student Study Guide. Many other goals are possible. We identify these because they are short term, specific, moderately challenging, and feedback is provided for each.

6.46:   Using the goal of answering each of the margin questions, a simple form of self-observation would be to check off each question as you've answered it.

6.47:   For each of the goals identified in 6.45, feedback is given, so assessment merely means comparing your response to the feedback. However, your written responses won't be identical to those given in the feedback, so you will have to make some judgments about the quality of your responses. These judgments involve self assessment in the true sense of the word.

6.48   Mrs. Evans's caring manner was an unconditioned stimulus to which Carlos responded instinctively with a feeling of comfort. Mrs. Evans's room became associated with her manner, so her room became a conditioned stimulus to which Carlos also responded with a feeling of comfort.

6.49:   Since reinforcement is based on a predictable number of responses, it is a fixed-ratio schedule.

Application Exercises

Exercise 6.1

Look at Items 1 through 3. If the behavior described in the italicized portion of the example is primarily the result of learning, put an *L* in the space in front of the example. Otherwise leave the space blank.

_____ 1. Mrs. Smith is doing a demonstration with air pressure and blows up a balloon. The balloon bursts, and Cathy, sitting in the front row, *jerks her head back.*

_____ 2. Ronnie, age 8, is going in for some booster shots. He *cries* when he sees the nurse with the needle.

_____ 3. Donnell, a senior, wants to be a good football player. He was a bit slow last year, running a 5.4-sec 40-yd dash. He lifted weights all summer, and to his pleasure, he *now runs a 4.9-sec 40-yd dash.*

Read the following case study.

Duranna is a conscientious and good student, although she is a bit unsure of herself. She's typically very attentive in class, and her classmates regard her as someone who will usually be able to answer questions.

One day, Mr. Harkness, her American history teacher, was conducting a question-and-answer session, and Duranna jerked when she heard her name called, suddenly realizing that she hadn't heard the question. A couple of the boys giggled as Mr. Harkness stared at her. Her stomach clenched, and she felt her face turn red. She started to stammer, then fell silent.

Now Duranna is uneasy whenever Mr. Harkness starts calling on students in class, and she doesn't like geometry as well as she did either, because she never knows when Mrs. Drake might call on her. She's relieved when she's in the safe confines of Spanish class, where Mrs. Lopez always calls on students in order up and down each row.

Consider this scenario as an example of classical conditioning, and identify each of the following from it.

4. Unconditioned stimulus

5. Unconditioned response

6. Conditioned stimulus

7. Conditioned response

8. Generalization

9. Discrimination

10. Think about the concept of *extinction*. Describe how Mr. Harkness could help Duranna eliminate her conditioned response, that is, help it become extinct.

Exercise 6.2

Read the following scenario and answer the questions that follow it.

Miguel is an inquiring student who asks good, probing questions in class, and the other students seem to appreciate him because his questions often help clear up some of their uncertainties. However, Miguel's questioning periodically makes Mr. Orr uneasy because he doesn't always have the answers.

One day when Miguel started to ask his fourth question in a row, Mr. Orr responded derisively: "Well, look at the brain. He's at it again."

Miguel stopped in mid-sentence.

During class a couple days later, Miguel asked one question and raised his hand to ask another. Mr. Orr looked at him and sneered, "Let's hear from the brain again."

The following day, Miguel quietly took notes the entire period.

1. Explain Miguel's behavior (his question asking). Use information from the case study to defend your answer.

2. Explain Mr. Orr's behavior (his sarcasm). How do we know? Use information from the case study to defend your answer.

3. On page 204 of the text, the statement, "All right, as soon as you've finished identifying the longitude and latitude of the five cities I've given you, you can begin your map projects," was given as an example of a teacher using the Premack Principle. For the Premack Principle to be in effect, what must be true about the students' attitudes toward longitude and latitude problems compared to map work?

Exercise 6.3

Read each of the following short case studies. For each, select from the following concepts--*generalization, discrimination, potency, punishment, fixed-interval reinforcement, variable-interval reinforcement, variable-ratio reinforcement, satiation, extinction,* and *shaping*--the one that is *most clearly illustrated* in the example. In each case, explain the illustration.

1. Mrs. Thornton arrives at the door of her classroom at 7:35 a.m. She takes out her key, puts it in the lock, and attempts to open the door. The door won't budge. "Hmm," she says to herself. "That's never happened before." She jiggles the key a couple more times, and then heads for the workroom to try and find a janitor.

2. Mrs. Green's fifth-grade class is studying insects. They've examined grasshoppers, beetles, a roach, and a water strider. "Hey!" Mary exclaimed while looking at a spider. "This isn't an insect."

3. Ken, a senior, wants to be as well prepared as possible for college. He's taking analytic geometry, even though math is not his strong suit, and he plans to major in a foreign language in college. He studied very hard for his first analytic geometry test and got a low C. He tried hard on the second test too, but it came back a D. He's having a difficult time trying now and is spending less time on the homework. He studied only haphazardly for his last test.

4. "I always give partial credit at the beginning of the year," Jane Howe, a geometry teacher, commented. "The kids have so much trouble with proofs. As time goes on, I make them do more to earn points on the problems, and by the end of the year, they have to get the whole thing right for any credit."

5. "I'm quitting sending notes home to parents," Mrs. Starke, a fourth-grade teacher, commented to a colleague in the teachers' lounge one day. "We had a workshop in which we were encouraged to write positive notes to send home when the kids are good. I tried it, and the children responded for a while. Now they hardly react, and the notes don't seem to affect their behavior. I even saw one child throw the note away rather than take it home."

6. Steve Weiss, a chemistry teacher, gives his students one problem each day when they come to class that counts five points on their overall quiz grade for the 9 weeks. "Generally, they're doing well," he noted. "I always give back their papers the next day, and they're about to the point where they like it. They ask me stuff like, 'Is this going to be another easy one today?'"

Exercise 6.4

1. Think about the children's story about the three little pigs. What form of modeling described in Table 6.5 on page 220 of your text is demonstrated in the story? What happens to the reader when the two lazy little pigs get eaten by the wolf? Explain. When the conscientious little pig outwits the wolf, what effect on behavior is this intended to have on the reader? Explain.

2. Think about the book *A Tale of Two Cities*. We described it in Chapter 3 as a piece of literature that has a moral dilemma embedded in it. Explain the dilemma and its effect on readers using the concepts of *vicarious reinforcement* and *vicarious punishment* when the character Sidney Carton chooses to die in his friend's place. What form of modeling is demonstrated by Sidney Carton?

Read the following case study and answer the questions that follow.

Mrs. Holmes was working with her seventh-grade geography students on specifying geographical locations. They knew the concepts of longitude and latitude and could read the numbers on a map.
She stood next to a large world map.
1. "Look at the map, everyone," she began. "Today we're learning an important skill that we'll use throughout the course. To start, let's find ourselves. Where do we look first? Jody?"
2. "We're in the United States," Jody responded. "It's right there," she continued, pointing.
3. "Good," Mrs. Holmes smiled. "Now let's be more precise."
She had the students locate their state and city and went on.
4. "Next we're going to locate another city. Name a famous city."
Several examples were suggested, and she decided on Mexico City.
5. "Now watch," she commanded. "I'm looking at these numbers up here. They're what? Karen?"
6. ". . . Longitude."
7. "Excellent, Karen. Now look, everyone. I'm going to find one that runs as close to Mexico City as possible. Here we go," and she traced a line from the top of the map through Mexico City with her finger. "It's very close to 100°," she noted, pointing to the number at the top. "We see we're west of England, where we said the zero line of longitude is, so Mexico City is 100° west longitude."
8. She repeated the process to find Mexico City's latitude.
9. "Give me another city," she continued. Settling on Chicago, she said, "Okay. Put your own maps on your desk." After waiting a few seconds, she asked, "What is its longitude? Joanie?"
10. ". . . It looks like it's about 88°."
11. She smiled at Joan. "Okay. West or east? Jack?"
12. ". . . West."
Mrs. Holmes continued the process, helping the students locate Chicago's latitude and then the location of Paris. Finally, she had them work independently to locate three more cities, saying that they would get five points on their homework grade for correctly identifying all three.

Analyze Mrs. Holmes's lesson as an example of applying observational learning in the classroom by identifying each of the four processes of observational learning in the lesson. Using the numbers at the beginning of each paragraph of the case study, make specific reference to the case study in your analysis.

3.   Attention

4.   Retention

5.   Reproduction

6.   Motivation

Exercise 6.5

Read the following case study and answer the questions that follow.

> Joe, a junior-high teacher, has a faculty meeting every Wednesday at 2:00 p.m. One week, Karen, the assistant principal, arrived for the meeting at 1:55 p.m. with overheads and handouts, ready to go. Joe got up from his classroom desk at 1:55 prepared for the meeting. As he stepped out into the hall, he glanced through the lounge doorway and saw four other faculty members sitting working. "I'll wait for them to walk by," he said to himself, and he sat back down and scored some more tests. The others walked by about 2:10, so he went to the meeting then. Everyone was there and settled by 2:15, and the meeting began.
>   The next week, the meeting again got started at about 2:15, and the following week at about 2:20.
>   The fourth week, Joe was in his office at 2:15 on Wednesday when his friend Sue walked by. "Aren't you coming to the meeting?" she asked.
>   "I'll be there in a minute," Joe responded with a smile, as he always did in response to a question. He came to the meeting at 2:25.

1.   Identify an example of modeling in the scenario.

2.   Identify an example of contiguity in the scenario.

3.   We see that Joe started going to the meetings later and later. Which concept from operant conditioning--*positive reinforcement*, *negative reinforcement*, *presentation punishment* or *removal punishment* best explains why he is going later? How do you know it is that concept?

Feedback for Application Exercises

Exercise 6.1

1. Cathy jerking her head back in response to the bursting balloon is an example of a reflex, and therefore is not a learned behavior.

2. Ronnie's crying is a learned behavior, based on previous negative experiences with needles or other experiences associated with needles. (People are not instinctively or reflexively afraid of needles.)

3. Donnell's increased speed is primarily the result of his improved strength and physical conditioning rather than the result of learning.

4. The unconditioned stimulus is the situation that caused the embarrassing experience. This situation is a combination of being called on, being stared at, and the boys giggling. We can't be sure of the exact combination of the factors. It could be any one of them, two of them, or all three.

5. The unconditioned response was Duranna's stomach clenching and her face turning red. (This is a reflexive response to the situation.)

6. The conditioned stimulus is an environment where students are being questioned. It has become *associated* with the initial embarrassing situation.

7. Duranna's uneasiness is the conditioned response. Notice that uneasiness is a response that is *similar* to the unconditioned response--stomach clenching and face turning red.

Notice that the conditioned and unconditioned stimuli are not necessarily *related* in any way (just as Pavlov's assistants and the meat powder are not related), but they become *associated*. The conditioned and unconditioned stimuli are *similar* or *identical* (similar in Duranna's case; identical for Pavlov's dogs).

8. Her uneasiness has now generalized to geometry because the environment there is similar to the environment in American History.

9. Duranna discriminates between Spanish, where the questioning is patterned, and American History and geometry, where the process has been anxiety inducing.

10. Mr. Harkness needs to call on Duranna in a situation where he is certain that she is not taken by surprise. After Duranna is called on several times without incident (the conditioned stimulus occurring repeatedly in the absence of the unconditioned stimulus), her uneasiness should begin to disappear. He also needs to make and enforce a rule that forbids students from laughing at each other's embarrassment.

Exercise 6.2

1. Miguel is being punished for speaking out in class, which is evidenced by the decreasing incidence of question-asking behavior. This is a form of presentation punishment, since an undesired consequence is being given, rather than something desirable being taken away.

2. Mr. Orr's behavior is being negatively reinforced. Miguel's questions make him uncomfortable since he can't always answer them. His sarcasm stops Miguel's behavior which removes an undesirable situation (being asked questions he may not be able to answer). As a result we see his sarcasm increasing.

3. For this statement to be true, the students would have to prefer doing map work rather than longitude and latitude problems. The map work (the preferred activity) could then be used as a reinforcer for the less preferred activity (doing longitude and latitude problems).

Exercise 6.3

1. The concept is *extinction*--the rapid reduction in behavior after a continuous reinforcement schedule. Normally, the door opens every time (continuous reinforcement) as evidenced by Mrs. Thornton's comment, "That's never happened before." The door opening each time is a reinforcer for putting the key in and attempting to open the door. This time when it didn't open, Mrs. Thornton quickly gave up, which is characteristic of behavior when a continuous reinforcement schedule is used and the reinforcers are removed. If the door had been "balky," meaning she had to struggle to get it open (an intermittent schedule) she would have persevered longer.

2. The concept being demonstrated in this example is *discrimination*. Mary is discriminating between the spider and the other animals, which are insects.

3. The example illustrates *punishment* (specifically presentation punishment). Ken is receiving something that is reducing his behavior. (To clarify how this answer is different from extinction, look again at page 211-212 of your text. In the example on page 211-212, Renita received nothing for her efforts--no reinforcer or punisher.) Ken, in contrast, received the low grade.

4. Mrs. Howe is making an effort to *shape* her students' behavior by reinforcing behaviors that are successive approximations of the desired behavior.

5. The case study is an example of *satiation*. Mrs. Starke has apparently sent too many positive notes home to the point that they've lost their potency as reinforcers.

6. Mr. Weiss was applying a *fixed-interval schedule of reinforcement* to his classroom. While this can have disadvantages, as discussed in the text of the chapter, his giving a problem every day kept the interval short, so student effort remained high. This is not an example of continuous reinforcement, because *not every studying behavior is reinforced*. The students are reinforced on the interval of one day.

Exercise 6.4

1. The story is a form of *symbolic modeling*. When the two lazy little pigs get eaten, the readers are *vicariously punished*; the readers observe the consequences of the little pigs actions, and perhaps adjust their own behavior accordingly. When the conscientious little pig outwits the wolf, the readers are *vicariously reinforced*. The effect on behavior that this is intended to have is to *facilitate existing behaviors*. The students know how to be conscientious, and the combination of the symbolic modeling of the conscientious little pig and vicarious reinforcement is intended to increased conscientiousness.

2. Readers are caught in a dilemma between vicarious reinforcement and vicarious punishment. They are vicariously reinforced through the Sidney Carton's noble act, but they are vicariously punished through the fact that he gave his life under the guillotine. It is a form of symbolic modeling.

3. Attention is illustrated in 1–4 of the case study. Mrs. Holmes pulled down a map, referred the students to it and has them find themselves on it. She then asked for another city.

4. She promoted retention by modeling the process of finding the location of longitude and latitude (beginning at 5). She continued the process through 8 of the case study.

5. Reproduction began at 9 when she asked Joanie to locate the longitude of Chicago. This continued through the locations of each city.

6. Motivation was illustrated in several places. She began the lesson by explaining that the skill was an important one, used throughout the course. During the course of the lesson she reinforced with comments like, "Good", and "Excellent." Finally, students received points for completing their homework.

Exercise 6.5

1. Joe imitated the behavior he saw in his colleagues by sitting back down and working when he saw them sitting and working.

2. His smile in response to the question "as he always did in response to a question" is an example of contiguity.

3. Joe is being positively reinforced for coming late. He is not in an aversive situation prior to demonstrating the behavior (going to the meeting), so nothing undesirable is being removed. It is therefore not negative reinforcement. We know his lateness is being reinforced because he is coming later and later (his behavior is increasing, not decreasing, so it cannot be punishment.)

Self-Help Quiz_____

TRUE/FALSE QUESTIONS. Write T in the blank if the statement is true, and write F if the statement is false.

_____ 1.   For operantly conditioned behaviors the influence of the environment (stimulus) precedes the behavior, but for classically conditioned behaviors it follows the behavior.
_____ 2.   Operantly conditioned behaviors must be reinforced to prevent extinction, but classically conditioned behaviors do not become extinct.
_____ 3.   Generalization occurs with operantly conditioned behaviors but not with classically conditioned behaviors.
_____ 4.   While positive reinforcement is an increase in behavior, negative reinforcement is a decrease in behavior.
_____ 5.   When classically conditioned learning takes place, the unconditioned and the conditioned stimuli will be similar to each other.

MULTIPLE-CHOICE QUESTIONS. Circle the best response in each case.

6. You're anticipating taking a test from an instructor with a reputation for being "tough." As you wait for the test, you feel jittery and your mouth is dry. Your jitters and dry mouth are best described as:
    a.   unconditioned stimuli.
    b.   conditioned stimuli.
    c.   unconditioned responses.
    d.   conditioned responses.

7. Mr. Powell's students are getting a bit rowdy as the end of the day nears. He comments, "If the trash around your desks isn't picked up, and if you're not quiet in one minute, we'll be spending 10 minutes after school." The students immediately pick up the papers around their desk and are sitting quietly as the bell rings. Mr. Powell's technique would be best described as:
    a.   negative reinforcement.
    b.   presentation punishment.
    c.   removal punishment.
    d.   discrimination.
    e.   satiation.

8. Mr. Allen tries to be judicious in praising his students. He wants to praise them enough but not too much. To implement this process, he praises his students when he feels like they give an insightful response or a response reflecting considerable effort. His schedule would be best described as:
    a.   continuous.
    b.   fixed ratio.
    c.   variable ratio.
    d.   fixed interval.
    e.   variable interval.

9. Mr. Allen's desire (in Item 8) to give "enough praise" but not "too much" indicates that he's aware of two concepts. The two concepts are best described as:
   a. potency and satiation.
   b. potency and extinction.
   c. generalization and discrimination.
   d. extinction and satiation.
   e. generalization and extinction.

10. In a lesson on place value, Kim sees the numbers 42 and 24 and says, "In the first number the four is in the tens column, and in the second it's in the ones column." Kim's comment best illustrates which of the following?
   a. Classical conditioning
   b. Discrimination
   c. Generalization
   d. Vicarious conditioning

11. In item 10, Kim's learning would be best classified in which of the following categories?
   a. Contiguity
   b. Classical conditioning
   c. Operant conditioning
   d. Symbolic modeling

12. Joanne is being disruptive in Mrs. Henderson's class. Exasperated, Mrs. Henderson tells Joanne to pull her desk out into the hall and sit there until she is told otherwise. Mrs. Henderson's technique is best describe as an attempt to administer:
   a. negative reinforcement.
   b. presentation punishment.
   c. removal punishment.
   d. vicarious punishment.

13. Two of your students are whispering instead of doing their assigned seatwork. You go to them and tell them to stop whispering. They comply. This incident best illustrates:
   a. negative reinforcement.
   b. presentation punishment.
   c. removal punishment.
   d. satiation.

14. Mr. Parker comments to his second graders as they are beginning a seat work assignment, "I'm very pleased to see that Debbie is already working and has finished the first two problems." Mr. Parker's comment is best described as an attempt to implement which of the following with his class?
   a. Positive reinforcement
   b. Negative reinforcement
   c. Vicarious reinforcement
   d. The Premack Principle

15. Which of the following most accurately describes Mr. Parker's behavior in Item 14?
   a. He is attempting to be a model for both Debbie and the rest of the students.
   b. He is attempting to be a model for Debbie but not necessarily be a model for the rest of the students.
   c. He is attempting to be a model for the rest of the students but not necessarily be a model for Debbie.
   d. He is attempting to use Debbie as a model for the rest of the students.

Tim is in kindergarten. His mother takes him to school. Tim is happy when his mother is there but is upset when she leaves. Mr. Soo begins to talk and joke with Tim while his mother is there, and now Tim is satisfied when his mother leaves.

Consider this situation to be a case of classical conditioning.

16. The unconditioned stimulus would be:
    a.   the school.
    b.   Mr. Soo talking and joking with Tim.
    c.   Tim's mother.
    d.   happiness.
    e.   upset.

17. The unconditioned response would be:
    a.   the school.
    b.   happiness.
    c.   upset.
    d.   satisfaction.
    e.   Tim's mother.

Martina is very uneasy in anticipating the beginning of her junior high school experience. Sensing her uneasiness, her dad drove her to school the first morning. They have a close relationship, and Martina feels very warm when she's with him. Martina's dad dropped her off at school, and she walked uncertainly into her homeroom. As she came through the door, Mrs. Hafner smiled broadly, put her arm around Martina and said, "Welcome to our school. Your records tell us that you're new here. I know you're going to like it." Martina felt instant relief. Mrs. Hafner proved to be consistent in her manner. Now, as she goes into the school each day, Martina is quite at ease.

18. The best illustration of the conditioned stimulus would be:
    a.   the school.
    b.   Mrs. Hafner's warmth.
    c.   feeling at ease.
    d.   feeling instant relief.

19. The conditioned response would be:
    a.   the warm feeling she has with her father.
    b.   relief.
    c.   Mrs. Hafter's manner.
    d.   feeling at ease.

"This test was impossible. They're always so tricky," Mr. Tuff's students complain as he finishes his discussion of a test he had just handed back. "And they're so long," they continue.

Mr. Tuff then consciously makes his next test easier and shorter, hoping his students won't complain so much. He gives the test, scores it, and returns it.

"Not again," some students comment about half way through the discussion of the test. "Yes, you must love to write tricky items," some others add.

Again, in preparing his next test, he reduces the application level of the items and makes the test still shorter.

20. In its impact on Mr. Tuff's behavior, the case study best illustrates:
   a. positive reinforcement.
   b. negative reinforcement.
   c. presentation punishment.
   d. removal punishment.
   e. a conditioned response.

21. In its impact on the students' behavior, the case study best illustrates:
   a. positive reinforcement.
   b. negative reinforcement.
   c. presentation punishment.
   d. removal punishment.
   e. a conditioned response.

22. Mrs. Batton gets up from her reading group every few minutes to go and circulate among the students who are doing seatwork to offer encouragement. In its influence on the behavior of the students doing seatwork, her actions best illustrate an application of:
   a. fixed-interval reinforcement.
   b. variable-interval reinforcement.
   c. variable-ratio reinforcement.
   d. vicarious reinforcement.

23. Your instructor assigns a written project to be turned in and says that it will be graded. You work conscientiously on the project, but your friend does a haphazard job the night before it is due. The instructor simply puts a check mark on the project, indicating that it has been turned in, and you and your friend each receive 5 points for having done the project. Based on *social cognitive theory*, which of the following best explains the outcome of yours and your friend's behaviors?
   a. You are both reinforced since you both received credit for having completed the project.
   b. You are both punished, since the instructor gave you points instead of a letter grade.
   c. You are being directly reinforced because you worked hard on the project, whereas your friend is being vicariously reinforced since he or she worked less hard.
   d. You are being punished, whereas your friend is being reinforced, since you got the same number of points on the project.

24. In a question and answer session, Mr. Hanson says, "Now what is the first step in the problem, Jimmy?"
   ". . . I'm not sure," Jimmy responds after sitting and looking at the problem for several seconds.
   "Help him out, Kelly," Mr. Hanson smiles.
   "We first must find the common denominator," Kelly answers. Later in the lesson, Mr. Hanson is examining another problem.
   "OK, now what do we do? Jimmy?"
   "I don't know," Jimmy says after glancing at the problem.
   "Help him out once more, Kelly," Mr. Hanson says supportively.
a) Explain Jimmy's behavior, identifying the specific concept or concepts from behaviorism that best apply. (Support your statements with evidence from the example.) b) What is Jimmy likely to do the next time he is called on? c) Describe what Mr. Kelly might have done differently that would have been more effective.

25. A middle-aged man who has become a little rotund would like to get in shape but is very uneasy about going to a fitness center, since he has long ago lost his "athletic appearance." At the urging of a friend, he finally goes to a fitness club near where he lives just to take a look.

Upon arriving at the club he is surprised to see several people about his age and build, laboring over the machines and free weights. The man is now consistently working out.

Using social cognitive theory, provide a *detailed* and *complete* explanation for the man's behavior (the fact that he is now working out). Include 1) the form of modeling (p. 220 of your text), 2) the effect of modeling on behavior (p. 221 of your text), and 3) the effectiveness of models (p. 224 of your text) in your explanation.

Self-Help Quiz Answers_____

1.	f	
2.	f	
3.	f	
4.	f	
5.	f	
6.	d	You are displaying a conditioned response. (Remember, an unconditioned response is *unlearned*. We don't respond reflexively or instinctively to tests.)
7.	a	The students displayed the desired behavior (picking up the trash and sitting quietly). Notice also that while Mr. Powell threatened the students with punishment, he didn't actually punish them.
8.	c	The students are praised based on their responses, and they are praised on an unpredictable basis.
9.	a	Mr. Allen is trying to maintain his praise as potent reinforcers. Too much praise could lead to satiation, which means that the praise could lose its potency.
10.	b	Kim is discriminating between the tens (10s) place and the units place.
11.	c	Kim had been reinforced for discriminating between the two. The behavior is more complex than simple contiguity, it is a voluntary response, so it can't be classical conditioning, and while we don't have evidence that modeling took place, it is unlikely that the modeling would be on film or in cartoons.
12.	c	Joanne is being removed from the classroom, and she is put in a situation where presumably she is unable to get positive reinforcement.
13.	b	The students were given something (your reprimand), which decreased their behavior.
14	c	Mr. Parker is attempting to vicariously reinforce the class by directly reinforcing Debbie, and using her as a model for the rest of the class.
15.	d	(See the feedback for item 14.)
16.	c	Tim is already happy with his mother. (This analysis is based on the assumption that children's love for their parents is innate.)
17.	b	(See the feedback for item 16.)
18.	a	Mrs. Hafner's warmth is an unconditioned stimulus which resulted in the unconditioned response-- relief. The school becomes associated with Mrs. Hafner's warmth, so it is the conditioned stimulus. (Since Martina's father merely drops her off, neither Mrs. Hafner nor the school have become associated with him, so he is *not* the unconditioned stimulus. Notice how this situation is different from the one with Tim, his mother, and Mr. Soo. In that case Mr. Soo became associated with Tim's mother, because they all stood together and talked. In that problem, Mr. Soo becomes the conditioned stimulus and satisfaction is the conditioned response.)
19.	d	Martina feels at-ease when she enters the school, so this feeling is the conditioned response. Notice that this is a response *to the school*. As we saw in Item 18, the school is the conditioned stimulus.
20.	c	His behavior is being reduced--he reduces the length and difficulty of the test, so it is punishment. The students are *presenting* him with their complaints. (The behavior is voluntary, so it is not a conditioned response.)

21.   b   A situation (typically considered undesirable when working with humans)--the length and difficulty of the test--is being reduced, so the students' complaints are being negatively reinforced. (Their complaints occur sooner, so their complaining behavior is increasing.)

22.   b   Her encouragement is a form of reinforcement, and "every few minutes" is a variable interval.

23.   d   This situation is best explained through "nonoccurrence of expected consequences." You expect to receive more credit for your hard work than your friend should receive, since you worked harder. This doesn't occur, so the nonoccurrence serves as a punisher for you. The exact opposite occurs for your friend.

24.   a) Since Jimmy's behavior is increasing--he says "I don't know," sooner the second time than he did the first time, he is being reinforced. The reinforcer is Mr. Hanson "removing" the question from him (taking him off the "hook"), so it is an example of negative reinforcement. b) Jimmy is likely to say, "I don't know," even sooner than he did before. c) Mr. Hanson should give Jimmy some prompts or cues that will allow him to answer instead of turning the question to another student.

25.   *Direct modeling* is illustrated--the man directly observes others working out. The situation illustrates the effectiveness of *perceived similarity*--the other people he observes are similar in age and build, and the effect on behavior is *facilitating an existing behavior*. (Changing inhibitions typically refers to socially unacceptable behavior, so we wouldn't conclude that his inhibitions about working out have been reduced.)

CHAPTER 7: COGNITIVE VIEWS OF LEARNING

Chapter Outline

I.   Cognitive views of learning
II. Information processing
    A.   Models: Aids to understanding
    B.   Sensory memory
    C.   Working memory
        1.   Working memory as a screen
        2.   Limitations of working memory
            a.   Increasing processing efficiency: Chunking
            b.   Increasing processing efficiency: Automaticity
            c.   Limitations of working memory: Implications for instruction
    D.   Long-term memory
    E.   Representing knowledge in long-term memory
        1.   Declarative and procedural knowledge
            a.   Representing declarative knowledge
            b.   Schemas: Combinations of propositions, images, and linear orderings
            c.   Schemas as scripts
            d.   Schemas: implications for teaching
            e.   Representing procedural knowledge in memory: Conditions and actions
            f.   Acquiring procedural knowledge
            g.   Importance of context in acquiring procedural knowledge
    F.   Cognitive processes
        1.   Attention: The beginning of information processing
            a.   Attracting and maintaining student attention
        2.   Perception: Finding meaning in stimuli
            a.   Background knowledge affects perception
        3.   Rehearsal: Retaining information through practice
        4.   Meaningful encoding: Making connections in long-term memory
            1.   Making information meaningful
                a. Organization
                b. Elaboration
                c. Activity
            2.   Levels of processing: An alternate view of meaningful encoding
        5.   Forgetting
            a.   Forgetting as interference
            b.   Forgetting as retrieval failure
            c.   The role of context in retrieval
            d.   Problems as contexts
    G.   Metacognition: Knowledge and control of cognitive processes
        1.   The development of metacognition
            a.   Meta-attention: Development of attention strategies
            b.   Metamemory: Development of memory strategies
    H.   Impact of diversity on information processing
        1.   Diversity and perception
        2.   Diversity, encoding, and retrieval
        3.   Instructional adaptations for background diversity
    I.   Putting information processing into perspective

III.   Constructivism
     A.   Emerging role of constructivism in education
     B.   Different views of constructivism
     C.   Characteristics of constructivism
          1.   Learners construct understanding
          2.   New learning depends on current understanding
          3.   Learning is facilitated by social interaction
               a.   Importance of dialogue in learning
          4.   Meaningful learning occurs within authentic learning tasks
     D.   Putting constructivism into perspective
          1.   Constructivist controversies
               a.   Situated learning
               b.   The nature of knowledge
          2.   Constructivist cautions

Chapter Objectives

- Understand the components of information processing, including sensory memory, working memory, and long-term memory.

- Explain the role of cognitive processes in learning.

- Explain how teachers can help students develop metacognitive abilities.

- Identify the essential elements of constructivist views of learning.

- Describe the implications that constructivism has for teaching.

Chapter Overview

In Chapter 6 we saw that behaviorists focus exclusively on observable behaviors as they are influenced by experience. In addition, we analyzed learning from a social cognitive perspective, focusing on the internal processes learners use as they observe other individuals' actions. In this chapter we continue our focus on cognitive views of learning, and we begin with information processing, a view of learning that stresses internal stores and processes. We cannot directly observe these information stores and internal processes so we create a model to help us visualize how information proceeds through the system, much in the same way as we create models to help us visualize the structure of atoms and molecules.

The Information Processing Model is composed of information stores, which store knowledge, cognitive processes, which move information from one store to another, and metacognition, which monitors and regulates our cognitive processes.

Metacognition is developmental; for example, older learners are better than younger ones at purposefully directing their attention toward important information (a form of meta-attention) and using strategies to encode information into long-term memory (a form of metamemory). When learners develop their metacognitive abilities they can become self-regulated, meaning they are equipped to learn effectively on their own.

Meaningfulness can be increased, and encoding made more efficient, if information is carefully organized, if new learning is consciously attached to old through elaboration in the form of reviews and comparisons, and if learners are put in active roles during learning activities.

Constructivism is a cognitive view of learning based on the views of Piaget and Vygotsky, which were described in Chapter Two. Characteristics of constructivism include: 1) learners construct their own understanding of information and events; 2) new learning depends on current understandings; 3) learning is facilitated by social interaction; and 4) meaningful learning occurs within authentic learning tasks. As teachers implement constructivism in their classrooms they must have clear goals in mind and adapt instruction to meet the learning needs of their students.

Feedback for Margin Questions

7.1:   Behaviorist theories contend that mental processes are not necessary to explain learning; rather they focus on behaviors and stimuli, such as reinforcers.

7.2:   The globe is intended as a miniature representation of the earth, similar in shape with the proportions of landforms and water represented on the globe similar to the earth's actual proportions. The model of the atom is only intended to help us visualize what we cannot directly observe. The information processing model is more like the model of the atom than like the globe.

7.3:   The lines represent the flow of information. Fewer lines between attention and perception suggest that some information is lost from sensory memory if we don't immediately attend to the stimuli.

7.4:   "Unorganized" means that the information exists in sensory memory in the same form as it exists in the environment. It is basically a perceptual copy of the objects and events in the outside world. "Organization" takes place in working memory as we will see in the next section.

7.5:   Though sensory memory is virtually unlimited in capacity, if the incoming information isn't quickly processed--beginning with attention--it gets lost. Asking a second question without giving students time to attend to the first will probably result in the first question being lost from sensory memory, or if the learner attends to the first question, the second will be lost. In any case, learning suffers.

7.6:   The information was moved to long-term memory. Information in working memory is lost in a matter of seconds unless it is rehearsed, and you wouldn't have been able to rehearse the information overnight. As you thought about these questions, the thinking took place in your working memory. Working memory is where deliberate thinking takes place. It is the conscious part of our information processing system.

7.7:   The loop helps us visualize that information can be retained in working memory through rehearsal. The arrow means our responses come from working memory. This again reminds us that working memory is the conscious part of our processing system.

7.8:   2HEALTH has chunked seven bits of information into two; the number 2 and the word "health." Also, the word "health" is more meaningful than the six numbers 4 3 2 5 8 4. The combination of chunking and meaningfulness makes the number much easier to remember.

7.9:   Since our working memories have limited capacity, and we use algebra skills to solve physics problems, the better algebra student will have more working memory space to devote to solving the physics problem than will the weaker student, since more of the algebra skills have become automatic for the better student.

7.10: "Processing bottleneck" means that there are limits to the amount of information that students can process in working memory. If this limit is exceeded, the information is lost instead of being transferred into long-term memory. Teachers can help accommodate the bottleneck by: 1) presenting information in small chunks, 2) facilitating transfer to long-term memory by putting the students into an active role by questioning them and giving them practice exercises, and 3) using visual displays such as the chalkboard or overhead projector that help maintain information until it can be processed further.

7.11: Making the statement represents declarative knowledge. Procedural knowledge would be required to actually use adjectives and nouns correctly in writing.

7.12: First, your schema will have more items of information in it, and second, the items in your schema will be more interconnected than will be the items in your friend's schema. The more interconnected the individual items, the better your understanding.

7.13: There would be fewer (or no) interconnections between the different bits of information. The items of information would sit separately and in isolation.

7.14: High SES students often have a richer background of school-related experiences than do low SES students. This means they have more items of information in their schemas, and their schemas are more elaborate (there are more links between the items). These elaborate schemas provide more available links to which new information can be attached.

7.15: The conditions involve recognizing that the problem involves adding fractions with unlike denominators. The actions require finding a lowest common denominator and adding the fractions. The declarative knowledge required is knowing that when you add fractions with unlike denominators you must find a lowest common denominator and knowing the rules for finding them.

7.16: You could give the students a series of word problems, some requiring adding fractions and others of that do not. Of those that require adding fractions, some should have like denominators and others should have unlike denominators. The key to helping students develop their abilities is to change the conditions. Changing the conditions requires putting the problems in context, which is why word problems are so important.

7.17: This example first implies that many stimuli enter our information processing systems even though we're not conscious of them. In addition to the example with conversations at parties, we often are unaware of "white noise," such as the whisper of an air conditioner in a room. If someone calls our attention to it, we then hear the air conditioner, for example. These examples suggest that the information enters our sensory memory, but it is lost unless we attend (pay attention) to it. When our attention is attracted, we begin to process the information.

7.18: Information processing theorists would say that students are more likely to pay attention to enthusiastic teachers. Social cognitive theorists would say that enthusiastic teachers are effective models, which would increase the likelihood that students would imitate their behavior.

7.19: "John, why do you think people are fascinated with the legends of King Arthur?" is a powerful attention getter for John, but it takes the rest of the class "off the hook." The second sequence is more effective for maintaining the attention of the whole class.

7.20: Our background knowledge is organized in the form of schemas. These schemas allow us to make inferences about new information. These inferences are our perceptions of the objects and events we observe. Each experience is either linked to an existing schema or is lost. The more complex our schemas the more "hooks" that can be used to perceive and attach new information to old.

7.21:   You would be most likely to use maintenance rehearsal as a strategy--simply repeat the number a few times. If you wanted to remember it for a longer period of time, you might use elaborative rehearsal--linking the number to information already in long-term memory, or you might try to find meaning in the number. For example the number 246-3487 can be made meaningful by recognizing that the 2, 4, and 6 are in an even-numbered sequence, and the 4 is one more than 3, 8 is twice as much as 4, and 7 is one less than 8. Obviously, numbers can be made meaningful in a countless number of ways.

7.22:   We see a rehearsal arrow going from working memory to long-term memory. This arrow is intended to help us visualize the process of moving information from working memory to long-term memory through rehearsal.

7.23:   While the line between elaborative rehearsal and encoding is fine and can be blurred, the primary difference is in the kind of information that is transferred to long-term memory. Rehearsal--both maintenance and elaborative--involves fact-level learning, whereas encoding is required for more complex forms of information, such as schemas.

7.24:   Complex schemas are meaningful (they have many connections in them), and they are stored as "chunks," so they don't overload working memory. Less interconnected schemas actually take up more working memory space, since many of the pieces tend to be stored in isolation, and each piece takes up some working memory space.

7.25:   Some of the patterns include: in both cases the immigrants had economic difficulties in their home country, the immigrants from both tended to be from low socioeconomic classes, and they had tight family structures. Also, in both cases, the immigrants initially had little contact outside their own groups. (As time went on the Italians tended to assimilate more rapidly than did the Chinese.)

7.26:   You could have them compare different verbals in the context of sentences, and you could also have them produce examples of verbals (also in the context of sentences). Both situations would also put the students in an active mode (which we discuss later in this section). You could also encourage students to visualize the hierarchy to form an image of the way you've organized the information about verbals.

7.27:   Charts, matrices and outlines can serve as attention getters. As is the theme of this section, they serve as ways of organizing information, which makes it meaningful and aids encoding and later retrieval.

7.28:   This does not imply that the information is not organized. In fact, the information is well integrated into larger schemas suggesting that all living things get their food from the environment. This is one reason that misconceptions are so hard to eliminate.

7.29:   They help us visualize what is meant by schemas. The give us a visual image of a schema as an organizer.

7.30:   In both cases, new information can be added to prior knowledge by associating the new information with the prior understanding. The primary difference is that elaborative rehearsal operates primarily with factual level information, whereas elaboration deals with more complex forms of understanding.

7.31:   You would capitalize on elaboration by beginning the lesson with a review of direct objects, then linking indirect objects to them.

7.32:   Virtually all mnemonic devices are designed to help students memorize factual information. While memorizing some facts is necessary, thinking skills, problem solving and understanding concepts and the relationships among them are much more important learning goals.

7.33:   The second one. She is making decisions about what is most important to highlight. Making decisions is an active process. (It is the most important part of the process.)

7.34:   Questions that promote deep processing include:
        . "Why," such as "Why is Mercury so hot on one side and cold on the other?"
        . "What would happen if. . . ?" such as "What would happen if Mercury had a period of rotation similar to that of the Earth?"
        . "How are these alike or different?" such as "How are the 'inner planets' alike, and how are they different from the 'outer planets?'
        Questions that simply call for factual or memorized information promote only shallow processing.

7.35:   Interference is more common when studying closely related ideas because learners often confuse the characteristics of the ideas. This suggests that interference is more likely when teaching similes and metaphors, since they are much more closely related than are figures of speech and parts of speech. This is one of the reasons teaching closely related ideas together and explicitly pointing out differences is helpful.

7.36:   Meaningfulness describes the number of associations between ideas. More meaningful ideas have more associations between them than do less meaningful ideas. More associations makes retrieval easier, meaning that ideas on "the tip of the tongue" would be easier to access.

7.37:   Encoding specificity can have an negative affect on classroom learning because it suggests that knowledge must be retrieved in the same way as it was encoded, making it narrowly accessible. To minimize this potential problem, teachers should present information from multiple perspectives, encouraging students to encode information in different ways. As we will see in Chapter 8, this is one reason a variety of examples, problems, and situations is so important in promoting learning.

7.38:   A variety of problems could be presented. One example could be the following: "Scientists have discovered something unusual about the planets in our solar system. All of them revolve around our sun in a plane like this (showing the plane). All except for one--Pluto. Why do you think this might be the case? Today we're going to explore some possible explanations.

7.39:   Yes, your behavior is strategic. A strategy is a plan for accomplishing a goal. Your goal is to understand the word, and you used the context of the sentence in an effort to do so. This is strategic behavior.

7.40:   While you may use different strategies, note taking and highlighting (or underlining) are two common ones. In each case the goal is to better remember and understand the information you hear from your instructor or read in your text.

7.41:   Mrs. Mahera was focusing primarily on helping the children develop their *awareness* of the need to pay attention. *Control over* their attention would be the next step.

7.42:   Quizzical looks on students' faces are one indication that the students realize that the information isn't making sense to them, and they're not likely to remember it. Students raising their hands asking for clarification or additional information is another indication. A third is note-taking. Presumably, students realize that they will remember and understand more about the topic if they take notes. Teachers can encourage metacognitive growth by talking about it and modeling it in the classroom.

7.43:   While taking notes could illustrate both, it more likely illustrates metamemory. College students typically take notes to help them remember the information they're hearing and studying. If a college student took notes to help him or her pay attention in class, it would illustrate meta-attention.

7.44:   "Different schemas" is probably more accurate. Because students don't have elaborate school-related schemas doesn't mean that the schemas they do have are not well developed. However, since school-related schemas are important for academic success, our task as teachers is to help them build on their school-related schemas to promote learning.

7.45:   "Rich" examples and representations contain all the information in them that learners need to understand an idea. The analogy between the school and nationalism is an illustration. The students could relate to the idea of school spirit, pride in the school, and traditions, which could be linked to similar feelings in a country. The example with the teacher having the students stand on both feet and then one foot (presented in the Classroom Connections on p. 265) is another instance. The students can "see" that their weight doesn't change, but the amount of surface area over which it is distributed is twice as great on two feet as it is on one. This provides a concrete and understandable illustration of the concept pressure.

7.46:   In cognitive constructivism, which is based on Piaget's work, social interaction serves as a way to test the validity of schemes. In the process of interaction, individuals' test their schemes against the ideas of others. However, reconstruction of the schemes, if it occurs, is an individual process.

        In contrast, social constructivists argue that knowledge is initially socially shared. Understanding proceeds from socially shared understanding to individual understanding. The idea of socially shared knowledge doesn't exist for cognitive constructivism.

7.47:   Suzie's thinking illustrates *centration*. She was centering on the number of blocks and not considering their location on the balance. The number is a more salient feature than the location.

7.48:   Both information processing and constructivism are based on the premise that learners are active. They also both emphasize the importance of background knowledge in new learning. An important difference is the emphasis they place (or don't place) on social interaction. Both cognitive and social constructivism emphasize the role of social interaction (although for different reasons, as we saw in 7.46). Information processing doesn't address the role of social interaction. (Also, information processing doesn't emphasize the process of knowledge construction, although its emphasis on organization and encoding could be inferred to be a "constructive" process.)

7.49:   Some different ways background knowledge can be organized include propositional networks, images, linear orderings and schemas. As we saw earlier in the chapter, schemas are combinations of the others. When we introduce new topics we want to activate these frameworks to encourage meaningful connections. The way we activate background knowledge is by asking students to describe their understanding of the topic being discussed, presenting information and asking their perceptions of it, and then building on these perceptions and understandings.

7.50:   Piaget would say that change disrupts their equilibrium. This would explain why learners are often resistant to change.

7.51:   David's teaching was quite strongly teacher-directed. Most of the whole-group interaction was teacher-student-teacher-student. Ideally, social interaction involves a significant amount of student-student interaction. Placing students in small groups encourages students to take a more active role in their learning and David did some of that. However, even in whole-group activities, constructivists would encourage as much student-student interaction as possible.

   Guiding student-student interaction is very sophisticated, however. Teacher-student interaction is vastly superior to instruction that is primarily teacher lecture.

7.52:   The information in this section would suggest that constructivism has more implications for instruction than it does for curriculum development. Constructivism impacts *how* information is taught more than *what* is taught. Constructivism does have implications for curriculum development, however, in that an emphasis on problem solving and authentic tasks will increase the emphasis on topics that allow for a problem solving and authentic orientation and a decrease in emphasis on topics that don't lend themselves to this orientation.

7.53:   Your analysis of the cases at the end of the chapters are a form of authentic task. You are asked to think as a teacher would think and analyze instruction based on this thinking. Many of the margin questions are authentic tasks in that they ask you to respond to practical teaching problems.

Application Exercises

Exercise 7.1

1. Identify at least two characteristics that behaviorism and cognitive learning theory have in common and at least two others that they do not have in common.

2. A pre-algebra teacher has written the following on the chalkboard:

   $$4 + 5(7-3) - 9/3$$

   She then asks, "What are we going to do first to simplify this expression? What is important to remember whenever we simplify something like this?" Criticize her questioning based on your understanding of sensory memory.

3. Describe a simple alternative to improve the teacher's questioning.

4. You are introducing a unit on the Far East in your world history class. You present information outlining the impact of religion on life in Japan in the early 20th century, exploitation by the British and other Western nations, the indignation Japan felt after World War I, Japan's overpopulation and scarce natural resources in the 1920s and 1930s, and how all these factors led to Japan's decision that it had no choice but to attack the United States. The students seem interested, watching you attentively as you present the information.

   However, the next day when you begin your review of the previous day's information, it's as if they hadn't listened after all. Using your understanding of working memory as a basis, explain why this might have happened.

5. Based on what we know about working memory, why is a textbook an important supplement to teacher lectures?

6. Two high school teachers were discussing their classes. The physics teacher commented,

   "I'm having a terrible time. The kids seem to understand the problems when I explain them, but they get wrapped up in their algebra when they try to do the problems on their own, so they wind up confused."

   Relate the physics teacher's description to our discussion of working memory, and explain why her students are having difficulty. Include the concept of automaticity in your explanation.

7. Students with good vocabularies have two important advantages in listening to lectures over those whose vocabularies are limited? What are these advantages? Explain.

8. When students perform each of the following, which type of knowledge--declarative or procedural--is primarily being demonstrated? Explain.
   a. State that Abraham Lincoln was the president of the United States during the Civil War.
   b. Ride a bicycle.
   c. State that isosceles triangles have two equal sides.
   d. Identify isosceles triangles in a group of plane figures.
   e. Calculate the areas of a right triangle and an isosceles triangle.

9. Consider these definitions:
    a. Common nouns are parts of speech that name persons, places, and things.
    b. Proper nouns name specific persons, places, and things.

Create a propositional network that would incorporate the two definitions.

Exercise 7.2

For Items 1 through 3, look at the topics and describe lesson beginnings that could be used to attract the students' attention and pull them into the lesson. (A variety of lesson beginnings are possible. Suggest at least two different ways of beginning each.)

1. You are beginning a unit on longitude and latitude in your geography class.

2. You want your students to understand the rule for punctuating possessive nouns--a singular possessive uses an apostrophe *s*, and a plural possessive uses only an apostrophe if the plural noun ends in *s* and an apostrophe *s* if the plural noun does not end in *s*.

3. You are beginning a lesson on the skeletal system with your science students.

4. You have taught your students about direct and indirect objects and you begin a review by writing the following sentence on the chalkboard:

    Kathy handed Tim the papers.

    What question could you now ask that would be an excellent way of diagnosing the students' perceptions. (Be specific. Either write down or say to yourself the exact question you would ask.)

5. Explain why teachers are discouraged from sitting down or standing behind a podium when they teach, based on the information in this section.

6. What is the simplest and most effective way a teacher can check the accuracy of student perceptions?

7. Read the following case study and explain the difference in the two teachers' reactions based on the information you've studied in this section.

    Two young teachers were interviewed by a principal for jobs at the same school. (There were two openings, so they each hoped to get a job.) They were very excited about the prospect of working together, so they went to lunch and discussed their respective interviews.
    "How was it?" Marianne asked.
    "Awful," Katarina responded. "He grilled me and made me feel like I was the dumbest thing in the world. How about you?"
    "I thought mine went really well," Marianne said tentatively, with a puzzled look on her face. "He asked me a lot of questions, but it seemed to me that he was just trying to see if I knew what I wanted from teaching."
    "I should never have applied for this job," Katarina continued disconsolately. "Donna (a friend of hers who teaches at the school) warned me about this guy. After today, I don't think I could ever work for him."
    "Gosh, I'm really looking forward to it," Marianne responded. "I went to a workshop last week on what to do in an interview. They said we'd be asked a lot of questions, and it's the interviewer's way of finding out how we think, so I guess I was sort of ready for it."

8. Suppose we look up a telephone number, follow it by looking up several others, and find that we cannot remember the first one. Offer two different explanations for why we cannot remember the first number.

9. Think again about the rule, "A singular possessive uses an apostrophe *s*, and a plural possessive uses only an apostrophe if the plural noun ends in *s* and an apostrophe *s* if the plural noun does not end in *s*." Describe a context in which the rule could be taught that would aid meaningfulness and retrieval.

10. We would predict that Juan would be able to retrieve information about the solar system more readily than would Randy. Explain why we would make this prediction based on the information in this section.

Exercise 7.3

1. A first- and a sixth-grade student are each asked to give directions about some building blocks to one of their classmates whose vision is blocked by a screen. Each student has a round red block, a square red block, and a blue block. The first grader is directed to tell her counterpart to put the round red block on the blue block. She responds, "Pick up the red one and put it on the blue one." Her classmate scans his display of blocks, sees two red ones, and picks one up. The sixth-grader, in contrast, says, "Pick up the round red block, and put it on the blue block."

Explain the difference in the first-grader's and the sixth-grader's directions based on the information in this section.

2. Look at the following examples and explain what they have in common.

a. Mrs. Jensen was giving directions for the social studies test on Friday. Marissa raised her hand and asked, "I'm sorry, but I'm not sure what you said about the second part of the test. Will it be multiple choice or essay?

b. Steve was doing his homework while listening to the radio. He noticed that he was periodically listening to the radio instead of focusing on his work, so he got up and turned off the radio.

c. Billy was reporting on the major exports of the southern colonies. As he looked up from his paper, he saw some confused looks on his classmates' faces. He paused and asked, "Are there any questions?"

d. Claudia was studying her notes for her science test. "Why can't I remember the difference between spring tide and neap tide?" she mumbles to herself. "I'll read it once more." She then went back to her text and highlighted the description of each.

e. A high school sophomore was up late baby-sitting on a school night and knew that she was going to have a rough time staying awake at school the next day. As she walked into her English class, she said to herself, "I'll sit in the most uncomfortable position I can, and that will keep me awake."

Exercise 7.4

In Items 1 through 4, decide which of the following concepts are best illustrated in each case: (a) organization, (b) elaboration, or (c) rehearsal. Explain your answers.

1. Nikki was confused about the solution to a force and acceleration problem involving friction. She went back to a problem she had worked in which no friction was involved, and then went through a sample problem in the book involving friction. She then used the information from the first two to help her understand the new problem.

2. Tanya knew there would be an essay question on the strengths and weaknesses of the Colonial and British armies during the Revolutionary War. To prepare for the test, she drew a matrix with England and the Colonies on one side and advantages and disadvantages on the top.

3. Meg knew there would be names and dates on the test on Wednesday, so she got some 3 x 5 index cards, wrote the important facts on the cards, and used them as flash cards to study on the bus ride to and from school.

4. To remember the correct order of the different phases of mitosis (prophase, metaphase, anaphase, telophase), Juan formed the word *Pmat* and used it as a retrieval guide.

5. Students--particularly young children--often believe that mammals are warm-blooded animals that live on land and have four legs, and they further believe that anything that lives in the water is a fish. Are these conceptions meaningful to them? Explain. Explain how they might come to these conclusions based on the information in this section.

6. You're teaching your students about the North and South prior to the Civil War. Describe how you might organize the information in your unit to help make it meaningful for the students.

7. You have been doing a unit on the areas of plane figures with your math students. They understand how to find the areas of squares, rectangles, and triangles. How might you use this information to capitalize on the process of elaboration as you move to a discussion of the areas of parallelograms and trapezoids?

Exercise 7.5

In the middle of a class discussion, Natalie, one of Sandy Clark's students raised her hand and said, "I don't get this 'division by zero is undefined.' I just don't understand what they mean by 'undefined.'"

"Yeah," Jeremy added. "Division is division. You divide, you get an answer. Everybody knows that. So, 'undefined' is . . . I don't get it."

Sandy thought a moment, wrote the number 12 on the chalkboard and assigned each of the students successively smaller numbers to divide into 12. (The 12 was arbitrary. Any number would work as well.)

As the students reported their answers, Sandy made a table on the chalkboard, which appeared as follows:

12 Divided by	Answer
6	2
2	6
.03	400
.01	1,200
.002	6,000
.0004	30,000
.000006	2,000,000
.000000002	6,000,000,000

"So, let's look at the patterns we have here," Sandy directed. "What do you notice about the left column? . . . Terry?"

"The numbers are getting smaller and smaller."

"Good. So imagine now that we kept going with those numbers. Eventually we would be approaching what? . . . Leah?"

". . . I . . . I'm not . . . quite . . . following you."

"Imagine that we have several more numbers in the left column," Sandy prompted, "and they continue to get smaller and smaller. Eventually, they would be nearly what?"

"... Zero?"

"Yes, exactly. Good," she nodded and smiled at Terry.

"Now look at the right column. What pattern do you see there? . . . Someone? . . . Rene?"

"They're getting bigger and bigger."

"Now imagine that the numbers in the left column get incredibly small; so small that we can hardly imagine. What would happen to the numbers on the right?"

"... They would be huge," Brent volunteered.

"And ultimately if we actually GOT to zero, what would happen to those on the right? . . . They would sort of what?" Sandy shrugged.

"... They would sort of blow up?" Dennis responded uncertainly.

"... Sensible enough idea," Sandy nodded. "So what do you mean, 'blow up?' Anyone, what does that term mean?"

"... It sort of means get huge all of a sudden I think," Veronica offered.

"It doesn't mean anything really," Cal put in. "I sort of know what you mean, but we can't really say 'Gets huge all of a sudden.'"

"So, what do you think?" Sandy probed. "What *does* it mean?"

"... That must be what 'undefined' is," Troy offered after thinking about it for several seconds.

"Good," Sandy nodded. "Good thinking everyone. Now, does "undefined" make sense to everyone?"

Identify the characteristics of constructivism that were illustrated in the case study. In what ways was the lesson *not* constructivist? How could it have been made more constructivist?

Feedback for Application Exercises_____

Exercise 7.1

1. Cognitive and behavioral theories both focus on learning and they both focus on stimuli and responses. They differ in their definition of learning--behaviorism describing learning as a change in behavior and cognitive theories defining learning as a change in learners' internal capacities which in turn can produce a change in behavior. Behaviorism focuses only on behavior, while cognitive psychology focuses on processes internal to the learner.

2. The teacher posed the question, "What are we going to do first to simplify this expression?" and before the students had a chance to answer, she posed a second question, "What is important to remember whenever we simplify something like this?" Because information is quickly lost from sensory memory if processing doesn't begin (through attention), one of two things is likely to happen: 1) The students will attend to the first question and lose the second one from sensory memory, or 2) their attention to the first question will be disrupted by the second question, so their attention to the first one will be incomplete. Either situation has a negative impact on learning.

3. She should ask the first question, wait for a response from a student, and then asked the second question.

4. Working memory has only limited capacity. You have introduced a great deal of information in the lesson-- religion, exploitation, indignation, overpopulation, scarce natural resources, and how all the details of these factors led to the Japanese attack on the United States. Since the students seemed attentive, it is likely that their working memories were overloaded, and rather than being able to encode the information into long-term memory, it was lost from their working memories.

5. Because of working memory's limited capacity and the rate at which information is transferred into long-term memory, it is likely that students "miss" some of the presentation, i.e., their working memory capacities are exceeded, and some information is lost. A textbook is then used to "fill in the gaps."

6. Too much working memory space is taken up by the algebraic manipulations involved in the problems, as evidenced by the teacher's comment, "They get wrapped up in the algebra," leaving inadequate space for the actual physics involved. To overcome the difficulty, the algebra skills should be automatic, so the amount of working memory space they occupy is reduced, leaving more working memory that can be devoted to focusing on the physics in the problems.

7. First, for students who have good vocabularies more of the content of the lectures will be meaningful, since they will be able to attach the content of the lectures to their already existing schemas. Second, many of the word meanings will be automatic for students with good vocabularies, which frees working memory space that can be focused on processing the information in the lecture.

8. Choices a, c, and d require declarative knowledge, since the tasks require "knowledge of facts, definitions, generalizations, and rules." Choices b and e require procedural knowledge, since they involve "knowledge of how to perform activities." Remember, procedural knowledge involves conditions and actions, and riding a bicycle and solving for the areas of the triangles involves taking an action based on the conditions.

9.   A propositional network could appear as follows:

```
                    place
                      |
           person- - -common- -thing
                      |
                    noun
                      |
     specific- -proper- -specific
     person         |           thing
               specific
               place
```

We must keep in mind, however, that propositional networks are individual and idiosyncratic, meaning the network for one learner can be different from that of another. An improperly constructed network is a source of learner misconceptions.

Another reminder: When we see a network presented in visual form, such as it does above, it helps us visualize the idea that we tend to associate items of information in memory. In this way it is a model.

Exercise 7.2

1. You could begin the lesson by asking the students what they would do if they met a new friend and they wanted to tell the friend exactly where they live. How might they describe their location for their friend. A second option could be to bring in a globe, have the students describe its characteristics, and then ask the students how we might describe a location on it.

2. Present the students with a paragraph in which the rules are embedded. Then ask the students why words such as boy's, girls', and children's are punctuated the way they are.

A second option would be to have the students describe some things that belong to one or more of them. Write their descriptions on the board properly punctuating the possessives. Then ask them why different words are punctuated the way they are.

3. Bring in a model skeleton and have the students describe it. Then tell them that the class needs to explain why the skeleton exists the way it does, e.g., closed skull, curved ribs, large upper leg bone, etc.

Have the students feel their own skeletons and describe them. Then ask them to explain why their skeletons exist the way they do.

4. An ideal question would be, "Describe what you see in this sentence." The students' answers would give you insight into the meaning they attach to the sentence, and perception is the meaning learners attach to stimuli.

5. Students tend to pay attention to teachers who move around and are animated in their presentations and explanations, which means that teacher animation and movement are attention getters. Standing behind a podium and sitting are not effective attention getters.

6. The simplest way of checking student perceptions is by asking an open-ended question such as, "What do you see?", "What do you notice?", or "Describe the information for us." The question ensures that the students will be successful, and the responses will give you indicators of their perceptions.

7. The case study illustrates the impact that expectations have on the perception of an event. The two teachers went into the experience with very different expectations, and as a result they interpreted their experience very differently.

8. One theory would suggest that the other numbers *interfered* with remembering the first one. A second theory would suggest that you were unable to retrieve the first one, primarily because it had not been encoded effectively enough to allow the retrieval.

9. Embedding examples of rules in a paragraph would the best way to capitalize on context.

10. Juan's schema for the solar system was more complete and interconnected than Randy's. Because there were more links in his schema, retrieval would be easier for him. (Look again at Figures 7.4 and 7.5 on page 251 of your text for a visual comparison the two students' networks.)

Exercise 7.3

1. Young children don't have well-developed metacognitive abilities. The first-grader is unlikely to realize that her message isn't clear. (She is not aware of the clarity of her communication, and she doesn't demonstrate control over it.) The sixth-graders metacognition (metacommunication in this case) is more developed.

2. The students are all demonstrating metacognition. The specific types vary, but each is an example of metacognition. We might describe each example as follows:

a.   Marissa is demonstrating metacommunication. She realizes that she may not have understood what Mrs. Jensen was saying, and she demonstrated control over her communication (listening) by asking Mrs. Jensen to repeat the question.

b.   Steve is demonstrating meta-attention. He is aware that he is attending to the radio instead of his homework, and he controls his behavior by turning off the radio.

c.   Billy is demonstrating metacommunication. He is aware that he may not be communicating clearly, and he governs his behavior by asking for questions.

d.   Claudia is demonstrating metamemory. She realizes that she doesn't remember the difference between neap and spring tide, and she adopts a strategy to help her remember.

e.   The student is demonstrating meta-attention--awareness that she would have difficulty attending and demonstrating control over her attention.

Exercise 7.4

1. Nikki was using elaboration. She had a "force and acceleration problem without friction" schema, which together with the sample problem served as the foundation from which elaboration could take place.

2. Tanya's matrix was a form of organization which would make the information more meaningful, thereby aiding its coding into long-term memory.

3. Meg's flash cards are a form of rehearsal.

4. Juan's nonsense word "Pmat" is a mnemonic device, which is a form of elaboration.

5. These conceptions are meaningful for the students, even though they're invalid. Meaningfulness means that associations exist. Associating the concept *mammal* with four legs, warmth, and land, is meaningful, as is associating fish and water. Students can easily come to these conclusions, because many examples are consistent with the ideas; for example, the majority of the animals in water *are* fish.

6. A matrix in which, for example, the geography, climate, economics and people's lifestyles in the South is compared to those in the North would be an excellent way to organize the information. Table 7.4 on page 260 of your text illustrates a matrix comparing two immigrant groups.

7. You could begin by reviewing finding areas of squares, rectangles, and triangles, then "cutting" parallelograms and trapezoids into rectangles and triangles, adding the areas to find the total area of each, and finally combining the formulas to derive a formula for finding the area for each.

Exercise 7.5

Constructivism has four characteristics:
.   Learners construct their own understanding.
.   New learning depends on current understanding.
.   Learning is facilitated by social interaction.
.   Meaningful learning occurs within authentic learning tasks.

As with many other aspects of teaching and learning, teaching according to constructivism is on a continuum, i.e., lessons are relatively more constructivist, or relatively less constructivist; they aren't "constructivist" or "non-constructivist."

From this perspective, the lesson was quite constructivist. For example, the students' confusion about division by zero being undefined was based on their prior understanding of division. Then, instead of trying to explain why division by zero was undefined, Sandy guided the students into "constructing" their own understanding by first having them divide 12 by a series of smaller and smaller numbers and looking for patterns in the results. As a result, the students developed understanding that made sense to them rather than trying to rely on Sandy's explanation. Also, throughout the lesson a considerable amount of interaction took place.

Finally, while trying to understand that division by zero is undefined isn't technically an "authentic" task, understanding the idea is fundamental to understanding mathematics. So, we see that the characteristics of constructivism were quite well illustrated in the lesson.

TRUE/FALSE QUESTIONS. Write T in the blank if the statement is true, and write F if the statement is false.

_____ 1. While information in working memory is in the form of perceived reality, information in long-term memory is in the form of objective, or true, reality.

_____ 2. Since working memory is what we call consciousness, its capacity is larger than that of long-term memory, which is unconscious.

_____ 3. Information that is not accurately perceived is lost from working memory.

_____ 4. Information is normally quickly lost from sensory memory, but it can be retained there with rehearsal.

_____ 5. Much of the information from sensory memory enters working memory even though we're not consciously aware of it.

MULTIPLE-CHOICE QUESTIONS. Circle the best response in each case.

6. Which of the following is the best definition of learning from a cognitive point of view?
   a. A change in individuals' mental structures that provides the capacity to demonstrate changes in behavior.
   b. A change in behavior that occurs as a result of experience.
   c. A change in the way we visualize and perceive information as a result of experience.
   d. A change in mental structures that occurs as a result of retrieving previously unconscious information.

7. A teacher is giving a lecture on the differences in the way the Spanish interacted with the natives in the Americas compared to the way the English and French interacted with them, and she included some graphic pictures depicting various forms of mistreatment from all parties. In an effort to cover all the factors in a class period, she lectures quite rapidly. Based on the case study, of the following, which is the most likely result?
   a. The information she is presenting won't enter sensory memory.
   b. The students' attention won't be attracted.
   c. The information is likely to be misperceived.
   d. Some of the information will be lost from working memory.

8. You are showing a film about bats to your third graders. Afterward one of the students comments, "I didn't know that birds have teeth." Of the following, the process most closely related to the third grader's comment is:
   a. attention.
   b. perception.
   c. rehearsal.
   d. encoding.

9. A teacher wants his students to know the most common prepositions, so he gives them a list and tells them that they have to know all the prepositions by the following week. The process the students will most likely use to learn the prepositions is:
   a. perception.
   b. rehearsal.
   c. elaboration.
   d. organization.

Use the following information for Items 10 and 11.

10. A third grade teacher in continuing her work with place value is introducing the concept of the 100s column. She begins the lesson by having them make several numbers, such as 24, with interlocking cubes. She then uses the cubes to demonstrate 124 for them and asks them to compare it to the other numbers they made. Of the following, the process she is most trying to capitalize on to make the information meaningful is:
    a.   attention.
    b.   perception.
    c.   organization.
    d.   elaboration.

11. In conducting the lesson the way she did, she is also attempting to capitalize on another process used to make the information meaningful. Of the following, her efforts best illustrate attempts to capitalize on:
    a.   attention.
    b.   perception.
    c.   rehearsal.
    d.   activity.

12. You find that your algebra students are having problems solving equations, because they get mixed up on simplifying simple arithmetic expressions. You decide to give them some additional practice. Of the following, which is the most desirable schedule?
    a.   25 minutes every Monday to kick off the week
    b.   10 minutes on Tuesday and 15 minutes on Thursday
    c.   15 minutes on Monday and 10 minutes on Friday
    d.   5 minutes every day

13. Consider the concept of interference. For which of the following pairs of ideas is interference most likely?
    a.   Nouns and verbs
    b.   Nouns and adverbs
    c.   Verbs and direct objects
    d.   Direct objects and indirect objects

14. Research indicates that teachers who move around the room, make eye contact with the students, gesture, and display other related behaviors have students who learn more than teachers who don't demonstrate these behaviors. Of the following, the process in the information processing model that most closely relates to these behaviors is:
    a.   attention.
    b.   perception.
    c.   rehearsal.
    d.   encoding.

15. Mr. Hunt always follows his presentations in his Algebra I class with an assignment where the students practice the skills and ideas he has presented. Research supports the technique of following presentations with student practice. Of the following, the aspect of promoting meaningful learning that most closely relates to Mr. Hunt's approach is:
    a.   activity.
    b.   attention.
    c.   perception.
    d.   organization.

16. Ben Johnson has had his analytic geometry students working on finding the formulas for parabolas, and is now moving to formulas for ellipses. He starts by reviewing the features of parabolas, such as the focal point, and he then moves to similar features in ellipses, such as having the students note that they have two focal points. Of the following, the concept related to making information meaningful that most closely relates to Ben's technique is:

    a.   discrepant events as attention-getters, since two focal points compared to one is discrepant.
    b.   expectations influencing perception. The students don't expect to see two focal points.
    c.   mnemonic devices to make information meaningful.
    d.   elaboration to make information meaningful.
    e.   activity to make information meaningful.

17. The research says that in order to learn concepts most effectively students should be provided with both a *definition* of the concept and *examples* of the concept. This research is most closely related to:

    a.   attention-getters in the information processing model.
    b.   rehearsal in the information processing model.
    c.   perception in the information processing model.
    d.   forming an association to make information meaningful.

You are using the *information processing model* as a basis for guiding your instruction and you are teaching your students about direct and indirect objects. Use this idea for Items 18 and 19.

18. Based on the information processing model, which of the following would be the best way to *begin* your lesson?

    a.   Take a ball out from behind your desk and throw it to one of the students.
    b.   Ask the students to describe what direct and indirect objects mean to them.
    c.   Write a sentence on the board and underline the direct and indirect object in it.
    d.   Tell the students that the topic for the day is direct and indirect objects, and that they will use these parts of speech in their writing.

19. Based on the information processing model, which of the following should you do as the *second* step in your lesson?

    a.   Ask students questions that will check their understanding of your examples.
    b.   Have the students rehearse the information you first give them to help retain it in working memory
    c.   Devise a means of getting the information into the sensory registers.
    d.   Have the students practice the information so it will be encoded into long-term memory.

Luis Garcia is teaching his fifth graders about the Northern and Southern colonies prior to the Civil War. He prepares a chart, which is outlined as follows:

	Landforms	Climate	Economy	Lifestyle
Northern Colonies				
Southern Colonies				

He assigns teams of two to gather information about each of the cells in the chart (such as the economy in the Northern Colonies). The students provide the information, Luis helps them organize it and they put it on the chart.

20. Luis's use of the chart in his lesson best illustrates which of the following as an attempt to help the students encode the information into long-term memory by making it more meaningful?
   a.   Activity
   b.   Organization
   c.   Elaboration
   d.   Perception
   e.   Mnemonics

21. A teacher complains, "I stood there for 15 minutes and explained the procedure for solving the problems until I was blue in the face. I know the procedure was a little hard, but this morning they came in and it was if they had only heard half of what I said. I don't get it." Of the following, the component of the information processing model that most closely relates to this problem is:
   a.   perception.
   b.   the sensory registers.
   c.   working memory.
   d.   rehearsal.
   e.   long-term memory.

22. The primary purpose in preparing practice exercises such as the ones you're now analyzing is to:
   a.   attract and maintain your attention.
   b.   be certain that you're perceiving the exercises properly.
   c.   be sure that your working memory isn't overloaded when you take a quiz or test.
   d.   help you encode this information by putting you in an active role.
   e.   give you practice in rehearsing the information we're now studying.

23. Brandon and Giselle are studying for a test. "What are you doing?" Brandon asks.
   "I always write out the answers, rather than simply read the answer given in the book," Giselle responds. "I remember the information way better if I do that."
   Of the following, Giselle is most demonstrating:
   a.   elaboration.
   b.   meta-attention.
   c.   proactive facilitation.
   d.   metamemory.

Four teachers are teaching the concepts of adjective and adverb to their language arts students.

   Mrs. Ortega presents a paragraph which contains three underlined adjectives and three italicized adverbs in the sentences that make up the paragraph. The class discusses the common features of the underlined and italicized words and what they modify, and they arrive at a definition of adjectives and adverbs. The students then write a paragraph containing at least two adjectives and two adverbs.

   Mr. Anderson displays several sentences--some of which contain adjectives and others of which that contain adverbs--on the overhead. He points out the adjectives, underlines them, and points to the noun they modify. He does essentially the same thing with the sentences containing the adverbs. He then gives the students several sentences for practice, directing them to underline the adjective and adverb, and circle the word it modifies.

   Mr. Weiss presents several sentences which contain underlined adjectives and adverbs. He asks the students to look for the word that each modifies and identify it as a noun or a verb. He then asks them what the words that modify nouns must be, and when no one answers he asks them what modifies nouns. They respond, "Adjectives," and he points out that these are adjectives. He does the same thing with adverbs, and he then has them work several exercises identifying the part of the sentence each adjective and adverb modifies in each case.   Mrs. Sanderson presents a passage in which several examples of adjectives and adverbs are embedded. She asks the students to describe the passages, and after they have made several observations, she underlines the adjectives, pointing out that they modify a noun in each case. She circles the noun they modify to be sure that the students focus on the relationship between the noun and the adjective. She then repeats the process with the adverbs.

24. The teacher who was <u>most</u> consistent with constructivist views of learning in his or her instruction was:
   a. Mrs. Ortega.
   b. Mr. Anderson.
   c. Mr. Weiss.
   d. Mrs. Sanderson.

25. The teacher who was <u>least</u> consistent with constructivist views of learning in his or her instruction was:
   a. Mrs. Ortega.
   b. Mr. Anderson.
   c. Mr. Weiss.
   d. Mrs. Sanderson.

Self-Help Quiz Answers

1. f
2. f
3. f
4. f
5. f
6. a   Choice b is the definition of learning according to behaviorism. Choice c is related, since changes in our mental structures can change the way we perceive information, but it is an incomplete description. Choice d is also related, but it focuses on retrieval, which is only one aspect of cognitive learning.
7. d   Lecturing rapidly is likely to result in the amount of information exceeding the capacity of working memory. Information enters sensory memory, whether or not we're aware of it, and the graphic pictures would be likely to attract the students' attention. We don't have evidence one way or the other to conclude whether or not the information will be misperceived.
8. b   The child perceives the bat as a bird, which results in his comment. (This child has encoded flying animals as birds (choice d), so encoding is involved as well. However, the information in the item focuses on perception. We see no evidence of the encoding process presently taking place, so the best answer is b.
9. b   Since the students are merely given a list, they will likely memorize it, which employs rehearsal.
10. d   She is attempting to have the children "elaborate" from two-digit numbers to three-digit numbers.
11. d   By having the students make the numbers with their cubes, she is attempting to put them in an "active" role.
12. d   Spaced practice is more effective than massed practice. Five minutes a day provides the most spaced practice.
13. d   Direct and indirect objects are most closely related to each other, and closely related ideas are more likely to interfere with each other than are ideas that are not closely related. (Teaching the two ideas at the same time is one way to try to prevent interference.)
14. a   Moving around the room, making eye contact, gesturing, and displaying other energetic behaviors are attention-getters.
15. a   Practice puts the students in an active role. Attention and perception are not regarded as "techniques" to promote meaningfulness, and we have no evidence one way or the other about organization.
16. d   Elaboration, organization, and activity are the strategies that help make information meaningful. Mnemonics are forms of elaboration, but we have no evidence of either mnemonics or activity in this example.
17. d   Having a definition and examples allow the students to form associations--between the examples and the definition, and the examples with each other. Forming associations promotes meaningfulness. We have no evidence one way or the other about attention, perception, or rehearsal, based on the information in the item.
18. a   Based on the information processing model, learning begins with attention, and of the choices given, throwing a ball is the best attention-getter.

19. a Asking students questions that check their understanding of the examples you've provided is the most effective way to check their perceptions, and perception is the second process that occurs in the information processing model.

20. b The matrix serves as an organizer.

21. c Students behaving as if they only heard half of what the teacher said, particularly since she stood there and "explained the procedure for solving the problems until I was blue in the face," suggests that the learners' working memories had become overloaded.

22. d While attention is involved (choice a), this isn't the primary purpose. Perception is also involved (choice b), but another technique would be used if accurate perception was the goal. Your working memory isn't being overload (choice c), because you can take as much time as you need to process the information, and you're doing much more than rehearsing (choice e) when you practice the exercises.

23. d Giselle is demonstrating knowledge of, and control over, her memory. Metamemory is a form of metacognition.

24. a In Mrs. Ortega's lesson, "The class discusses the common features of the underlined and italicized words and what they modify, and they arrive at a definition of adjectives and adverbs." The students are constructing their own understanding, and social interaction is prominent to a greater extent than it is with the other three teachers. (We have little evidence of prior understanding in any of the cases, and identifying adjectives and adverbs is the goal for all four teachers. [Identifying adjectives and adverbs isn't an authentic task.])

25. b Mr. Anderson "points out the adjectives, underlines them, and points to the noun they modify. He does essentially the same thing with the sentences containing the adverbs." He puts the students in a passive role, and there is little evidence of social interaction in the lesson.

CHAPTER 8: COMPLEX COGNITIVE PROCESSES

Chapter Outline

I. Concept learning
   A. Concepts: Categories that simplify the world
      1. Characteristics: The defining features of concepts
      2. Factors influencing the ease of learning concepts
      3. Examples: The key to learning and teaching concepts
   B. Strategies for teaching concepts
      1. Rule-Example: An expository concept-teaching strategy
      2. Example-rule: An inductive concept-teaching strategy
      3. Concept mapping: Embedding concepts in complex schemas
   C. Concept learning: Misconceptions and conceptual change
   D. Relating concepts to each other: Principles, generalizations, and academic rules
   E. Adaptive instruction: Dealing with diversity in students' thinking
      1. Accommodating differences in background experiences
      2. Accommodating differences in patterns of interaction
II. Problem solving
   A. Problem solving: Theoretical perspectives
   B. Well-defined and ill-defined problems
   C. Routine and nonroutine problems
   D. A general problem-solving model
      1. Identifying the problem
         a. Lack of experience in defining problems
         b. Tendency to rush toward a solution
         c. Tendency to think convergently
         d. Lack of domain-specific knowledge
      2. Representing the problem
      3. Selecting a strategy: Algorithms and hueristics
         a. Trial and error
         b. Means-ends analysis
         c. Working backward
         d. Drawing analogies
      4. Implementing the strategy
      5. Evaluating the results
   E. Expert-novice differences in problem solving ability
      1. Developing expertise: The role of deliberate practice
      2. Acquiring expertise: The importance of motivation
   F. Cognitive approaches to problem solving: Helping learners become better problem solvers
      1. Capitalize on social interaction
      2. Present problems in meaningful contexts
      3. Provide practice in problem finding
      4. Provide scaffolding for novice problem solvers
         a. Analyzing worked examples
         b. Visually representing problems
         c. Cognitive apprenticeship
      5. Teach general problem-solving strategies
III. The strategic learner
   A. Cognitive strategies, concept learning and problem solving: How are they different?
   B. Characteristics of effective strategy users
      1. Broad background knowledge
      2. A repertoire of strategies
      3. Well-developed metacognitive abilities

C.   Study strategies
   1.   Basic study skills
   2.   Comprehension monitoring
      a.   Summarizing
      b.   Self-questioning
   3.   Strategies for improving comprehension monitoring
      a.   SQ4R
      b.   MURDER
   4.   Helping students become effective strategy users
D.   Thinking skills
   1.   Teaching thinking: Within or outside the regular curriculum?
   2.   Basic processes
   3.   Domain-specific knowledge
   4.   Metacognitive knowledge
   5.   Motivational factors
IV.   Transfer of learning
A.   Positive and negative transfer
B.   General and specific transfer
C.   Factors affecting the transfer of learning
   1.   Similarity between the two learning situations
   2.   Variety of learning experiences
   3.   Quality of learning experiences
   4.   Context of learning experiences
   5.   Depth of understanding and practice
   6.   Dispositions, metacognition, and general transfer

Chapter Objectives

■   Explain the application of concept learning to classroom activities.

■   Apply problem-solving strategies to well-defined and ill-defined problems.

■   Explain how thinking skills can be used in classroom learning activities.

■   Describe how study strategies can be used to increase student learning.

■   Discuss ways of increasing transfer of learning.

Chapter Overview

In Chapter 7 we examined cognitive views of learning in detail and explored their implications for teaching. As part of our study we learned that the contents of long-term memory as well as the processes used to encode information into long-term memory influence not only retention but usefulness. In this chapter we examine complex processes such as concept learning, problem solving, learning strategies and transfer.

Because content exists in different forms, it is learned differently, and must be taught differently. Concepts are one type of content; principles, generalizations, and academic rules describe relationships among concepts.

Problem solving begins with identifying a problem, and proceeds to representing the problem, selecting and implementing a strategy and evaluating the results. Strategies for solving problems include trial and error, means-end analysis, working backwards and drawing analogies.

Expert problem solvers are better at representing problems, solve them more holistically and strategically and monitor their progress more effectively than do novices. Constructivist approaches to teaching problem solving capitalize on social interaction, present problems in meaningful contexts, include practice in problem finding and provide instructional scaffolding.

Cognitive strategies are plans for accomplishing learning goals. Effective strategy users have a repertoire of strategies, they are aware of where and when the strategies should be used, and they have thorough background knowledge.

Critical thinking is the ability to accurately and efficiently gather, interpret and evaluate information. It incorporates basic processes, such as comparing, hypothesizing and generalizing, together with domain-specific and metacognitive knowledge, and attitudes and dispositions.

Transfer occurs when learners are able to use information or skills they've learned in a new context. Factors affecting transfer include the similarity between two learning situations, the variety, context, and quality of learners' experience, depth of understanding and practice, and the metacognitive dispositions to look for opportunities to use information. The key to all forms of transfer is a variety of high-quality examples presented in realistic contexts.

Feedback for Margin Questions

8.1:   If you have studied the chapters in the order they've been written, you've been involved in a great deal of concept learning. Some examples of concepts you would have studied include equilibrium, centration, zone of proximal development, scaffolding, moral dilemma, psychosocial crisis, intelligence, socioeconomic status, specific learning disabilities, negative reinforcement, modeling, vicarious learning, perception, working memory, and metacognition, among many others.

8.2:   Some concepts in each of these areas include: music--pitch and rhythm; art--line and perspective; physical education--aerobic exercise and endurance.

8.3:   The characteristics of adjective are: modifies noun or pronoun. The characteristics of conifer are: needle-shaped leaves, exposed seeds, and resinous wood.

8.4:   Noun should be easier to learn, because it has fewer characteristics--name of a person, place, or thing-- and they are more concrete than are the characteristics of culture.

8.5:   Concepts such as culture, which we saw in 8.4, have "fuzzy boundaries." We have trouble identifying the precise characteristics of culture, whereas identifying the characteristics of concepts such as noun or rectangle is easy. A great many other concepts, such as impressionism in art, classicism or romanticism in literature, and socialism in social studies also have "fuzzy boundaries."

8.6:   Nonexamples only tell what the concept "is not," and don't give any information about what the concept "is." For this reason, positive examples are generally presented first. A teacher might have a rationale for presenting a nonexample first, however, such as using them to establish a context or to review, and this would be perfectly acceptable.

8.7:   *Parts of speech* would the superordinate concept to the concept adjective. It is a larger category into which the concept adjective can be classified.

The "concept" *adjective* is a mental idea. We can have a "schema" for adjective, for example. The name is merely a label used for communication. For instance, in our example with "snurfs," we could have used any label. The distinction between the concept and the name is important, because examples and nonexamples are required to learn the concept, whereas rehearsal is used to learn the label. Teachers sometimes make the mistake of trying to teach concepts with labels and definitions alone.

8.8: An adverb would generally be the best negative example because adjectives and adverbs are more likely to be confused than are adjectives and nouns or adjectives and verbs. Since examples and nonexamples help learners create schemas that incorporate the concepts, they most closely relate to the process of encoding.

8.9: While more than one network could be valid for the concept operant conditioning, a possible network might appear as follows:

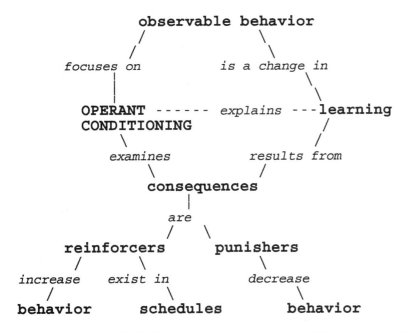

8.10: One way of eliminating the misconception would be to present the students with specific and concrete illustrations of the characteristics of each, such as common ownership of property being a characteristic of Communism but not a characteristic of Fascism. It would also be valuable to have the students describe a personalized example of what common ownership means, such as all their parents' houses being owned by the government.

8.11: *Equilibrium* is the concept that best explains people's reluctance to give up misconceptions. Retaining misconceptions allows learners to remain at equilibrium. Reconceptualization requires disrupting and reestablishing equilibrium.

8.12: The statement would be called more accurately a generalization. Teachers have seen students' behavior decrease after they've been praised, for example, so there are exceptions to the pattern described in the statement. To be accepted as a principle, we view the statement as true for all known cases.

8.13: All three--principles, generalizations, and academic rules--describe patterns and relationships between concepts. The difference between a generalization and an academic rule is that we describe the pattern in a generalization based on our observations, while the pattern in an academic rule is arbitrarily created by people.

8.14: Experience is the factor that best explains the learners' preconceptions. Students who have seen live, dry snakes will have very different preconceptions than those who have seen live, wet snakes, and both will have different ideas than those that have never seen a live snake.

Social interaction is an important factor in helping learners change their preconceptions. A learner's equilibrium can be disrupted during social interaction, when it is pointed out that his or her scheme is inadequate to explain the object or event being discussed. The result is accommodation, and new and revised schemes that make the learner better able to function in the world, and development occurs.

8.15: The concept of "schemas" best helps us understand why the students' responses vary so much. The students' scripts guide their patterns of interaction, and their schemas and scripts depend in part on their cultural background. As teachers, we need to help students form school-related schemas and scripts that help them function effectively in classroom settings. (You might note that we're using Piaget's concept of schemes slightly differently from the concept of schemas in Chapter 7. Piaget's schemes are mechanisms that are used to process information in the world. Schemas, as they're used in Chapter 7, are complex knowledge structures. The differences for purposes of instruction are not critical.)

8.16: Not knowing the meaning of the word would not be considered a problem under these conditions, since you simply look up the word in the dictionary.

Not knowing the definition could be a problem, however, if you didn't have access to a dictionary. Then you would have to search for an alternate solution, such as asking someone what the word means, or trying to infer the meaning of the word from the context of the sentence in which it appears. An important characteristic of a problem is the extent to which you must search for solution path to the goal, and this is an intuitively sensible idea. You could even imagine saying something, such as, "I've got a problem. I don't know the meaning of this word, and I don't have a dictionary."

8.17: This was a well-defined problem. The students knew that they were trying to determine how much carpet they needed, and to determine the amount, they had to find the area of the mapped portion of the classroom.

8.18: This is an ill-defined problem. You are probably not completely clear on what a "satisfying relationship" would be, and it's unlikely that you have a clear idea as to how a satisfying relationship would be achieved, even if you had a clear idea of what it meant.

8.19: Laura didn't give her students a great deal of experience in identifying problems. She told the students ". . . your job is going to be to figure out how much carpet we need." She would have been more effective in helping them identify problems by discussing the fact that they were going to carpet the room but that the carpet would be likely to quickly wear out under where the computers are. She could then ask them what could be done to deal with that factor. She could guide them into suggesting that linoleum might be placed under the computers, which would then lead to identifying the problem of the amount of carpet needed.

8.20: Social interaction is the most effective way to prevent students from rushing toward a solution. Discussing the problem in detail, including asking for estimates, helps the teacher determine whether or not the problem makes sense to the students. Teacher questioning is the primary processing that would be used to promote the discussion.

8.21: While more than one algorithm can be used in some cases, a common algorithm for your problem would be:
1. Measure the length and width of your living room in feet.
2. Convert inches to fractional portions of a foot.
3. Multiply the length times the width the get the area of the room.
4. Multiply your answer by $21.99.

8.22: The first step in using means-ends analyses to solve ill-defined problems is to identify a clear goal state. Often, this will require operationally defining the goal. Then, a series of subgoals might be identified to reach the overall goal, and solution paths identified to reach each of the subgoals. For instance, a "satisfying" relationship would have to be defined. This might mean the partner demonstrates affection and acts of caring. One subgoal might then be "improved communication."

8.23: Lack of domain-specific knowledge in either the problem domain or the analogy domain. They must have knowledge in both, or it won't work.

8.24: A variety of possibilities exist. For example, you could draw the six jugs and show each being two-thirds full. Then ask a series of specific questions that would require the boy to reconsider his thinking, such as, "How much would we have if all the jugs were full?" "Must we have more or less than that amount?" "How do we know?"

An alternative series of questions might be, "Based on what we see, how much in two jugs?" "In three?" "Must we have more or less than six pints altogether?" and "How do we know?"

8.25: The teacher could ask questions or pose problems that would help learners see new relationships or connections between old ideas, and thereby the students' "expertise" would be increased.

8.26: As we saw in the section on "deliberate practice," practice and experience (assuming that they have enough domain-specific knowledge) are keys to developing expertise. Motivation can be an obstacle, since only a motivated learner will make the effort to acquire enough practice and experience to become an expert.

8.27: Yes. If the knowledge is in the form of facts and isolated pieces of information, one could be an expert. The notion of "amount" is admittedly arguable. It could be argued that if one has organized, generative knowledge, and another has knowledge in isolated pieces, that the "amount" of knowledge the first has is greater. However, if "amount" means individual, "unchunked" pieces, they could have the same amount, and one still have more expertise.

8.28: First, all new learning depends on current understanding. Second, if learners have misconceptions about aspects of the topic they're studying, deliberate practice will exacerbate the misconceptions. The misconceptions must be directly confronted and hopefully eliminated. Both of these factors makes taking existing knowledge into account important.

8.29: Discussing problems qualitatively helps students form schemas to which numerical results can be attached. This makes the quantitative aspects of the problem more meaningful, because they are attached to concrete information.

8.30: Procedural knowledge involves "conditions" and "actions." In order to perform the appropriate actions, learners must identify the conditions congruent with the actions. Context provides situations that allow learners to practice identifying "conditions."

Laura's students needed declarative knowledge about the concept *area* and the formulas for finding the areas of different geometric shapes. They demonstrated procedural knowledge when they devised techniques for measuring the room and when they did the actual calculations of the areas.

8.31: Almost all problems presented in schools are well-defined, and they're laid out by the teacher, so the students get little practice. They acquire little experience with any form of ill-defined problem.

8:32: First, Laura presented an overhead of the problem-solving model. Then she provided prompts and cues, such as the note "remember the linoleum" to help guide the students as they worked, and she also gave each group a diagram of the room to further guide them as they attempted to find the areas.

8.33: Constructivism emphasizes the role of social interaction in learning. As students interact with the teacher and with each other learning progresses from shared to individual understanding. Without the discussion, learners can't capitalize on the perspectives of others, and individual internalization is less likely.

8.34: Questioning to promote learner involvement was the primary aspect of cognitive apprenticeship that Laura demonstrated. She also coached the students as they worked on finding the areas.

8.35: Within a particular domain, learners will have a store of knowledge to which the strategies can be linked. Having a concrete link to each of the steps in the general problem-solving model increases the likelihood of the model being meaningful.

8.36: This is an ill-defined problem, in spite of the fact that we have defined self-regulation. Self-regulation includes setting goals, as well as monitoring and assessing those goals. Uncertainty exists in monitoring and assessing goals, and the solution paths to setting, monitoring, and assessing goals are not clearly specified.

8.37: Since concepts are declarative knowledge and strategies are procedural knowledge, they will be taught differently. In teaching concepts the teacher will provide examples and non-examples and a definition to help learners form a schema for the concept.

Teaching a strategy requires that the learners acquire declarative knowledge about the strategy and then be put in a variety of situations that give them practice in identifying the conditions in which the strategy will be most effective. Finally, they need additional practice in using the strategy when the conditions are appropriate.

8.38: Well-developed metacognitive abilities and background knowledge are characteristics of expertise in problem solving.

8.39: If students have background knowledge, they have a number of points to which new information can be attached. This makes the new information meaningful. If the information is meaningful, they are better able to determine whether or not it's important.

8.40: The difference between effective and ineffective highlighting and notetaking best relates to the concept of "activity." Students who avoid the decision about what is most important by highlighting whole sections put themselves in a somewhat passive role, whereas those who make decisions about what is most important to highlight put themselves into a much more active role.

8.41: "Organization" is one of the factors that makes information meaningful.

8.42: ". . . creates links between new information and knowledge in long term memory" refers to the concept of meaningfulness.

8.43: While beneficial to both, the strategy should be most helpful in studying DNA. Since the study of DNA is probably more cognitively demanding than merely reading an article in a news magazine, constructing questions, trying to relate DNA to other topics in biology, answering questions about DNA and restudying difficult material would all be more beneficial than constructing and answering questions, etc., about the news article.

8.44: MURDER should probably be more effective. Processes such as paraphrasing content, trying to apply information, and analyzing errors on quizzes--all parts of MURDER--put learners into a more active role than they would be in using SQ4R.

8.45: The most obvious application of information processing was Donna's effort to promote metacognitive awareness in the students. Second, by having the students practice the skill, she put them in an active role, which promotes encoding, and with enough practice, can lead to automaticity. She also provided feedback, which gave the students information about the accuracy of their encoding.

Donna modeled the skill, and modeling is part of social cognitive theory. Also, expectations of reinforcement, and feedback are related to social cognitive theory. (Feedback is important in virtually all theories of learning.) Feedback is important in social cognitive theory, so learners know what behaviors will be reinforced, and according to social cognitive theory, reinforcement works only when learners know what behaviors will be reinforced.

8.46: As with virtually all aspects of learning, "thinking" requires background knowledge. In general, the more background knowledge a learner has, the more effective his or her thinking will be. Trying to teach thinking outside the context of the regular curriculum fails to take background knowledge into account. A good critical thinker in geography isn't necessarily a good critical thinker in science, for instance.

8.47: The answer to this question isn't cut and dried, because it depends on the topic being studied. However, in general, preoperational learners could use any processes that are essentially perceptual, such as recalling, recognizing, comparing and contrasting, and classifying. They can also infer, predict, and confirm conclusions with facts if concrete ideas are involved, such as, "We know that animal is a mammal because it is warm and furry." In addition to the processes already identified, concrete thinkers can hypothesize, identify relevant and irrelevant information, and check consistency. Critical-thinking skills such as identifying bias, stereotypes, and unstated assumptions are abstract and require formal thinking. The ability to recognize over- or undergeneralizing depends on the topic.

8.48: Attitude would be best indicated by a person's inclination to study math beyond the requirements set by the teacher. The inclination to use a thinking skill without being prompted to do so would be the best indicator of a person's attitude toward it.

8.49: The schema of the one for whom transfer occurs is more complex and interrelated. This means that there are more points to which the new situation can be related, increasing the possibilities for transfer.

8.50: The theme is the preeminence of domain-specific knowledge (background knowledge in a specific area, such as geometry, American literature, flowering plants, and many others). Transfer without a rich background of domain-specific knowledge is unlikely. This idea is similar to the question asked in 8.46, which also emphasizes the role of knowledge.

8.51: David represented information about the solar system using his demonstration with the socks, his model of the solar system, and a detailed matrix related to the planets. These demonstrate considerable variety in his representations.

8.52: The first representation is of higher quality. In it we can see that "quickly" modifies "jumped." The words alone provide no context, which will result in merely memorizing that they're adverbs.

8.53: Quality of examples is very good. For instance, we know that "counties" is plural because the passage says "several counties." The same is true for each of the other examples.
    Variety is quite good. For instance, we have at least three examples of nouns ending in 'y' preceded by a consonant, at least two examples of nouns ending in 'y' preceded by a vowel, and at least three examples of nouns ending in consonants. We also have three examples of where the form of the word is changed (e.g., woman/women), but we have only one example of nouns ending in a vowel (tree/trees).

8.54:   First, they're modeled. Second, students know that they will be reinforced for displaying the behaviors, and they are put in situations where they can demonstrate the disposition and receive feedback. Again, we see that social cognitive theory helps us understand why it works.

Application Exercises

Exercise 8.1

For Items 1 through 5, read the episode and decide whether the lesson was aimed primarily at a *concept*, a *principle*, a *generalization*, an *academic rule*, or a combination of two or more of these forms of content. Explain how you know in each case.

1. Mary Jo Fernandez wanted her students to understand the theory of continental drift. She began by giving an overview of the theory, complete with an outline and slides. Then the students broke into study groups to investigate geological formations, fossil forms, magnetic clues, and data from the sea floor. As each group gathered information, they put it on a chart that the class discussed at the end of the unit.

2. Bill Stanton wanted his art students to know how color influences depth perspective in paintings. To reach his goal he displayed and asked students to compare a series of color prints, ultimately guiding them to the conclusion that "dark colors appear to recede" and "light and bright colors look closer."

3. Dan Shafer wanted his language arts students to be able to identify inferences in written essays. He began by defining inferences and explaining why they're important. He then displayed a paragraph on the overhead and went through it line by line, underlining each inference and explaining his thinking. Finally, he displayed a second paragraph and had the students identify inferences and explain their thinking.

4. Juanita Kennedy was teaching a unit on farm animals to her kindergarten class, most of whom had never been to a farm. Juanita wanted her students to know the names of both the animals and their babies, what they eat, and the products they give us. In teaching the unit, she used pictures, stories, such as *The Little Red Hen* and *The Ugly Duckling*, and songs. She completed the unit with a trip to the zoo and petting farm.

5. Kathy Connor's prealgebra students were having trouble simplifying simple arithmetic expressions such as $8/4+6(8-2)/9$. She presented several examples, explained and demonstrated each step in the process, and then gave the students several problems on which to practice. Each was discussed and explained.

Read the following case study and answer the questions that follow it.

> Jan Schwartz's fifth-grade music class was learning a ballad about cowboys. As they turned to the page in the music book, a hand went up.
> "What's a dogie?"
> "Actually, Kim, it's pronounced dōgee, long 'e'. It does kind of look like the word *doggy*, doesn't it? Who knows what a dogie is? . . . Anyone? . . . Well, let's look at the sentence and see if we can find out. It says, 'Get along, little dogie.' What are the cowboys doing? Jed?"
> ". . . They're herding cattle."
> "Good, and so a little cow would be a? . . . Tanya?"
> ". . . Calf."
> "Very good! A dogie is a calf, but a special kind of calf--one that's lost its mother. Why would that be important to a cowboy? Shannon?"
> ". . . Because they wouldn't know who to follow or where to go."
> "Excellent, Shannon! Class, look at the picture of the cattle drive on the front of the album. Can you see any potential dogies?" she asked, holding the picture up for them.

Identify each of the following:

6. The concept being taught

7. A superordinate concept

8. A coordinate concept

9. A characteristic of the concept

10. An example of the concept

11. How "easy" was this concept to learn? Explain why.

Exercise 8.2

Read the following descriptions of a class involved in problem solving and answer the questions that follow:

Jack Watson's algebra class was working on applications of problem solving. To begin the class, Jack put the following problem on an overhead:

A goat is tied to the corner of a 40-ft-square barn with a 30-ft rope. If it can graze everywhere outside of the barn that its rope allows it to reach, what is the size of its grazing area?

"What do we need to do first?" he began. "Taffy?"
" . . . Figure out what we know and need to find out."
"Good, Taffy. Let's start with givens. What do we know? Betty?"
"Well, we know how big the sides of the barn are . . . 40 ft, and . . . we know that the rope is 30 ft long."
"Okay. Now would anyone like to come up and draw us a picture to help us see what we are trying to figure out?. . . Shanda?"
" . . . Well, I think the problem looks like this. We have a circle with a radius of 30 ft. But the barn is here. It cuts out part of that circle. We have to find the area of the circle that's not in the barn because no grass grows in the barn, and he couldn't get in to eat it anyway."
"Excellent drawing, Shanda. So how do we translate this into a formula? Kerry?"
"The formula for the area of a circle is A equals pi times the radius squared. So we need to find that and subtract 1/4 from it . . . to allow for the barn."
"Who can do that on their calculator and then share with us on the board? Brad?"
"Hmmm . . . Okay. I think the answer is 2,826."
"It's 2,826 what, Brad?"
"Oh, right! Square feet. Does that sound about right?"
"Is that what everyone else got? Kim?"
" . . . I don't think so. I think . . . he forgot to subtract the quarter of a circle in the barn. So it should be 2,119.5 square ft, I think," Kim responded hesitantly.
"How about anyone else?" Jack queried. "Check it out."
Several other students rechecked and confirmed Kim's results.

Jack then continued, "Good, everyone. . . . Now, two things we can learn from this problem. First, always go back to the notes you took when you set up the problem. If Brad had checked with the diagram we drew, he would have caught his mistake. Second, make sure you have the right units. If it's area, it needs to be square something."

1. Identify steps from the general problem-solving model that are illustrated in the description. Make direct reference to the information in the description in identifying the steps.

2. Are any of the steps from the general problem-solving model missing? If so, identify those steps.

3. Is the problem well-defined or ill-defined. Explain.

4. Did the students use an algorithm to solve the problem or did they use a heuristic? Explain.

136

5. How effectively did Jack implement the suggestions for helping students become better problem solvers in his activity? Explain.

Exercise 8.3

Read the following example and answer the questions that follow it.

Kendra Phillips is working with her class on the development of their study strategies. She begins the activity by saying, "Today we're going to learn a new way to check whether we understand what we're reading. There are several steps in the process. After every paragraph that we read, we need to make a statement that summarizes the main ideas in it. Then we'll make a question about the material in that paragraph. Our passage for today is about snakes. I'll read the first paragraph out loud and then try to summarize.

"'The snake's skeleton and parts of its body are very flexible--almost like a rubber hose with bones. A snake's backbone can have almost 300 vertebrae, almost ten times as many as a human's. These vertebrae are connected by cartilage that allows easy movement. Because of this bendable, twistable spinal construction, a snake can turn its body in almost any direction at almost any point.

"Hmmm. Let's see--what would be a sentence that summarizes this paragraph? How about, 'Snakes have lots of bones'? Hmmm, that's okay, but it doesn't tell why it's important. How about, 'Snakes have lots of bones in their backbones, and that allows them to move and bend'?

"Yes, that's better. Now I need a good question. 'How,' 'why,' and 'when' words are often helpful. How about this one: 'Why do snakes have so many bones in their backbones?' That's a good one because it aims at the main idea in the paragraph.'

"Now, let's see. Are there any ideas in the paragraph that aren't clear? . . . What is cartilage? . . . Oh, yes. It's the flexible material between bones, like the cartilage in our knees between the bones in our upper leg and our lower leg.

"What will the next paragraph be about? . . . I wonder if it will explain how snakes' flexible spines help them to survive and hunt. . . . Now let's try another paragraph, and I want one of you to try these four steps." (adapted from Brown & Palinscar, 1985).

1. Was Kendra's focus on basic study strategies or on comprehension monitoring? Explain how you know based on information taken directly from the case study.

2. Based on the information in the chapter, how effectively did Kendra implement the suggestions for "Helping students become effective strategy users?"

Look at the following statements:
   "Japanese-made cars are better than American-made cars."
   "Candidate Smith has a better position on tax reform than candidate Jones."
   "A square is a kind of rectangle."

3. If an individual "spontaneously" asks, "How do you know?" in response to any one or more of the three statements, which of the Elements of Thinking is best illustrated by this behavior? (Spontaneously asking the question.)

4. If a person answers the question ("How do you know?") which basic process and which subprocess are being best illustrated? Explain.

Exercise 8.4

1. The following descriptions show how three teachers taught their students about reptiles. Analyze the three episodes in terms of the discussion of transfer in the chapter and decide which teacher's students would have the highest likelihood of transfer and which would be least likely to transfer. Explain your reasoning in the analysis.

Mrs. Jung carefully explained what reptiles are, where they live, and what they eat. She then told her students that animals such as alligators, crocodiles, turtles, and snakes are reptiles.

Mrs. McManus brought her son's pet snake to class. She also showed the students colored pictures of an alligator, a turtle, and a horned toad. She had the students observe the snake and the pictures and discuss the characteristics they all had in common.

Mr. Hume explained what reptiles are and told the students that snakes, lizards, alligators, and turtles are reptiles. He also showed the students a picture of a sea turtle, so they knew that some reptiles live in water.

2.　Identify one important aspect of concept teaching that each of the teachers neglected to do in the lesson.

Feedback for Application Exercises

Exercise 8.1

1. This lesson focused on a combinations of concepts, generalizations, and principles (together with facts). For example, *fossil* is a concept, "Mountains are formed by pressure within the earth's crust" is a generalization." Often in science, social studies, literature, and health, we want students to remember large, integrated bodies of information (which will be discussed in detail in Chapter 12), not isolated facts, concepts, generalizations, or principles. Mary Jo Fernandez attempted this by providing a structured overview at the beginning of the lesson and a comprehensive review with a chart at the end of the unit.

2. Bill Stanton was teaching his students a generalization that related the concepts *color* and *depth perspective*. "Dark colors appear to recede and light and bright colors look closer," is a generalization. His examples (the paintings) illustrated the relationship. Illustrating the relationship is critical when a generalization is being taught.

3. Dan Shafer was teaching the concept *inference*. He gave the students a definition and a series of examples, which were embedded in the context of a paragraph. He then reinforced the concept by having the students identify examples of inference in another paragraph.

4. Juanita Kennedy was teaching her students a combination of facts, concepts, and generalizations. For example, each of the animals are concepts, and what they eat and the products they provide are generalizations.

5. Kathy Connor's students were learning the *rule* for simplifying arithmetic expressions. She demonstrated the rule with examples and she had the students apply the rule with several more examples.

6. The concept being taught was "dogie." Note how the teacher helped her students use context clues to teach the concept. This is a helpful and widely applicable concept learning strategy for use with printed material.

7. The superordinate concept could be either cows (cattle) or calves in general. Both are larger, more inclusive concepts in which the target concept is embedded.

8. A coordinate concept would be calves *with* mothers. A coordinate concept is another concept that is also a subset of the superordinate concept. For example, adverbs and adjectives are coordinate concepts, since they are both subsets of "modifiers," and similes and metaphors are coordinate concepts since they are subsets of "figures of speech."

9. The essential characteristic mentioned in the episode was "motherless." From student responses we could infer that other characteristics such as "four-legged" and "nurses from mother" were present in the students' schemas for calf, but these are not the essential characteristics.

10. The teacher used the picture of a cattle drive to present a positive example of the concept. This is an essential component of concept learning, but one that is often by-passed because examples for some concepts are hard to find or create.

11. This concept would be easy to learn, because it only had one essential characteristic, and the characteristic is concrete.

Exercise 8.2

1. The different problem solving stages occurred as follows:

Identifying and representing the problem: The following part of the dialogue illustrates these first two phases of the process:

> "What do we need to do first?" he began. "Taffy?"
> " . . . Figure out what we know and need to find out."
> "Good, Taffy. Let's start with givens. What do we know? Betty?"
> "Well, we know how big the sides of the barn are--40 ft--and we know that the rope is 30 ft long."
> "Okay. Now would anyone like to come up and draw us a picture to help us see what we are trying to figure out? Shanda?"
> "Well, I think the problem looks like this. We have a circle with a radius of 30 ft. But the barn is here. It cuts out part of that circle. We have to find the area of the circle that's not in the barn because no grass grows in the barn, and he couldn't get in to eat it anyway."

Selecting and implementing a strategy: Selecting and implementing a strategy were illustrated in the following part of the dialogue:

> "Excellent drawing, Shanda. So how do we translate this into a formula? Kerry?"
> "The formula for the area of a circle is A equals pi times the radius squared. So we need to find that and subtract 1/4 from it . . . to allow for the barn."
> "Who can do that on their calculator and then share with us on the board? Brad?"
> "Hmmm . . . Okay. I think the answer is 2,826."
> "It's 2,826 what, Brad?"
> "Oh, right! Square feet. Does that sound about right?"

Evaluating the results: Evaluating the results occurred in the following part of the dialogue.

> "Is that what everyone else got? Kim?"
> ". . . I don't think so. I think . . . he forgot to subtract the quarter of a circle in the barn. So it should be 2,119.5 square ft, I think," Kim responded hesitantly.
> "How about anyone else?" Jack queried. "Check it out."
> Several other students rechecked and confirmed Kim's results.

2. All the steps in the general problem-solving model were present. The students didn't get much practice in "problem finding," but this is typical of instruction in problem solving.

3. This was a well-defined problem. The problem asked for the area of the grazing area, which is a clear goal state, and clear solution paths existed for reaching the goal state.

4. The students used an algorithm. The formula for finding the area of a circle involves an algorithm.

5. Jack presented a fairly traditional approach to problem solving. The problem was in context, but it could have been personalized to make it more meaningful for the students. Finding the area of a portion of the room, or the students' desks, for example, would have been a more meaningful context.

There was a moderate amount of social interaction involved in the lesson, and the students were given adequate scaffolding. For example, Brad received immediate feedback about his solution.

Jack made some effort at teaching general problem solving strategies when he commented, "Good, everyone. . . . Now, two things we can learn from this problem. First, always go back to the notes you took when you set up the problem. If Brad had checked with the diagram we drew, he would have caught his mistake. Second, make sure you have the right units. If it's area, it needs to be square something."

Exercise 8.3

1. Kendra's focus was primarily on comprehension monitoring. For example, she said, "After every paragraph that we read, we need to make a statement that summarizes the main ideas in it. Then we'll make a question about the material in that paragraph." This comment relates to summarizing and self-questioning, both comprehension monitoring strategies.

2. Kendra was quite effective in implementing the suggestions for helping students become effective strategy users. She modeled the process, thinking aloud throughout the modeling. She then planned to have the students practice the strategy.

3. "Spontaneously" asking the question suggests an attitude or a disposition. This suggests the disposition to ask for evidence for conclusions.

4. The process being illustrated in answering the question is, "Assessing conclusions based on observation," and the subprocess is "Confirming conclusions with facts."

Exercise 8.4

1. Three criteria for effective transfer are *quality*, *variety*, and *context*. We have little evidence about the context in any of the three episodes. The quality of Mrs. Jung's examples wasn't good, since she only used verbal descriptions. The quality of Mr. Hume's examples was a bit better, since he used a picture of a sea turtle. Mrs. McManus clearly had the best quality examples, and even though Mr. Hume had the added variety of the sea turtle, Mrs. McManus's quality would more than make up for this deficit, so the likelihood of transfer would be the greatest in her case. The poor quality examples in Mrs. Jung's case would make transfer least likely for her students.

2. In addition to neglecting *context*, none of the teachers used any *nonexamples*.

TRUE/FALSE QUESTIONS. Write T in the blank if the statement is true, and write F if the statement is false.

_____ 1. The rule-eg teaching strategy is one example of an approach to teaching problem solving.
_____ 2. Generalizations and principles differ in that principles describe relationships between concepts, but no relationship is implied with a generalization.
_____ 3. "Raise your hand when you wish to speak" is an example of an academic rule.
_____ 4. Research indicates that students learn most of the study skills that they are able to use without formal instruction from a teacher.
_____ 5. Dispositions are one element of the critical-thinking process that transfer in a general sense, as opposed to domain-specific knowledge which transfers poorly to new situations.

MULTIPLE-CHOICE QUESTIONS: Circle the best response in each case.

6. You want your students to understand what *fractions* are. You introduce the topic by saying, "Fractions are numbers that you use to describe what you have when you break a whole number or thing into smaller parts. If I break a cookie into two pieces that are the same size, I have two halves of a cookie." The first sentence of the statement to the students can also be called a:
    a. discrimination.
    b. definition.
    c. characteristic.
    d. rule.
    e. principle.

7. In Item 6, "numbers" is most precisely described as the:
    a. concept.
    b. subordinate concept.
    c. coordinate concept.
    d. superordinate concept.
    e. characteristic.

8. The statement, "In writing possessives, the apostrophe is written before the 's' if the noun is singular but is written after the 's' if the noun is plural," best describes a(n):
    a. concept.
    b. principle.
    c. definition.
    d. academic rule.
    e. discrimination.

9. Which of the following best illustrates a cognitive strategy?
    a. Reading an assigned passage in history
    b. Finding the lowest common denominator when adding fractions
    c. Identifying an example of an inference in a written paragraph
    d. Writing notes in the margins of your textbook

10. You want to teach your students about prepositions. Of the following, which is most effective for promoting transfer?
   a. Present a list of prepositions and explain how they're used.
   b. Present a list of sentences that have prepositions in them and guide the students to identifying the prepositions in each case.
   c. Present a paragraph that includes several prepositions and guide the students to identifying the prepositions in each case.
   d. Explain to the students that prepositions are always in phrases, and all they have to do is identify the phrase. Then show them several prepositional phrases.

11. The aspect of transfer that is the focus of Item 10 is:
   a. variety of examples.
   b. quality of examples.
   c. context for examples.
   d. both variety and quality of examples.

12. Maurice has learned to add fractions in math. When he encounters a word problem in science he is able to use fractions to solve it. This situation most closely relates to:
   a. hierarchical learning.
   b. a study skill.
   c. discovery learning.
   d. specific transfer.

13. You have taught your students the concept rhombus (figures with four equal sides and opposite angles equal). Of the following, which is the best way to determine if transfer has occurred?
   a. Show them a parallelogram, square, trapezoid, and hexagon, and ask them which is a rhombus.
   b. Show them a square and ask if it is a rhombus.
   c. Ask them to write a definition of rhombus on a sheet of paper.
   d. Show them a regular hexagon (six equal sides and six equal angles) and ask if it is a rhombus.

Three teachers were teaching their students about *adverbs*.

Mrs. Evans told the students that adverbs modify verbs, adjectives, and other adverbs, and went on to say words, such as *quickly, openly, very,* and *rapidly* were adverbs and wrote the words on the board.

Mrs. D'Armas showed the students the sentences:

"Joe quickly jumped into the straight lunch line when Mrs. Smith reminded him."
"Ronnie very openly described his strong feelings about the incident."
"Jim has extra large biceps."

She pointed out that the underlined words were adverbs, and the class determined what they modified. They then formed a definition of adverbs and she wrote it on the board.

Mrs. Voltaire wrote the statement, "Adverbs are parts of speech that modify verbs, adjectives, and other adverbs," on the board and showed the students the following sentence:

"Jo powerfully made her argument by stating the facts in the matter."

She then had Susan walk across the floor, and prompted the students to state, "Susan walked quickly across the floor," she wrote the sentence on the board, and she underlined the word *quickly*. She then pointed out that the underlined word in the sentence was an adverb.

14. The type of content the teachers were attempting to teach would best be described as:
   a. generalizations.
   b. concepts.
   c. academic rules.
   d. cognitive strategies.

15. The next day, Mrs. D'Armas showed the students the sentence:

Steve is rapidly improving in his work in advanced math,

and asked the students to identify what *rapidly* was in the sentence. They said, "It's an adverb." The type of learning represented by their answer is best described as:
   a.   concepts.
   b.   academic rules.
   c.   concepts and generalizations.
   d.   generalizations.

16.   Ken, a student in Mrs. D'Armas' class noted that in each of the sentences the adjective came before the noun that it modified. The type of learning that this best represents is:
   a.   discriminations.
   b.   concepts.
   c.   academic rules.
   d.   principles.
   e.   cognitive strategies.

17.   Think about the three teachers. The one whose students are *most* likely to *transfer* the information is:
   a.   Mrs. Evans.
   b.   Mrs. D'Armas.
   c.   Mrs. Voltaire.

18.   The one whose students are *least* likely to *transfer* the information is:
   a.   Mrs. Evans.
   b.   Mrs. D'Armas.
   c.   Mrs. Voltaire.

19.   Of the following, which is the best example for teaching the concept *adjective*?
   a.   The word *big* written on the chalkboard
   b.   The statement, "Adjectives modify nouns and pronouns," written on the chalkboard
   c.   A picture of a large building with a small building beside it
   d.   The sentence, "The <u>heavy</u> truck nearly ran over the <u>small</u> car," written on the chalkboard

20.   You want to teach the students, "Objects expand when they're heated." If successful, this would result in the students learning:
   a.   concepts.
   b.   academic rules.
   c.   principles.
   d.   generalizations.

21.   Of the following, which is the best example for teaching, "Objects expand when they're heated?"
   a.   Ask the students why they suppose bridges have expansion joints in them.
   b.   Ask the students to think about a sidewalk. Prompt them to notice that a sidewalk is not a solid piece of concrete; rather it is in sections. Ask them why they think the sections exist.
   c.   Fill two identical balloons with similar amounts of air. Put one in hot water and put the other in ice.
   d.   Write the statement, "Objects expand when they're heated," on the board. Ask the students if they can think of cases where they've seen heated objects expand.

22. Three students are discussing their approaches to understanding the information being taught in their economics class.

"I always read economics before I go to class," Kim comments. "Mrs. Hernandez sometimes blasts through the stuff. If I've already read it, I don't get lost."

"I always read my economics before I do English," Albert shrugs. "That gets it out of the way, and then I can enjoy myself. I like English."

"I never miss a homework assignment in that class," Sandra adds. "You know how Mrs. Hernandez is about homework. I'd never go to that class without doing it."

The student that is illustrating the most "strategic" behavior is:
   a. Kim.
   b. Albert.
   c. Sandra.

Steve Fraser displays a drawing of an island on the overhead projector. The drawing includes landforms, ocean currents, and the prevailing wind direction.

"Now," he says after the students have looked at the drawing, "How do you suppose we could determine what the best location for a city would be on this island? What factors should we take into account in making our decision?"

"I think we need to consider how good a harbor it might have," Natalie suggested.

The class considers several factors and decides that point C on the map is the best location.

"I don't think that's a good choice," Kathy comments. "That's not on any river and it's not near the coast, and it isn't even around good land."

The discussion then continues and the class reconsiders it's choice.

23. Steve's question, "How do you suppose we could determine what the best location for a city would be on this island? . . ." best illustrates his attempt to help his students with which step in the problem-solving process?
   a. Identifying the problem
   b. Representing the problem
   c. Selecting a strategy
   d. Implementing a strategy
   e. Evaluating the results

24. Kathy's comment is most closely related to which step in the problem-solving process?
   a. Identifying the problem
   b. Representing the problem
   c. Selecting a strategy
   d. Implementing a strategy
   e. Evaluating the results

Four people see a drawing showing the path of the cue ball (the ball driven into the other balls in pool) before striking the object ball, and the paths of both the cue ball and the object ball after the object ball has been struck.

25. Jerome says, "The cue ball went off to the left and the other ball went off to the right."

Sharon says, "It's a conservation of momentum problem."

Steve says, "The cue ball must have hit the other ball at an angle."

Linda says, "The harder you hit the cue ball, the faster the other ball will go. This cue ball must have been struck fairly hard."

If the students demonstrate the characteristics of expertise identified by research, the one whose comments indicate the most expertise is:
   a. Jerome.
   b. Sharon.
   c. Steve.
   d. Linda.

1. f
2. f
3. f
4. t
5. t
6. b   The statement, "Fractions are numbers that you use to describe what you have when you break a whole number or thing into smaller parts," includes the concept--fractions, a superordinate concept--numbers, and characteristics--"what you have when you break a whole number or thing into smaller parts."
7. d   "Numbers" is a larger class into which fractions fit.
8. d   This is a convention that has been arbitrarily derived by humans. (Rules are necessary, however, for the sake of consistency in communication.)
9. d   Writing notes in the margin of your book is a "plan for accomplishing a learning goal," and it goes beyond the processes involved in directly carrying out the task.
10. c   Presenting the prepositions in the paragraph provides the most effective context, and guiding the students to identify the prepositions in the paragraph provides practice and results in the deepest understanding. (Based on information from Chapter 7, it also puts the students in the most active role.)
11. c   We have little information about either the variety of examples or the quality of the examples based on the information in the description.
12. d   He is performing the task in a slightly different context.
13. a   The ability to identify an example is a good measure of transfer of concept learning. Having them draw a rhombus would also be a good way of indicating that their understanding of the concept has transferred.
14. b   "Adverb" is a concept.
15. a   Being able to identify "rapidly" as an adverb indicates that they understand the concept. (Remember, a rule involves a relationship, such as the singular/plural and spelling, as in the rule for forming plural nouns.)
16. c   Adjectives preceding the nouns they modify illustrates an arbitrary relationship. (For example, adjectives follow the nouns they modify in French and Spanish.)
17. b   Mrs. D'Armas provided a definition, an example of each of the forms of adverbs, and the adverbs were in the context of sentences. Mrs. Evans provided only words, and Mrs. Voltaire only illustrated adverbs that modify verbs, both with her sentence and having Susan walk across the floor.
18. a   Mrs. Evans had very poor quality examples, and they were not in any form of context.
19. d   The word "big" is presented in the abstract, the statement in choice b only describes adjectives; it isn't an example, and choice c merely illustrates a large and small house. It doesn't illustrate the characteristics of adjectives.
20. d   This one is admittedly a little tricky. Most commonly we think of objects expanding when they're heated as true for all cases, which is the characteristic of a principle. However, water near freezing, doesn't expand when it's heated (which is why we put antifreeze in car radiators in the winter), so there are exceptions to the statement. This example is another case that illustrates the importance of domain-specific knowledge.
21. c   This choice is the only true illustration. Each of the other choices requires background knowledge that the learners may not possess. (This idea is very important when considering the diversity in our students.)
22. a   Kim is demonstrating the most "strategic" behavior. Reading the information ahead of time is a "plan for accomplishing a learning goal."
23. a   Steve's question is most closely related to identifying the problem.
24. e   Kathy's comment best illustrates "evaluating the results."
25. b   Sharon's comment indicates that she sees the illustration as an interconnected relationship. Experts see patterns and relationships to a greater extent than do novices.

CHAPTER 9: COGNITION IN THE CONTENT AREAS

Chapter Outline

I. Learning to read and teaching reading
 - A. Learning to read
   1. Reading as a developmental process
   2. Background knowledge
   3. Linguistic knowledge
   4. Conflicting conceptions of learning to read
     a. Meaning-emphasis approaches
     b. Code-emphasis approaches
     c. Phonemic awareness
     d. Decoding
 - B. Reading to learn
   1. Components of comprehension
     a. Background knowledge
     b. Comprehension strategies
     c. Metacognition

II. Learning to write and teaching writing
 - A. Writing as problem solving
 - B. The writing process
   1. Planning
   2. Translating
   3. Revising
 - C. Helping students learn to write
   1. A cognitively oriented writing classroom
     a. Teach specific strategies
     b. Embed strategies in a larger context
     c. Provide opportunities for practice and feedback
     d. Create a community of writers

III. The challenges of diversity in learning to read and write
 - A. Creating a supportive and language-rich learning environment
 - B. Providing scaffolding in literacy activities
   1. Background knowledge
   2. Linguistic scaffolds
   3. Meaningful learning activities

IV. Learning and teaching mathematics
 - A. Changing views of learning mathematics
   1. Historical views of learning
   2. Culture of the classroom
     a. Beliefs about learning mathematics
     b. Learner strategies
   3. Learning mathematics: cognitive perspectives
 - B. Cognitive views of learning: Implications for instruction
   1. Characteristics of effective math instruction
     a. A focus on problem solving
     b. Real-world application
     c. Emphasis on reasoning
     d. High levels of interaction
   2. Cognitive views of learning: Experimental programs
 - C. Putting reform into perspective

V.   Learning and teaching science
    A.   Difficulties in learning science
        1.   Life experiences and naive theories
            a.   Naive theories: Theoretical explanations
        2.   Curriculum and instruction
    B.   Helping learners understand science
        1.   Adapting the curriculum
        2.   Refocusing instruction
            a.   Assessing current understanding
            b.   Representing content
            c.   Effective interaction
            d.   Real-world interaction
VI. Looking across the content areas
    A.   Common threads in learning and teaching
        1.   Learners' background knowledge
        2.   The use of learning strategies
        3.   Language and dialogue
        4.   Multiple representations of content and authentic tasks

Chapter Objectives

■   Explain the developmental process of learning to read and how teachers can implement strategies to help students learn to read.

■   Analyze cognitive factors influencing the process of learning to write and explain how teachers can facilitate students in this process.

■   Describe current views of learning in mathematics and explain implications for instruction in math.

■   Explain how students' conceptions of science content influence learning in that area and describe instructional strategies to confront those conceptions.

Chapter Overview

While many principles of learning span most teaching situations, individual content areas present unique learning and teaching challenges. This chapter examines learning and teaching in four of these areas: reading, writing, math, and science.

Learning to read is a developmental process that requires both background and linguistic knowledge. *Meaning-emphasis* approaches to learning to read, such as whole language, emphasize the relationships between reading and speaking and listening, and *code-emphasis* approaches, such as phonics, teach letter-sound patterns and rules for sounding out words.

About the third or fourth grade the emphasis changes from learning to read to using reading to learn content. *Data-driven models* of reading to learn emphasize decoding and the analysis of text; *conceptually-driven models* stress reader background knowledge, expectations, and beliefs.

Learning to write requires both background knowledge and discourse knowledge. Discourse knowledge, similar to linguistic knowledge, involves understanding of how language can be used to communicate.

Writing occurs in three stages: planning, translating, and revising. Views on teaching writing have changed from a project to process-driven emphasis. Writing is now viewed as a communication process in which the writer attempts to communicate ideas.

Diversity presents special challenges to learning to read and write because of their heavy reliance on language. Strategies to accommodate diversity include providing a supportive and language-rich learning environment, and providing content and linguistic scaffolds.

Mathematics education has changed from an emphasis on proceduralized algorithms to an emphasis on understanding. Current views emphasize creating a classroom culture that stresses problem solving, reasoning, application, and interaction.

NCTM standards have been influential in shaping reforms in math education. These reforms include a number of experimental programs, all of which stress authentic problems, problem solving, and interactive instruction.

Reform efforts in science education have focused on the naive theories that students bring with them to the classroom. These naive theories, constructed from learners' day-to-day experiences often result in misconceptions about the way the world operates.

Experts recommend two adaptations to address student misconceptions. The curriculum needs to be narrowed to allow more in-depth coverage of content, and instruction needs to assess current student understanding, represent content in multiple ways, show real-world applications, and allow students to share ideas through classroom interaction.

Despite their differences, the learning in these four content areas has several commonalities. Background knowledge influences learning in each. Learning strategies and language and dialogue are important in each. Finally, authentic tasks and multiple representations of content facilitate learning in all four areas.

Feedback for Margin Questions

9.1: A trip to the zoo develops background knowledge by exposing learners to new information about animals. It develops linguistic knowledge to the extent that they read and talk with others.

9.2: Your knowledge of piggy banks was a form of declarative knowledge that was stored in schemas about money, banks, or piggy banks.

9.3: Both were formed through experiences and both are stored in schemas. Background knowledge is much more domain specific (knowledge about a specific content area).

9.4: Code-emphasis approaches explain how you recognize individual words. Meaning-emphasis approaches explain how you apply your background knowledge of piggy banks to the passage.

9.5: Both are meaning-emphasis approaches to reading. Whole language is a more comprehensive and inclusive strategy.

9.6: Phonemic awareness is a form of procedural knowledge because it involves knowing how to do things. This suggests that phonemic awareness can be taught through modeling with practice and feedback.

9.7: Phrend becomes "friend" because of the generalization that "when p and h go together they are pronounced like "f". Nale becomes "nail" because of the generalization, "a vowel consonant combination followed by an e makes the vowel long and the e silent."

9.8: Background knowledge is more important for meaning-emphasis approaches because they emphasize schema activation. Linguistic knowledge helps readers contextualize the codes they are trying to break within sentences by embedding individual words into meaningful sentences.

9.9:   For activation of prior knowledge to work relevant schema have to exist in long-term memory. For example, if you have never washed clothes or watched someone do this, telling you what this passage is about would be much less effective.

9.10:   You could activate (discuss) their schemas for geography and climate prior to the lesson. During the lesson you could give them a matrix that has geography and climate at the top and the agricultural products on the side.

9.11:   Discussing students' own ecological environments both activates and develops their schemas for ecology.

9.12:   The text uses the following to highlight important information: headings, margin questions, bold-facing important concepts in text, defining them in italics, and listing them at the end of each chapter.

9.13:   Outlining involves two important comprehension skills. It requires learners to identify important ideas and also wrestle with the organization of the text.

9.14:   Rereading a passage indicates that the reader didn't understand the passage the first time. Knowing when text makes sense is a fundamental metacognitive reading strategy. Older students do this naturally; younger students have to be taught to do so.

9.15:   The teacher provided instructional scaffolding through modeling and by asking questions to remind students of the next strategy to use.

9.16:   Predicting might be difficult to do if social studies texts are conceptually or chronologically organized. (This problem doesn't occur in narrative stories that have a plot line.) Density might influence clarifying because of task overload; the amount of information could make the task overwhelming.

9.17:   Dave identified the problem as getting an assignment over with, represented it as a quick brainstorming activity, and the strategy he selected was to write down his first thoughts on paper. Luis, by contrast, identified the problem as telling something about himself, represented the task as one of communicating with others, and selected the strategy of writing and organizing his thoughts on paper.

9.18:   The availability of resources such as books, notes, and being able to collaborate with other people drastically changes the cognitive load demands on you. Being able to use these resources would, in all likelihood, result in a longer, deeper and more coherent essay.

9.19:   Both involve knowledge of how language works. Discourse knowledge is more oriented to applying this knowledge to communicate. Both are developed in a language-rich classroom that provides students with tasks that require these forms of knowledge to be used.

9.20:   The arrows go both ways to indicate that the three processes are interconnected. For example, our planning influences our translating and during the process of putting our ideas down on paper we often revise our original plans. In addition, translation influences what we revise and our revisions also influence what we've translated down on paper.

9:21:   Their writing assignment was authentic in that it served the real function of providing an opportunity to talk about themselves. It would have been more authentic if they would have been allowed to choose the particular aspect about themselves to write about.

9:22:   Poor writers may have poorly developed schemas in long-term memory--both for the planning process itself and for the particular topic they are writing about.

9.23: Probably the most effective way to overcome the limitations of working memory during writing is to use external notes as supplemental aids. A second way to deal with working memory limitations is to overlearn the topic you are writing about so information is readily retrievable from long-term memory. Also, basics skills must be automatic, so that working memory space isn't required to perform these skills.

9.24: Semantic and textual challenges can be addressed by better planning to produce clearer and more coherent text. Teachers can help students with graphic and syntactic challenges in two ways. One, which should occur prior to the writing task, involves overlearning to the point of automaticity. The other strategy is to de-emphasize these during writing which allows developing writers to focus on semantic and textual tasks (Bruning et al, 1995).

9.25: Automaticity with micro-processes like grammar and punctuation free working-memory space to focus on larger, more structural issues. In addition teachers can develop learners' schemas for effective revision strategies.

9.26: Jennifer emphasized writing as a problem-solving process when she said, "When we write something new, it's like thinking on paper, but before we put our ideas on paper we need to think about what we're going to say." She stressed communication when she called attention to the audience's knowledge of bicycles. The planning sheet encouraged students to transform information rather than just putting original ideas down on paper.

9.27: Jennifer promoted transfer by explaining the logic behind the strategies (versus rote memorization) and by asking students to apply the planning strategies to a second topic, making a sandwich.

9.28: Both times when she worked on planning strategies she embedded these strategies in the larger framework of communicating through the papers students were writing.

9.29: They might be confusing because their background experiences, upon which their schemas for classroom procedures are formed, may not match those of U.S. classrooms.

9.30: Invented spellings, because they make sense to the writer (and often to the reader), reflect large amounts of knowledge about how letters and language work to convey meaning.

9:31: Historical views of writing emphasized the accurate transmission of information and the correct application of procedures, such as grammar and spelling. (Look again at Table 9.1). This is consistent with the emphasis on procedures in developing an understanding of math.

9.32: The most likely belief is that math learned in school has nothing to do with the real world.

9.33: It takes time to develop complex lessons that emphasize problem solving and high levels of interaction. When preparation time is limited, teachers are likely to revert to simpler forms of instruction, such as lecture.

9.34: The simplest way to emphasize that math is communication is to encourage students to articulate their understanding of mathematical ideas in words. The more practice they get with articulating understanding, the better their communication with mathematics will be. They can also be encouraged to write about their understanding, i.e., describe problems and solutions in writing.

9.35: Jenny's lesson focused on the problem of how to put weights on the balance beam in order to make it level. The emphasis in the lesson was on *problem solving*. This was a *real-world application* that relates to teeter-totters and balancing in general. The lesson strongly emphasized *reasoning* in that the students were first directed to think about what it would take to make the beam balance, then discuss whose prediction they wanted to try first and then finally try it and explain why it did or did not balance. Finally, there was a great deal of *interaction* between Jenny and the students and the students with each other.

9.36: In each case, emphasis is placed on interaction and discussion between the teacher and students and students with each other. (Interaction and discussion are implied in guided discovery approaches to instruction.)

9.37: When we stand closer to a fireplace, or move our hand closer to a hot stove burner, it feels warmer than when we're farther away. Based on these experiences, it makes sense that it would be warmer in the summer because we're closer to the sun. (In fact, it's warmer in the summer because the sun's rays are more direct than they are in winter.)

9.38: As with 9.37, if an object is moving in one direction, it makes sense intuitively that the forces in that direction are greater than the forces in the opposite direction. Also, in order to make an object move, we must push or pull on the object.

9.39: Constructivism best explains why learner understanding varies dramatically. Since learners construct understanding, and they construct this understanding based on what they already know, the constructions will be unique to each individual.

9.40: The naive theories allow learners to remain at equilibrium. Modifying the naive theories disrupts learners' equilibria, so they will be reluctant to do so unless their existing understanding becomes untenable to them. This requires that the naive theories are directly confronted.

9.41: One representation will be meaningful to some learners but not others. Additional representations increase the likelihood that all the learners will be able to construct a meaningful understanding of the topic.

9.42: Nussbaum and Novick would describe this as an exposing *event*. It's purpose is to assess learners' current understanding of the topic.

9.43: The teacher is applying the concept of *social interaction* when she asks questions and helps students arrive at valid understandings of the topic. "Learning depends on social interaction" is a characteristic of constructivism.

Application Exercises_____

Exercise 9.1

1. Explain how background knowledge and linguistic knowledge influence your comprehension of each of the following sentences?
    a. When phosphoenolpyruvate is converted in pyruvate during glycolysis, only one ATP is generated from ADP.
    b. The clunker binked the flandy hoder.
    c. Das bier ist sehr gut.

2. Identify the following as indicating: a) print awareness, b) graphic awareness, c) phonemic awareness, or d) syntactic awareness.
    a. A child can hear the distinction between "bad" and "had."
    b. A pre-schooler points to his favorite box of cereal in the store.
    c. A third grader correctly pronounces lead in the sentence, "He was the lead dog."
    d. A first grader has difficulties distinguishing between d and b.
    e. A three-year-old says "Stop!" whenever she encounters a stop sign while riding in her car seat.

3. Explain how language experience and whole language are both *meaning-emphasis* approaches to reading.

4. Why is phonemic awareness essential to phonics? In your answer, include an example.

5. What can readers do when letter combinations like "gh" (e.g., ghost, through, and rough) don't make the same sound?

Exercise 9.2

1. Read the following passage from the perspective of either a wrestler or convict. How is your comprehension influenced by background knowledge in the form of schemas?

> Tony got up slowly from the mat, planning his escape. He hesitated a moment and thought. Things were not going well. What bothered him most was being held, especially because the charge against him had been weak. He considered his present situation. The lock that held him was strong, but he thought he could break it. He knew, however, that his timing would have to be perfect. Tony was aware that it was because of his early roughness that he had been penalized so severely--much too severely, from his point of view. The situation was becoming frustrating; the pressure had been grinding on him for too long. He was being ridden unmercifully. Tony was getting angry now. He felt he was ready to make his move. He know that his success or failure would depend on what he did in the next few seconds. (Anderson, Reynolds, Schallert, & Goetz, 1977, p. 372).

2. How is self-questioning related to metacognition?

3. How do the four steps in reciprocal teaching contribute to comprehension: summarize, construct a question, clarify, predict?

Exercise 9.3

1. How is writing like problem solving? (Refer to the problem-solving model in Chapter 8 which has the following five steps: 1) identify the problem, 2) represent the problem, 3) select a strategy, 4) implement the strategy, and 5) evaluate results.

2. Explain how teachers can influence the task environment to make the writing task easier or less demanding.

3. How is planning different for very young writers (5-6 years old) versus older (8-12 years old) ones? What implications do these differences have for instruction?

4. Classify the following in terms of: a) graphic challenges, b) syntactic challenges, c) semantic challenges, and d) textual challenges.
    a.   Maria, an ESL student, struggled with grammar in her writing.
    b.   Angie could write clear sentences but had problems integrating them into clear, organized paragraphs.
    c.   Alan, a third grader, had lot of ideas but struggled with his handwriting.
    d.   Bill had trouble "getting into the heads" of his audience.
    e.   Jessie could think faster than her word-processing skills.

5. Which of the following are true about the revision process?
    a.   Expert writers have to spend less writing time revising.
    b.   Expert writers use their revision time to fine tune grammar and spelling.
    c.   Expert writers have an easier time detecting problems in others' writing than their own.

Exercise 9.4

1. Look again at the problem described by Holt (1964) on page 314 of your text. Based on the information in the section on historical views of learning (p. 374), explain why the boy was so willing to accept an answer that didn't make sense.

2. Which of the beliefs about learning mathematics (p. 375) is most likely illustrated in the boy's thinking and conclusion?

3a. Jeremy, a third grader, is presented the following problem:

LeAnn has 24 jelly beans in a small package. She eats 5 of them and gives 3 to her friend, Andrea. Now, how many jelly beans does LeAnn have altogether?

Jeremy concludes that LeAnn now has 32 jelly beans. Based on research examining learning in math, what is the most likely reason for Jeremy's conclusion?

3b. What characteristic of constructivist views of learning would be most likely to help students such as Jeremy develop more valid understandings of problems like the one above.

Exercise 9.5

1. Evidence indicates that learning science is often more difficult than learning other content areas. Then, consider that some learners believe that both the sun and the moon revolve around the earth. Using the example of learners' beliefs about the sun and the moon, explain *why* science can be difficult to learn.

2. Teachers commonly hold two misconceptions about learning in science: 1) Hands-on activities are required for effective science learning, and 2) If learners are involved in hands-on activities, learning is taking place. Explain why these two ideas are often invalid.

Feedback for Application Exercises

Exercise 9.1

1a. Background knowledge (or the lack thereof) strongly influences comprehension.

b. Linguistic knowledge--your understanding of how language works--at least allows you to identify nouns, verbs, and adjectives, and the fact that this is a transitive sentence with an actor (clunker) doing something (binked) to something (the flondy hoder).

c. Your ability to comprehend this sentence in German, which translates into "The beer is very good" probably resulted from some background knowledge (e.g., recognizing bier and gut as their English equivalents) and linguistic knowledge (e.g., of sentence structure).

2a. Hearing different sounds is a component of phonemic awareness.

b. Recognizing symbols is an example of print awareness.

c. Understanding how sentence-level patterns influence meaning involves syntactic awareness.

d. This difficulty relates to graphic awareness--the ability to recognize that letters have different shapes or configurations.

e. This probably involves print awareness in which the child focuses on the shape and color of the sign versus individual letters.

3. Language experience is based upon the idea of learners reading about concrete experiences that they've had. Whole language is a more comprehensive approach that integrates reading into the total communication process. They both stress the functional or useful aspects of reading.

4. Phonics involves matching letter and letter combinations to sounds. If learners can't hear that a word like "sit" has three separate sounds--"s," "i," and "t," they'll have trouble linking their sounds to letters.

5. Readers use contextual clues from the other words in the sentence to make sense of words.

Exercise 9.2

1. Background knowledge in the form of schemas allows you to focus on various aspects of the text and make sense of them. For example in the first sentence "mat" can either be a sleeping pad in a cell or a wrestling mat. Your schemas for each of these allows you to bring up images that make the passage meaningful.

2. Self-questioning is a strategy that facilitates metacognitive monitoring of comprehension. Continually asking ourselves questions while we're reading allows us to gauge whether we understand what we're reading.

3. Summarizing encourages the reader to search for important information. Constructing a test question puts the reader in an active role. A clarifying question encourages metacognition, searching for possible areas of confusion. Prediction also places the reader in an active role, anticipating what will come next.

Exercise 9.3

1. The first two steps in problem solving involve identifying and representing the problem. This corresponds to deciding upon the goals of writing. Selecting a strategy, the third problem-solving step corresponds to organizing ideas. Implement the strategy corresponds to translation and evaluate results is similar to revision.

2. One element of the task environment is the writing task. Teachers can adapt this by shortening the assignment, providing more time, or choosing a topic with which students are familiar. A second element of the task environment includes resources. These include articles, books, and other students.

3. Young writers have trouble generating ideas, possibly as a result of lack of background knowledge Brainstorming and discussing a topic before writing could help here. Older writers have trouble organizing ideas. Modeling and think alouds are helpful here.

4a. Maria was struggling with a syntactic challenge which involves using appropriate grammar and punctuation.

b. Angie was wrestling with a textual challenge involving creating cohesive and organized paragraphs.

c. Struggling with printing and writing involves a graphic challenge.

d. Understanding what your audience knows is a semantic challenge.

e. This problem is a modern-day technological version of a graphic challenge.

5a. False. As writers improve they spend more time revising.

b. False. Expert writers spend more time on organization and other macro issues.

c. True. Even expert writers encounter problems detecting errors or problems in their own writing.

Exercise 9.4

1. The boy lacked a conceptual understanding of the problem. As a result, he accepted an answer that made no sense. He probably centered on the 3 in the 2/3, multiplied it by 6, got the answer of 18, and accepted the answer because he didn't understand the problem.

2. The belief most likely illustrated in the boy's thinking is that math learned in school has nothing to do with the real world. This belief helps us understand why learners will accept answers that make no sense.

3a. Jeremy is most likely using a superficial strategy to get the answer. Since the word *altogether* appears in the problem, Jeremy concludes that he must add.

3b. Social interaction is the characteristic of constructivism that is most likely to help students like Jeremy develop more valid understandings. The teacher could ask a series of questions that would require the students to think about the problem. Some possibilities include:
> "What did LeAnn do with her jelly beans?" (Ate some and gave some away)
> "Will she now have more or fewer jelly beans than the number she started with?" (Fewer)
> "How do you know?" (If you eat some, you can't have as many left as the number you started with)
> "How many fewer?" (Eight)
> "How do you know?" (If she ate five and gave three away, that's eight)

Many different questioning sequences could be effective. The important thing is that the students are required to think about the problem, generate answers that make sense, and ultimately arrive at a solution. Social interaction is the means to accomplishing that goal.

Exercise 9.5

1. In reality, the moon revolves around the earth, but the earth revolves around the sun. However, we see both the sun and the moon "come up" in the east and set in the west in the same way. It then makes sense that the behavior of the sun and the moon is similar, since what we see is similar. In fact, they behave very differently. Behavior that isn't consistent with our intuitive ideas is what makes science difficult to learn.

2. Two important keys to learning science are: 1) effective representations of the topics that are being studied, and 2) high levels of social interaction.

TRUE/FALSE QUESTIONS: Write T in the blank if the statement is true, and write F if the statement is false.

_____ 1. Teachers can improve learners' linguistic knowledge by activating their schemas before reading.

_____ 2. Phonetic generalizations are crucial to conceptually-driven views of reading.

_____ 3. First graders often have problems generating ideas during the planning phase of writing.

_____ 4. While learners in countries, such as Japan, score higher than their American counterparts on basic skills in mathematics, American students score higher on measures of mathematical reasoning.

_____ 5. Learning science is different from learning mathematics in that learners have many life experiences that lead to misconceptions in science.

MULTIPLE-CHOICE QUESTIONS: Circle the best response in each case.

6. Which of the following is least related to the other three?
   a. Emergent literacy
   b. Language experience
   c. Phonetic generalizations
   d. Whole language

7. Pre-schoolers who recognize their favorite book even though they can't read are most demonstrating:
   a. print awareness.
   b. graphic awareness.
   c. phonemic awareness.
   d. syntactic awareness.

8. First graders who experience difficulty differentiating "p" from "q" are wrestling with:
   a. print awareness.
   b. graphic awareness.
   c. phonemic awareness.
   d. syntactic awareness.

9. A child who can't hear that the word "hat" has three sounds is struggling with:
   a. print awareness.
   b. graphic awareness.
   c. phonemic awareness.
   d. syntactic awareness.

10. What of the following is NOT used to assess phonemic awareness?
   a. Segmenting words into constituent sounds
   b. Identifying capital from small letters
   c. Identifying the last sound in a word
   d. Substituting a different sound for an initial letter

11. Which of the following is NOT a component of reciprocal teaching?
   a. Predicting
   b. Inferring
   c. Summarizing
   d. Clarifying

12. Based on research examining children's metacognitive abilities during reading, which of the following statements is most valid?
    a. Third graders have problems identifying inconsistencies in text.
    b. Third graders can identify important ideas in text.
    c. Seventh graders have difficulties identifying important ideas in text.
    d. Sixth graders can't explain why they reread an unclear passage.

13. Which of the following is NOT part of the writing task environment?
    a. The writing assignment
    b. Books and articles
    c. The teacher
    d. Other people

14. Based on research examining planning for writing, which of the following statements is most valid?
    a. Five- and six-year-olds have trouble generating ideas.
    b. Eight to 12-year-olds have trouble generating ideas.
    c. Eight to 12-year-olds have trouble organizing ideas.
    d. Brainstorming improves the writing of college students.

15. When young students' ideas are produced faster than their ability to write them down they are encountering:
    a. graphic challenges.
    b. syntactic challenges.
    c. semantic challenges.
    d. textual challenges.

16. When writers have problems matching their writing to readers' background knowledge they are encountering:
    a. graphic challenges.
    b. syntactic challenges.
    c. semantic challenges.
    d. textual challenges.

17. When writers can't decide whether to end a sentence with a period or exclamation point they are encountering:
    a. graphic challenges.
    b. syntactic challenges.
    c. semantic challenges.
    d. textual challenges.

18. When writers wrestle with the overall organization and cohesiveness of their piece they are encountering:
    a. graphic challenges.
    b. syntactic challenges.
    c. semantic challenges.
    d. textual challenges.

19. When Calvin sees word problems asking for *how many more*, as a strategy he subtracts the smaller number in the problem from the larger number, and if he sees *altogether*, he adds. If his experience is consistent with patterns identified by research, which of the following conclusions is most valid:

    a.   He is likely to develop a generally good understanding of word problems if he uses the strategies consistently, and he is likely to be quite successful (in answering the problems correctly).

    b.   He is likely to be quite successful (in answering the problems correctly) with the strategies but develop very little understanding of the problems.

    c.   He is likely to be unsuccessful with the strategies, but in the process he will develop a generally good understanding of the word problems.

    d.   He is likely to be unsuccessful (in answering the problems correctly), and he is unlikely to develop a generally good understanding of word problems.

20. Of the following, the theory of learning most reflected in Calvin's strategies (in Item 19) is:

    a.   behaviorism.

    b.   social cognitive theory.

    c.   information processing.

    d.   constructivism.

21. Mr. Gomez emphasizes that his students understand and compute algorithms automatically (such as knowing that they have to borrow from the 3 when subtracting 19 from 34). He gives the students extensive practice in using the algorithm.

    Mrs. Layne focuses on problems, such as "What percentage of the students in this class have blonde hair?" The students discuss the problems and develop their strategies for solving the problems.

    Mr. Willouby also focuses on problems in the same way that Mrs. Layne does, but he spends five minutes each day having the students practice basic math facts, so they can use the facts automatically.

Which of the following conclusions is most consistent with research examining learning in mathematics?

    a.   Mr. Gomez's approach is likely to produce the most learning, because knowing the algorithms to automaticity will leave working memory space to focus on problem solving.

    b.   Mrs. Layne's approach is most consistent with learning and the NCTM standards, because she is focusing on problem solving.

    c.   Mr. Willouby's approach is likely to produce the most learning, because he emphasizes both problem solving and mastery of basic skills.

    d.   Mrs. Layne's approach is likely to produce the most learning, because she doesn't waste instructional time on factual level learning (such as basic math facts).

Use the following information for Items 22-24.

Karen, a sixth grader, believes that if a baseball and a marble are dropped simultaneously, the baseball will hit the floor first.

22. Of the following, which is the most likely explanation for Karen's belief?

    a.   Karen's life experiences with heavy and light objects have caused her to develop this misconception.

    b.   Karen's teachers before the fifth grade have failed to explain the acceleration of gravity to her in understandable ways, so she developed the misconception.

    c.   Karen's textbooks have failed to accurately describe the acceleration of gravity, so she developed the misconception.

    d.   Karen had learners' natural fear of science as a lower-elementary student, so she developed the misconception.

23. Of the following, the theory of learning that best explains Karen's conclusion is:
    a. behaviorism.
    b. social cognitive theory.
    c. information processing.
    d. constructivism.

24. Of the following, the most effective way to help Karen form a valid conclusion about the acceleration of gravity, is to:
    a. carefully explain that all objects fall at the same rate regardless of weight, being sure that Karen is paying attention while you explain.
    b. give her an assignment in which she has to explain that all objects fall at the same rate regardless of weight. Give her feedback and have her repeat the assignment if she explains it incorrectly.
    c. have a student who understands the acceleration of gravity explain it to Karen.
    d. drop the baseball and marble simultaneously, so that Karen can see that they hit the floor at the same time.

25. Which of the following is NOT important to learning in all four content areas?
    a. Teacher modeling and think-alouds
    b. Multiple representations of content
    c. Learners' background knowledge
    d. Language and dialogue

Self-Help Quiz Answers_____

1. f
2. f
3. t
4. f
5. t
6. c Phonetic generalizations. All the others are related to meaning-emphasis versus code-emphasis approaches to learning to read.
7. a Print awareness involves understanding that letters and symbols carry meaning.
8. b Graphic awareness involves recognizing that letters have different shapes or configurations.
9. c Phonemic awareness includes understanding that speech is composed of a series of separate sounds.
10. b All the others involve differentiating speech sounds--the essence of phonemic awareness.
11. b All the others (plus "construct a text question") are essential components of reciprocal teaching.
12. a Even when told to do so, third graders have difficulties identifying inconsistencies in text.
13. c The teacher is not part of the writing task environment (unless he or she assists the writer).
14. a Primary-age children have trouble generating ideas during the planning state of writing, presumably because of a lack of background knowledge.
15. a Graphic challenges are related to young writers' difficulties with printing and writing.
16. c Semantic challenges involve using ideas that make sense to the writing audience. This problem may be developmentally related to egocentricity.
17. b Syntactic challenges are related to problems with grammar and punctuation.
18. d Textual challenges focus on creating sentences and paragraphs that form a cohesive whole.
19. b Research indicates that when learners use superficial strategies to solve problems they often are quite successful, but the strategies often bypass understanding completely.
20. a Calvin is simply responding to a specific stimulus (the word *altogether*, or the words *how many more*)
21. c The NCTM standards emphasize problem solving and student reasoning, but students must also know basic facts.

22. a Learners' life experiences cause them to form naive theories about how the world works. We don't have any evidence about Karen's teachers or textbooks (Choices b and c), and children in the lower elementary grades don't have a natural fear of science (Choice d).

23. d Karen is constructing understanding based on her life experiences.

24. d Research indicates that naive theories must be directly confronted. Any form of explanation, either by the teacher, or by peers is unlikely to change her belief. (We should also note that it is critical that Karen actually believes that the baseball and marble hit the floor at the same time, or she is likely to retain her belief.)

25. a Teaching modeling and think-alouds while important in skill-heavy areas like reading, writing, and math are not central to learning in science.

CHAPTER 10: INCREASING LEARNER MOTIVATION

Chapter Outline

I. Extrinsic and intrinsic motivation
II. Theories of motivation
    A. Behaviorism: Motivation as reinforcement
        1. Effective reinforcers
        2. Criticisms of a behavioral approach to motivation
            a. Reinforcers decrease intrinsic motivation
            b. Learners' focus is narrowed
            c. Rewards present logistical problems
            d. Rewards ignore student cognitions
    B. Cognitive theories of motivation
        1. Cognitive theories: The need to understand
        2. Cognitive theories: The development of self-efficacy
        3. The influence of self-efficacy on behavior and cognition
        4. Factors influencing self-efficacy
    C. Humanistic views of motivation
        1. Humanistic psychology: The development of the whole person
        2. Motivation as growth
            a. Promoting growth: Implications for teaching
III. Personal factors in motivation
    A. Motivation and arousal
        1. Anxiety, motivation, and performance
        2. Capitalizing on arousal: Curiosity motivation
    B. Motivation and needs
        1. Motivation as a hierarchy of needs: The work of Maslow
            a. Deficiency needs
            b. Growth needs
            c. Implications of Maslow's work for teachers
        2. Cognitive learning needs
            a. The need for competence
            b. The need for control and self-determination
            c. The need to achieve
            d. Attribution theory
            e. Impact of attributions on behavior
            f. Attributions and self-efficacy
    C. Motivation and beliefs
        1. Beliefs about ability
        2. The need to protect self-worth
        3. Needs, beliefs, and self-worth: Conventional wisdom and research
    D. Motivation and goals
        1. Characteristics of effective goals
        2. Learning versus performance goals
    E. Motivation and self-regulated learning
        1. Motivational control
IV. The classroom: A model for promoting student motivation
    A. Class structure: Creating a learning-focused framework for motivation
    B. Teacher characteristics
        1. Teacher modeling
        2. Teacher enthusiasm: Communicating genuine interest
        3. Teacher caring
            a. Communicating caring

4.	Teacher expectations
            a.	How teachers form expectations
            b.	How expectations affect teacher behavior
            c.	Teacher expectations. Implications for motivation
       C.	Climate variables
            1.	Order and safety: Classrooms as secure places to learn
            2.	Success
            3.	Challenge
            4.	Task comprehension
       D.	Instructional variables
            1.	Introductory focus: Attracting students' attention
            2.	Personalization: Links to students' lives
            3.	Involvement
                 a.	Using open-ended questioning to promote involvement
                 b.	Involving students: Alternatives to questioning
            4.	Feedback
                 a.	Praise
       E.	Combining elements of the model for promoting student motivation
   V.	Motivation and diversity
       A.	Motivational problems: Student perspectives
       B.	Motivational problems: Possible solutions

Chapter Objectives

- Explain learner motivation on the basis of behavioral, cognitive, and humanistic theories.

- Explain the role of motivation in developing self-regulation.

- Explain how teacher-personal characteristics promote student motivation.

- Describe how classroom climate variables promote student motivation.

- Identify instructional factors that promote student motivation.

Chapter Overview

The core concept on which the study of your text has focused is *learning* and what we as teachers can do to increase it. In order to effectively promote learning we must understand the characteristics of the learners we're trying to teach--the content of Chapters 2-5. In Chapters 6-9 we examined the learning process itself, from behaviorist, social cognitive, information processing, and constructivist points of view. Now we turn to motivation. In this chapter we're trying to answer the question, "What is the nature of learner motivation and what can we as teachers do to increase it?"

Theories of motivation explain both extrinsic motivation to learn--motivation to engage in an activity as a means to an end--as well as intrinsic motivation to learn, which is motivation to engage in an activity for its own sake.

Behavioral theories describe motivation in terms of effective use of reinforcers, cognitive theories suggest that people are instinctively motivated by a need to understand the way the world works, and humanistic views of motivation assume human beings have an innate need for personal growth and development. The humanistic view focuses on the whole person, and personal growth is fundamental.

Personal factors--arousal, needs, beliefs, and goals--can also affect learner motivation.

Teachers can do much to promote motivation in their classrooms. Personal characteristics, such as modeling, enthusiasm, caring, and high expectations, together with promoting an orderly and safe environment all contribute to positive learner motivation. In addition, classrooms where learners feel safe, understand the learning task, are challenged, and are successful significantly increases motivation even in reluctant learners. Effective instructional variables that influence student motivation include introductory focus, personalization, involvement, and frequent and specific feedback.

Feedback for Margin Questions

10.1: Based on the information in the case study, it appears that Susan is high in intrinsic motivation and low in extrinsic motivation (at least in Kathy Brewster's history class) based on her comment, "I don't mind it all that much. Actually, it bothers me when I don't get something, and sometimes it's even sort of fun," suggests that she does her homework because she feels that its worthwhile for its own sake. We have no evidence from the case study that she studies and does her homework as a means to some end.

10.2: These examples are not inconsistent. As we see in this section, extrinsic and intrinsic motivation are on separate continuums. A person can be high in both, low in both, or high in one and low in another. Jim is demonstrating both intrinsic motivation (". . . it's sort of interesting the way Brewster's always telling us about the way we are 'cause of something that happened a zillion years ago") and extrinsic motivation ("You miss a homework assignment in this class, and you're dead.") in Kathy Brewster's history class.

10.3: One explanation might be as follows: If a task is intrinsically motivating, no reward is necessary. The task is an end in itself. Offering a reward can communicate to the learners that the task must not be intrinsically interesting or the offer of a reward wouldn't be necessary. As a result, intrinsic interest in the task declines.

10.4: Based on behaviorism, we would say that the praise has lost its potency because the learners have become satiated. To be effective, praise must be credible, and to be credible, the task must be praiseworthy in the perception of the receiver.

10.5: If the behavior that was praised increased, it was a reinforcer. If it decreased instead of increased, the praise acted as a punisher.

10.6: The child is responding to his need for equilibrium. If the story sounds the same each time it is read, he remains at equilibrium. If is sounds different, his equilibrium is disrupted, and he is motivated to reestablish it. Hearing the story as it has always been read is the easiest way to remain at equilibrium.

10.7: The key difference between the two is that self-efficacy is a cognitive appraisal of a person's capability of performing a certain task, whereas self-esteem, or self-worth, is an affective or emotional reaction to the self. People can believe, for example, that they are poor tennis players--they have low self-efficacy for tennis--but not have it affect their self-esteem, as long as tennis isn't overly important to them.

10.8: Self-efficacy describes the extent to which learners believe that they are capable of accomplishing a specific task. Learners with low self-efficacy tend to have lower intrinsic motivation than those with high self-efficacy. Praising students for accomplishment of a trivial task, such as praise for answering an easy question, communicates to the learner that he or she is not capable of accomplishing something more challenging. Communicating that the learner has low capability can lower the learner's self-efficacy, which in turn lowers intrinsic motivation.

10.9:   A model perceived to be similar in ability would likely increase self-efficacy the most. In Chapter 6 we saw that perceived similarity was one of the factors that influence a model's effectiveness. An observer would be more likely to imitate a model--such as seeing a model expend effort and persist on a challenging task--perceived as similar in ability than one perceived as either higher or lower in ability.

10.10: The phrase "provided only enough guidance to be sure that he made genuine progress toward the solution--essentially on his own," best describes the concept of *scaffolding* from Vygotsky's work. As we've seen in other parts of the text, there is a subtle but important difference between scaffolding and simply telling or explaining. In order for learners to increase self-efficacy, they must feel like they are the ones making progress, not someone doing it for them. Scaffolding provides the support to help them make that progress; simply telling or explaining does not provide the support.

10.11: Humanistic views of motivation views the concept of needs more broadly than do cognitive views of motivation. Humanistic views consider physical, emotional, intellectual, and interpersonal needs. Cognitive views of motivation, as the term cognitive implies, tends to focus on needs in the cognitive domain--the need to understand the way the world works.

10.12: By noticing that Jennifer had been a little quiet and asking her to move into the middle of the room, Kathy demonstrated sensitivity to Jennifer as a person. Even if Kathy misperceived Jennifer's behavior, she communicated an attitude of concern for Jennifer and her feelings. Kathy promoted a positive climate in at least two ways. First, she tried to include as many students as possible in the activity by calling on several of them by name. Second, she protected individuals' rights to be heard by admonishing Joe when he interrupted Nikki.

10.13: Cognitive theories best explain curiosity motivation. Events that arouse curiosity disrupt a learner's equilibrium, so the learner is motivated to re-establish it. Moderate discrepancies disrupt a learner's equilibrium enough to be motivating but not bewildering. Large discrepancies require a major--or perhaps even total--reorganization of the learner's schema. Rather than reorganize the schema, the learner may simply ignore the experience.

10.14: We would conclude that people with high need for aesthetic appreciation have high self-esteem. According to Maslow, in order to be at the level of growth needs, all the deficiency needs must be met, so to be at the level of aesthetic appreciation the need for self-esteem must be met.

        Their need for intellectual achievement has not been met. According to Maslow, growth needs are never "met" in the same sense that deficiency needs are.

10.15: Competence motivation suggests that learners have an intrinsic need to develop a sense of competence. This is consistent with the premise of a "need to know and understand," which is at the foundation of cognitive views of motivation.

10.16: Curiosity is the first source of intrinsic motivation that was described.

10.17: Behaviorists would describe achievement motivation as resulting from reinforcers that were given for achievement in the past. Behaviorists would measure achievement motivation by looking for observable learner behaviors that indicated striving for achievement, such as persevering on a task, solving additional problems, and making statements about questions and problems and answers and solutions.

10.18: She would likely select easier dives to perform in competition, and her inclination to avoid challenges would likely result in slower progress than she would make if she had a higher need for achievement.

10.19: Effort is unstable and within the learner's control, which means that the possibility exists for different outcomes in the future if effort is increased. In contrast, many people view ability as stable and out of a learner's control, which means that a different outcome in the future is unlikely.

10.20:   Ann commented, ". . . but I knew I wouldn't. I just didn't study hard enough. I knew I was going to be in trouble. I'll be ready next time." High-efficacy learners persevere when goals aren't initially reached, and they believe they're in control of their environment. Her determination suggests these characteristics.

10.21:   Of the students in the example, Bob is most likely to have an entity view of ability. He concluded, "I just can't do this stuff. I'm no good at writing the kind of essay she wants. Ann, in contrast, as we saw in 10.20, believes she is in control of her environment. She is most likely to have an incremental view of ability.

10.22:   Billy, with his comment, "That isn't bad considering how much I studied. I didn't crack a book for this one," illustrates a need to protect his self-worth. Uncertain about his ability to succeed on the test, he protected his self-worth by making a point of saying that he didn't study. This puts him in a "win-win" situation. If he did well in the test, he must have been "smart," since he was able to do well without studying. If he did poorly, he is still safe because he didn't make an effort.

10.23:   The most effective way to improve self-efficacy is for the student to see genuine evidence of improvement. You might help the student set specific goals, such as being able to solve and explain the solutions to ten math problems. You then provide only enough assistance to ensure success. As the student solves the problems, he or she will see evidence of progress and self-efficacy is likely to increase. Once completed, the student could be encouraged to set slightly more challenging goals, and again as progress is made toward them, improvement is evidence of progress and self-efficacy is further increased.

10.24:   Goal setting most closely relates to the motivational control component. The inclination to set goals indicates motivation. Self-observation and self-assessment most closely relate to the metacognitive component. It is awareness of the progress that is being made toward goals.

10.25:   This statement would not be recommended. It promotes a performance rather than a learning focus, an ego rather than a task orientation, and it compares learners' performances to each other.

10.26:   The statement demonstrates that the teacher studies and that she sometimes struggles in the process. Studying is a behavior that we want students to imitate, so it demonstrates modeling.

10.27:   The effects of enthusiasm can be best explained with cognitive views of motivation--specifically social cognitive theory. People tend to imitate behaviors they observe in others, and the likelihood that learners will be enthusiastic about studying a particular topic is increased if they observe a model who is enthusiastic about the topic. Further, as we saw in this section, research indicates that teachers who present information enthusiastically increase learners self-efficacy, attributions of effort and ability, self-confidence and achievement more than do less enthusiastic teachers. Self-efficacy is a concept from social cognitive theory, and attribution theory is cognitive in its orientation.

10.28:   Using Maslow's work as a basis for the explanation, students in a negative emotional climate may not feel safe. Further, being treated sarcastically can detract from self-esteem. If safety and/or self-esteem needs are not being met, students are less likely to progress to growth needs, such as intellectual achievement.

The effect of a negative emotional climate can also be explained on the basis of social cognitive theory. Criticism and sarcasm can lower self-efficacy, which lowers motivation, and in turn, achievement.

10.29: Cognitive theory (particularly social cognitive theory) best explain the effects of teacher expectations. Teacher expectations affect the ways teachers treat students. This treatment influences students' expectations for their own success. Appropriately high teacher expectations increase both the expectancy and the value component of the *expectancy x value* relationship. This results in increased self-efficacy, which improves motivation.

10.30: Behaviorists would explain the negative effects of criticism by saying that criticism is a punisher. Punished behaviors decrease, so learners who are criticized would be less likely to display the behavior (that was criticized) in the future. According to social cognitive theory, reinforcers and punishers cause learners to form expectations about what behaviors will be reinforced or punished in the future. If a student is criticized for a certain behavior, the student will expect to be criticized for similar behaviors in the future, and will be less likely to display the behavior.

10.31: When Nikki was offering a point in the discussion, Joe interrupted with his own point. Kathy then admonished him for his interruption, reminding him that they didn't have to agree, but they did have to listen.

10.32: One type of open-ended question merely calls for observation, such as, "What do you see here?", "Describe the hamster for us," "Tell us something about the hamster," and similar questions about the stone.

A second type of open-ended question calls for comparisons, such as, "How are the hamster and the stone different?" or "How are the hamster and the stone alike?"

10.33: Behaviorists would have difficulty explaining the positive influence of challenge. The best explanation they could offer would be to suggest that success on challenging tasks is more reinforcing than success on trivial tasks. Behaviorism has difficulty, however, in eliminating all cognitive aspects of the explanation.

Humanistic thinkers would explain the positive effects of challenge by saying that it responds to the need for intellectual achievement.

10.34: Self efficacy best explains this outcome. Self-efficacy refers to learners' beliefs about their capability of accomplishing certain tasks. If the task is perceived to be so difficult that they don't believe they have a chance of accomplishing it, they may be unwilling to try. Not being willing to try is an indicator of lowered motivation.

10.35: The statement promotes an ability/performance-focused classroom and an ego orientation rather than a learning-focused classroom with an achievement orientation. An ability focused classroom and an ego orientation can lower motivation for those who are not among the highest achievers.

10.36: First, introductory focus capitalizes on the effects of arousal and curiosity to attract students' attention. Second, it provides a conceptual umbrella under which the remainder of the lesson fits.

10.37: Personalization relates examples to the real world of the students. As both introductory focus and personalization the teacher might ask Reeanne and Edward to come to the front of the class and say something such as, "Look everyone. Now, why do you suppose Reeanne has blue eyes and Edward has brown ones? What does that tell us about their parents? This is what we're going to try and figure out today." If the same students were used as examples in the course of the lesson, they then serve only as a form of personalization.

10.38: Involvement and activity are closely related but not identical. First, the concept of activity exists in the context of learning. Activity is one way of increasing the meaningfulness of information, which in turn aids encoding. Involvement is cast in a motivational context. Involvement increases motivation, which in turn increases learning. Second, activity implies "conceptual" activity, and it can occur in a social or a solitary setting. Involvement means learners are "attending and actively participating in the learning activity," which implies a social setting.

10.39: To be willingly involved, learners must feel *safe*.

10.40: Individual items should be discussed, and model responses to essays should be provided. This information provides feedback.

10.41: Teacher characteristics include enthusiasm, caring and positive expectations. Climate variables include success, task comprehension and challenge. Positive instructional variables include personalization and involvement.

10.42: Disengagement suggests that the students are not inclined to be involved. Open-ended questioning is an effective questioning strategy for increasing the involvement of cultural minorities. Open-ended questioning allows learners to respond according to their own backgrounds, perceptions, and learning styles.

Application Exercises_____

Exercise 10.1

For each of the following items, be sure to carefully *defend your answer* based on the information you've studied in this section of the chapter.

1. In the chapter's opening case study, Jim's comment, "It's sort of interesting the way Brewster's always telling us about the way we are 'cause of something that happened a zillion years ago," indicates that his motivation has increased as a result of Kathy's teaching. Which approach to motivation--behaviorist, humanistic, or cognitive--best explains Jim's motivation?

2. Jim also commented, "Besides, you miss a homework assignment in this class, and you're dead. . . Nobody messes with Brewster." This comment gives us an indication of Kathy's expectations. Which theoretical view of motivation best explains the impact of teacher expectations on student motivation?

3. Later in the case study, we saw the following encounter:

    "Wait a minute!" Joe interrupted. "How about the new fighting techniques they learned? . . ."
    "Joe," Kathy began firmly, "what is one of the principles we operate on in here?"
    "We don't have to agree with someone else's point, but we do have to listen. Sorry, Nikki. It just slipped out."

    Which approach to motivation best explains the importance of the principle, "We don't have to agree, but we have to listen"?

Toward the end of the case study Kathy commented, "Now isn't that interesting! . . . See, here's another case where we see ourselves in the 20th century finding a relationship to people who lived a thousand years ago. That's what history is all about."

4. Explain the motivating effects of this comment from a cognitive point of view.

5. Explain the motivating effects of the comment from a humanistic point of view.

6. In the case study, David indicated to Kelly that he perceived that "Brewster loves this stuff." Which theory of motivation best explains the motivating effects of Kathy's behavior that led to David's comment?

Exercise 10.2

1. You are a language arts teacher and you're planning a lesson on direct and indirect objects. Offer a specific suggestion for what you might do to capitalize on the effect of *arousal* in motivation.

2. Think about Maslow's hierarchy of needs and identify two examples in the chapter's opening case study where Kathy Brewster attempted to meet a deficiency need in one of her students. Defend your answer with information taken from the case study.

3. Identify an example in the chapter's opening case study where Kathy Brewster attempted to meet students' needs for control and self-determination.

4. Kathy Brewster attempted to conduct her class so she emphasized the need for achievement and reduced the need to avoid failure. Citing specific evidence from the case study, explain how she attempted to accomplish this.

For Items 5 through 8, decide if attribution theorists would recommend (*R*) or would not recommend (*NR*) the teacher statement. Explain why in each case.

5. In handing out a test to her class, a teacher says, "Work hard on this test now. It's kind of a tough one."

6. In handing back a test, the teacher notices that Tommy has gotten an A on it. With a smile, he says, "Well done, Tommy. That was easy, wasn't it?"

7. Sympathetically, a teacher says to a student who has just received a D on a math quiz, "Try not to feel too bad about this, Billy. I know math is hard for you."

8. To a girl of average ability who has just received a B on a test, a teacher says, "Very well done, Susan. Your hard work is starting to pay off, isn't it?"

For Items 9, 10, and 11, decide on the basis of attribution theory whether or not the students would be likely to make the statements that appear in each case. Explain your reasoning.

9. "I'm generally pretty good in science, but I don't think I'll do well on this next test. I have a funny feeling about it."

10. "I'll never be able to get it. I have a mental block against Spanish. I've never been able to get it straight."

11. "I'm scared of this test. I guessed on four questions last time and got three right. I don't know if I can pull that off again."

Exercise 10.3

1. Identify a student behavior at the beginning of the opening case study that was the direct result of Kathy Brewster's modeling.

2. Identify the one student statement in the case study that best indicates a combination of Kathy Brewster's modeling and her enthusiasm.

3. What concept from the section on teacher characteristics do the statements, "You miss a homework assignment in this class, and you're dead" and "Nobody messes with Brewster," best indicate?

4. Consider the climate variable *order and safety*. Using the characteristics of the variable described in this section, identify a specific example in the case study that illustrates this variable.

5. Look at the ways teachers can promote student success (on pages 428 and 429 of your text). Other than reteaching, Kathy Brewster implemented at least three of the strategies with her class. Identify an instance in the case study that illustrates each of the strategies.

Exercise 10.4

1. Describe how Kathy Brewster capitalized on the concept of introductory focus when she began her unit on the Crusades.

2. How did Kathy attempt to personalize the content of her lesson?

3. Describe Kathy's techniques for promoting student involvement.

Feedback for Application Exercises_____

Exercise 10.1

1. The increase in Jim's motivation can best be explained on the basis of cognitive theories of motivation. His comment, "It's sort of interesting the way Brewster's always telling us about the way we are 'cause of something that happened a zillion years ago," best indicates a response to a need to understand the way the world works. We have some inferential evidence for Kathy's enthusiasm and modeling, but this evidence is more conjectural than the evidence for a need to understand.

2. The impact of teacher expectations are best explained on the basis of cognitive theories of motivation. Learners make inferences about the teacher's perception of their abilities based on the teacher's behavior. For example, when a student tries to answer a question, but is unable to do so, and the teacher exhorts and prompts the student, the student concludes that the teacher thinks he or she is capable of answering. This can result in an increased sense of self-efficacy, which in turn increases motivation.

3. The importance of the principle is best explained on the basis of humanistic views of motivation. Knowing that they will be allowed to respond without fear of interruption (or ridicule) increases a student's sense of safety, which is part of Maslow's Hierarchy of Needs. Maslow's work best fits humanistic views of motivation.

4. Cognitive theorists would suggest that Kathy's statement describing a relationship between a thousand years ago and the present appeals to learners' instinctive need for order, predictability, and how the world works.

Kathy is also modeling genuine interest in the content she is teaching, which is related to cognitive theory (specifically social cognitive theory).

5. Humanistic theorists would suggest that the description of the relationship appeals to Maslow's level of "Intellectual Achievement."

6. David's comment to Kelly was a response to Kathy's enthusiasm. The motivating effects of enthusiasm are best explained through modeling, which is consistent with cognitive views of motivation.

Exercise 10.2

1. One way to promote arousal is to begin a lesson with a question or problem. For example, the teacher might write a pair of sentences on the board, such as the following:

   Steve sketched Conchita a picture of his new house.

   Mom gave Sen a ride to school.

She could then ask the question, "What do Conchita and Sen have in common in the two sentences?" The students' search for the commonality would promote arousal.

2. Kathy was attempting to meet a need for belonging when she pulled Jennifer's desk into the middle of the row, and she was attempting to meet Nikki's need for safety when she admonished Joe for interrupting.

3. She helped meet a need for control and self-determination when she gave them the option of group presentations on the Renaissance or writing a paper on the Middle Ages. She also allowed them to decide the group order.

4. Kathy attempted to focus on a need for achievement by emphasizing that the quality of a student's paper depended on the quality of their argument, not a cut-and-dried answer. Second, she emphasized the long-range need for developing the skill of making and defending an argument, and finally, she allowed the students to revise the paragraphs based on the day's discussion.

5. Attribution theorists would recommend the statement. The teacher's statement puts students in a "win-win" situation. If they do well, they have the pride of accomplishment on a difficult task. If they do poorly, they can attribute the results to task difficulty rather than lack of ability or effort.

6. This statement would *not* be recommended. By contrast with Item 5, this statement encourages Tommy to attribute his success to an external source (ease of the task) thereby reducing his pride in the accomplishment.

7. This is *not* a recommended statement. The teacher is unwittingly inducing an attribution of low ability for Billy's poor performance which is precisely what teachers are encouraged to avoid.

8. This statement is recommended. The teacher is encouraging Susan to attribute her success to effort, which is the attribution most encouraged.

9. According to attribution theorists, this is an unlikely statement. The student attributes past success to ability which is a stable cause, leading to the expectation of similar results in the future.

10. The theory would suggest that this is a likely statement. The student attributes failure to a stable cause (ability), which, as in Item 9, leads to the expectation of similar results.

11. This is a likely statement. Success on the last test was attributed to luck, which is unstable, leading to the expectation of different results in the future.

Exercise 10.3

1. When Susan encouraged Jim to hurry to class because, ". . . you know how Brewster is about this class. She thinks it's *so* important," she was responding to Kathy's modeling.

2. David's comment, "Brewster loves this stuff," was a response to Kathy's enthusiasm and her modeling of the importance of what they were studying.

3. These comments best indicate Kathy's expectations for the students.

4. Kathy's admonishment of Joe for interrupting Nikki, helped meet Nikki's need for safety.

5. Kathy prompted Kim when Kim didn't respond to Kathy's question, "Now, how did we start? . . . Kim?"

Kathy used an example of a crusade with her suggestions that they would be going on a "crusade" to change people's minds about eliminating extracurricular activities. This was a high-quality example that was used to promote understanding.

Kathy provided for scaffolded practice by leading the discussion of whether or not the Crusades were a success.

Exercise 10.4

1. When Kathy began her unit, she brought pictures of the crusaders into class. This provided an eye-catching introduction.

2. She personalized the activity by drawing an analogy between the Crusades and the students "crusading" to change the leaders' minds about extracurricular activities in Lincoln High School.

3. She promoted involvement by calling on a variety of students and using their products as the basis for providing feedback.

TRUE/FALSE QUESTIONS: Write T in the blank if the statement is true, and write F if the statement is false.

_____ 1. Your students are finding out what kinds of materials are attracted to magnets and are very involved in the activity. According to research, offering them a reward for their participation would be unwise practice.

_____ 2. According to Maslow, people can become self-actualized after they've met their needs for intellectual achievement and aesthetic appreciation.

_____ 3. According to Maslow, belonging to a family or social group will not be a need for people until their need for safety is met.

_____ 4. According to research, people with a high need for achievement avoid challenging tasks in order to assure themselves of success.

_____ 5. According to Bandura, people achieve a sense of self-efficacy based primarily on the extent to which they're successful.

MULTIPLE-CHOICE QUESTIONS. Circle the best response in each case.

For Items 6-11, mark A if the example best fits a humanistic view of motivation, mark B if it fits a behaviorist view, and C for a cognitive view.

6. "I try to give my kids' tests back to them the next day. They try harder when they know how they're doing."

7. "Kenny is always seeking attention. I think he has a bad home life, so the attention makes him feel like he's 'in with the guys'."

8. "I needed that grade. When I do well, I try harder; when I do poorly, I don't try so hard."

9. "Steve is always acting up. He wouldn't do it except he gets the attention of the other kids in the class."

10. "I try get the kids to think they're learning something important and challenging. Then, I fix it so they can "get it," so they feel "smart.""

11. "I always try to start my lessons with a problem or something they don't quite expect. It helps keep the kids interested."

12. Janet enjoys living in a large city, because "It gives me a chance to go to a play now and then, a concert, and maybe even the opera." Based on Maslow's work, we would conclude from this information that:
    a. Janet's intellectual achievement need has been satisfied.
    b. Janet is a self-actualized person.
    c. Janet has reasonably high self-esteem.
    d. Janet often feels uneasy when she's alone.

13. Of the following, the concept most closely related to cognitive views of motivation is:
    a. reinforcement.
    b. competence.
    c. safety.
    d. self-esteem.

14. Susan is improving her ability in algebra, and she now is able to solve simultaneous equations with considerable skill. According to cognitive theories of motivation, what is the most likely outcome of this experience?
    a. Susan feels reinforced each time she correctly solves a problem.
    b. Susan will develop a sense of self-efficacy.
    c. Susan's self-esteem will improve.
    d. Susan's need for intellectual achievement will be met.

15. Leah seems to have a strong aesthetic need. She very much enjoys the symphony, ballet, and art openings. Based on Maslow's work, which of the following is the best conclusion?
    a. Leah's belonging need has been met.
    b. Leah's belonging, self-esteem and intellectual achievement needs have been met.
    c. Leah's intellectual achievement need has been met, but we don't know about her belonging and self-esteem needs.
    d. Leah's intellectual achievement need and all of her deficiency needs have been met.

Use the following example for Items 16-20.

Their teacher has returned a test, and the students are commenting on the results.

"I just can't do it," Kathy moaned slapping her test down on her desk after seeing a D on it. "I guess I just can't do French."

Billy nonchalantly shrugged, seeing a C-, "Not bad, considering how much I studied. I would have done fine, but I just couldn't get into studying for this one. I never opened my book."

"Weird," Jeff added. "I got a B and I really didn't understand this stuff. I must have been good at guessing or something. I don't know how I did it."

Seeing a C, Sandra said shaking her head, "I knew this test was going to be really rough, and I just wasn't ready. I will be next time though."

16. The student whose attribution has an external locus of control is:
    a. Kathy.
    b. Billy.
    c. Jeff.
    d. Sandra.

17. The student who is in the greatest danger of developing "learned helplessness" is:
    a. Kathy.
    b. Billy.
    c. Jeff.
    d. Sandra.

18. The student who is most likely to have an incremental view of ability is:
    a. Kathy.
    b. Billy.
    c. Jeff.
    d. Sandra.

19. The student who has the most fragile sense of competence and self worth based on a need to "look smart" is probably:
    a. Kathy.
    b. Billy.
    c. Jeff.
    d. Sandra.

20. The student with the most desirable attribution is:
   a.   Kathy.
   b.   Billy.
   c.   Jeff.
   d.   Sandra.

21. You have a student who has an incremental view of ability. He scores poorly on one of your tests. Based on this information, which of the following is most likely?
   a.   He will avoid challenging tasks in the future to protect his self-esteem.
   b.   He will develop a sense of learned helplessness.
   c.   He will consciously avoid trying, so he can attribute lack of success to lack of effort rather than lack of ability.
   d.   He will view his lack of success as lack of effort and will try harder in the future.

22. Mrs. Richards conducts help sessions for her students two nights a week after school. She also works with them before school and even during their lunch hour if they ask for help. The element of the Model for Promoting Motivation that these behaviors most closely relate to is:
   a.   modeling.
   b.   caring.
   c.   personalization.
   d.   feedback.

23. Mr. Moran always returns his quizzes the day after they're given and he goes over frequently missed items carefully. The characteristic of the Model for Promoting Motivation that this behavior most closely relates to is:
   a.   modeling.
   b.   expectations.
   c.   task comprehension.
   d.   enthusiasm.

24. Whenever students fail to respond to her questions, or they give an incorrect answer, Mrs. McDonald asks another, simpler question that the students are able to answer. The characteristic of the Model for Promoting Motivation that this behavior most closely relates to is:
   a.   enthusiasm.
   b.   modeling.
   c.   expectations.
   d.   caring.

25. Mrs. Kryzewski attempts to begin each of her lessons with a question or problem that sets the tone for the day. The feature of the Model for Promoting Motivation that best relates to her effort is:
   a.   involvement.
   b.   introductory focus.
   c.   task comprehension.
   d.   challenge.
   e.   personalization.

Self-Help Quiz Answers_____

   1.   t
   2.   f
   3.   t
   4.   f
   5.   f

6.   c   Knowing "how they're doing" relates to the "need to understand," which is a fundamental idea on which cognitive theories of motivation are based.

7.   a   A need to be "in with the guys" implies a belong need, and the consideration of needs such as belonging most closely relates to humanistic views of motivation.

8.   b   The example only describes a relationship between the grade and how hard the student tries. There is no implication of any internal needs or processes that are operating. The grade serves as a reinforcer.

9.   b   There isn't an implication of the attention meeting a need, such as a need for belonging. The attention serves instead as a reinforcer.

10.   c   The teacher in this case is trying to develop high self-efficacy in the students.

11.   c   The teacher is trying to capitalize on curiosity motivation, which is best explained with cognitive theories. Something that arouses curiosity relates to the "need to know," which is fundamental to cognitive theories of motivation.

12.   c   According to Maslow, in order to be at the level of growth needs, deficiency needs must have been met, and the example implies that Janet is at the level of aesthetic appreciation. Further, he suggests that growth needs are never "met." Therefore Janet's intellectual achievement need cannot have been met (choice a). We don't have enough information to determine whether or not she is a self-actualized person (choice b), and feeling uneasy is a form of not feeling safe. To be at aesthetic appreciation, she would have to have her safety needs met (choice d).

13.   b   Reinforcement is a behaviorist concept, and safety and self-esteem are most closely related to humanistic views of motivation.

14.   b   Self-efficacy is a concept related to cognitive views of motivation. Tangible evidence of improvement tends to increase self-efficacy. Reinforcement is a behaviorist concept and self-esteem and intellectual achievement are most closely related to humanistic views of motivation.

15.   a   Belonging is a deficiency need, which, according to Maslow, must be met before the individual proceeds to the growth needs. Intellectual achievement needs are never "met."

16.   c   Jeff is suggesting that he was lucky. Luck has an external locus of control.

17.   a   Kathy suggesting that she just can't do French attributes her performance to lack of ability. In extreme cases attributions of lack of ability can lead to learned helplessness.

18.   d   Sandra says, "I knew this test was going to be really rough, and I just wasn't ready. I will be next time though." She is making an attribution of effort (or lack of effort). Of the students in the example, she is most likely to believe that she can change her own ability through hard work.

19.   b   Billy makes a point of saying that he didn't study. This means that he must be quite "smart" in order to get a C- minus without exerting any effort. (Kathy makes no effort to look "smart." She admits that she has problems in French.)

20.   d   Sandra believes that she's in control and that she can improve her grade with effort. This belief can lead to sustained motivation.

21.   d   Learners with an incremental view of ability tend to believe that they can improve with effort.

22.   b   Being willing to spend time with students is an important indicator of caring. While she is "personally" involved with her students, "personalization" refers to representing the topics that are being taught in such a way that students can relate to them personally.

23.   c   Going over quizzes and tests provides students with "knowledge of results," which is characteristic of task comprehension. (Going over tests and quizzes of course provides feedback as well.)

24.   c   Prompting students until they're able to answer communicates that the teacher "expects" all students to be involved. (This also promotes success, another important variable.)

25.   b   Using a question or problem would be an attempt to initially get the students involved in the lesson, and a question that "sets the tone" would provide a conceptual umbrella for the remainder of the lesson.

CHAPTER 11: CREATING PRODUCTIVE LEARNING ENVIRONMENTS

Chapter Outline

I. Productive environments and learning-focused classrooms
II. Creating productive learning environments: Effective teaching
   A. Essential teaching skills
      1. Attitudes
         a. High-efficacy teachers
         b. Democratic teachers
      2. Use of time
      3. Organization
      4. Communication
         a. Precise terminology
         b. Connected discourse. Making relationships clear
         c. Transition signals
         d. Emphasis: Signalling important points
      5. Focus
      6. Feedback
         a. Verbal feedback
         b. Written feedback
      7. Questioning
         a. Cognitive levels of questions
      8. Review and closure
III. Creating productive learning environments: Classroom management
   A. Classroom management and discipline
   B. Cognitive approaches to management: Developing learner responsibility
   C. Planning for effective classroom management
      1. Student characteristics
      2. The physical environment
      3. Establishing procedures
      4. Creating effective rules
         a. Provide rationales for rules
         b. Allow student input
         c. Keep class and school rules consistent
         d. State rules clearly
         e. State rules positively
         f. Keep the list short
   D. Making rules and procedures work
      1. Beginning the school year
      2. Teaching rules and procedures
      3. Monitoring rules and procedures
   E. Dealing with misbehavior: Cognitive approaches to intervention
      1. Classroom interventions: Talking to students
         a. Verbal-nonverbal congruence
         b. I-messages
         c. Active listening
      2. Guidelines for successful intervention
         a. Withitness
         b. Preserve student dignity
         c. Be consistent
         d. Follow-through

   e. Keep interventions brief

   f. Avoid arguments

  3. Logical consequences

  4. Designing and maintaining a cognitive management system

 F. Dealing with misbehavior: Behavioral approaches to intervention

  1. Decisions about behavioral systems

   a. Reinforcers or punishers?

   b. Individual or group consequences?

  2. Assertive discipline: A structured approach to consequences

  3. Designing and maintaining a behavioral approach to management

 G. An intervention continuum

  1. Ignoring inappropriate behavior

  2. Praising desired behavior

  3. Using desists

  4. Applying consequences

 H. Serious management problems: Violence and aggression

  1. Short-term strategies

  2. Long-term solutions

IV. Accommodating diversity in productive learning environments

 A. Accommodating diversity: Teacher expectations

 B. Accommodating diversity: Communication with parents

  1. Benefits of communication

  2. Barriers to parental involvement

   a. Economic barriers

   b. Cultural barriers

   c. Language barriers

  3. Strategies for involving parents

   a. Early communication

   b. Maintaining communication

Chapter Objectives

- Explain how instruction and classroom management contribute to productive learning environments.

- Identify essential teaching skills that help create productive learning environments.

- Explain how effective planning can prevent management problems.

- Identify differences between cognitive and behavior approaches to management.

- Describe how effective intervention techniques can eliminate management problems.

Chapter Overview

In Chapters 2-5 your study centered on students, how they develop, and the ways they differ. Your efforts shifted in Chapters 6-8 to the nature of the learning process itself. With an understanding of the learner and the learning process as context, this section of the text has focused on learner motivation and what teachers can do to increase it. We now turn to the development of productive learning environments.

Productive learning environments focus on learning, and effective teachers, regardless of grade level, subject matter area, or topic, promote learning with personal characteristics and a repertoire of skills--called essential teaching skills--that increase student achievement. They use their time effectively, have a positive approach to their teaching, are well organized, communicate clearly, and begin their lessons in ways that attract learners' attention.

Effective teachers are responsive to students. They constantly monitor learners' verbal and nonverbal behaviors, they intervene at the first signs of uncertainty, confusion, or inattention, and they provide informative feedback.
Effective teachers maintain the flow of their lessons with questioning. They ask a large number of questions, call on volunteers and nonvolunteers equally, provide cues and prompts when students are unable to respond, and give students time to think about their answers.

Productive learning environments are orderly. Effectively managing classrooms promotes this order, which leads to increased achievement and improved motivation.

The cornerstone of efficient management is a well-designed system of procedures--the routines that students follow in their daily activities--and rules, which provide the standards for student behavior. To be most effective, teachers prepare a small number of clearly stated rules, they allow the students to provide input into their preparation, and they provide reasons for the rules' existence.

Effective managers are democratic--a combination of sincere caring for all students together with making students responsible for their own behavior and holding them accountable. They teach their procedures and rules just as they would teach any concept, principle, or skill.

When teachers must intervene to eliminate disruptive behavior, they keep the interventions brief, they follow through to be certain students comply with the rules, and rules are enforced consistently.

Severe management problems, such as defiance or violence, require both immediate, short-term attention and longer-term solutions that deal with the sources of the problem. Teachers should immediately get help in the case of a violent or defiant student, and they should not attempt to solve the problem alone.

Feedback for Margin Questions_____

11.1:   In Chapter 9, we saw that Japanese students spend less time doing seatwork than their American counterparts. Based on the research cited in the chapter, would the American learning environment be considered more or less productive than the Japanese environment? Explain.

Productive learning environments are orderly and learning focused. Students doing seatwork are likely to be quite orderly. However, as we saw in Chapters 7, 8, and 9, students' active involvement is critical in their learning, and learners are less active during seatwork than they are during class discussions. As a result the American environment would likely be less productive than the Japanese environment.

11.2:   The questioning skills of experts will be more nearly automatic than will the questioning skills of novices. This helps free their working memory space and leaves them able to monitor the students' behaviors while conducting interactive instruction, such as questioning. They quickly notice when a learning activity isn't working, and they adapt their instruction. Novices' routines are less well-established, they are more "mechanical" in their instruction, and they are less able to adapt when the activity isn't working. Experts acquire these skills through knowledge, experience and conscious effort.

11.3:   Glasser would suggest that a truly caring teacher would not accept excuses for misbehavior, regardless of student background and experience. A caring teacher communicates, "I care too much about your learning to allow you to harm yourself by being disruptive."

11.4: The allocated time would be the class time as stated in the schedule of classes. While instructors have no control over the allocated time for classes, they are in total control over the amount of time they allocate to specific topics.

To answer the question about the amount of time your instructor devotes to instruction, note when the instructor typically begins actual teaching and when he or she stops instruction. Also, note the time spent in noninstructional activities, such as explaining class procedures and collecting and passing back papers, which are the kinds of activities that compete with instructional time. The reason instructional time is important is that research indicates that instructors who devote as much of their time as possible to instruction have students who learn more than instructors who tend to lose time to noninstructional activities.

11.5: Feeling good about themselves and the material they're learning refers to the concept of self-efficacy. In order to feel a sense of self-efficacy, learners must perceive the task as worthwhile and moderately challenging. Success on trivial tasks doesn't lead to a sense of self-efficacy.

11.6: Precise terminology most closely relates to academic learning time. Precise terminology results in a greater degree of learner understanding. Understanding leads to success, which is one of the characteristics of academic learning time.

11.7: This *doesn't* imply that teachers should always avoid interjecting additional material into lessons. It suggests instead that they clearly describe how the new information relates to the topic or why diverging is appropriate.

11.8: *Elaboration* is the concept being illustrated when learners link new to past information or create new links in what they already understand. (Elaboration and encoding are closely related. When learners link new information to past information through the process of elaboration, they have encoded the new information. However, learners can encode information--form mental representations of it--without elaboration.)

11.9: Focus relates most closely to engaged time. When learners have something to focus on, they are more likely to be attentive and involved.

11.10: Introductory focus both provides the students with something to see, hear, or feel *and it provides context for the lesson that follows*. It is designed to attract attention and provide an umbrella for the lesson to follow. Sensory focus is something that merely attracts attention--it is something to see, hear, or touch. (It could also be something to taste or smell but *see, hear,* and *touch* are much more common).

11.11: Feedback is needed so learners will know what they are doing that results in reinforcement. According to social cognitive theory, reinforcement works only if the learner is *aware* of what behaviors are being reinforced. Feedback helps them understand *why* they were reinforced, which leads them to the expectation that they will be reinforced for similar behaviors in the future. This results in a change in behavior, because learners form expectations about what will be reinforced and adjust their behavior accordingly.

11.12: Safety is one of the variables in the Model for Promoting Student Motivation. Critical or harsh feedback detracts from this sense of safety, which in turn detracts from motivation to learn. Think about it intuitively. Would you be likely to try as hard if you knew that your efforts might be criticized? You would be more likely to adjust your behavior to avoid the criticism.

11.13: If the same students are answering all the questions, involvement of others is reduced, and achievement is lowered. Equitable distribution communicates that the teacher *expects all students* to be actively involved and to learn. Of the teacher characteristics discussed in Chapter 10--caring, enthusiasm, modeling, and high expectations--it most closely relates to expectations.

Teachers often ask questions that are *undirected*, meaning any students who choose to volunteer an answer are allowed to do so. This allows the most aggressive students to dominate the discussion and encourages others to remain passive, which reduces their involvement. Calling on students *by name* prevents volunteers from dominating the discussion.

11.14: Negative reinforcement best explains the student's behavior. Turning the question to someone else "removes" the situation from the student originally called on.

11.15: When automaticity is the goal, such as knowing multiplication facts, quick answers are desirable and wait-times should be short. Also, if a student appears nervous or anxious, a teacher may choose to intervene earlier.

On the other hand, students need more time when they're asked to apply, analyze, or evaluate information, and in general, increasing wait-time reduces rather than increases student anxiety, because a climate of support is established.

11.16: Shirley carefully reviewed the problems the class had discussed as closure in her lesson (the paragraphs near the end of the case study).

11.17: Some aspects of management that contribute to learning include: 1) maximizing time devoted to instruction, 2) lessons staying focused and uninterrupted, 3) students cooperating and answering questions, and 4) providing routines that help learners establish a sense of equilibrium about their experiences in school.

11.18: According to cognitive theories, we are motivated by a need for order and predictability, and well-managed classrooms are orderly. Also, learning is motivating in and of itself because, according to social cognitive theory, it leads to feelings of self-efficacy.

11.19: Behaviorist approaches treat learners as passive, i.e., learners change their behavior in response to reinforcers and punishers.

11.20: According to Piaget, younger children are more egocentric and are more perceptual and concrete than are their older counterparts. This is reflected in their need for rules that are explicitly taught and practiced. According to Erikson, students are motivated by an increasing desire to be independent, which is most manifested in adolescence during the crisis of identity vs. confusion. This is reflected in the need for a firm foundation of stability, explicit boundaries and predictable outcomes.

11.21: Teaching is very complex, sophisticated, and demanding. Beginning teachers' working memories can easily become overloaded with even the routine demands of teaching. This leaves little or no working memory space to consider aspects of the process, such as whether or not the students can see the print on the board.

11.22: The answer to this question will vary, but most procedures in college classrooms are less explicit than they are at the public school level, because there is less need for explicit procedures with college students. However, your instructor may have made some comments about procedures, such as starting times and how tests and papers will be returned.

11.23:   The thrust of the rule is twofold--listen when someone else has the floor, and when you have the floor you have the right to be listened to. Shirley handled Sondra's infraction of the rule by helping her understand how her actions were interfering with the process of teaching and learning.

11.24:   "Instantly knowing" best illustrates the concept of *automaticity* from our study of information processing. One of the reasons we keep lists of rules short is to make them manageable and easy to learn.

11.25:   With third graders, you could explain the rule, then explicitly model it yourself in a role play situation, which would be followed by pointing out examples in a learning activity. Seventh graders have usually been exposed to this rule and so it usually only needs to be clearly described. (Identifying examples of students raising their hands to speak during a learning activity might also be a good idea to reinforce and clarify the rule with seventh graders.)

11.26:   Effective concept teaching involves the use of positive and negative examples to teach abstract ideas. Martha effectively modeled desired behaviors (positive examples); if she had anticipated any common mistakes she might have modeled and discussed these as negative examples.

11.27:   If the students don't want to get caught breaking a rule, and they know that the teacher monitoring the rule increases the likelihood that they will get caught, they are operating at Stage 1. On the other hand, if they know the teacher is monitoring the rule and they don't want to disappoint her by misbehaving, they are operating at Stage 3.

11.28:   People tend to disregard the credibility of verbal behavior when they see inconsistency between verbal and non-verbal behavior. Making this decision requires internal processing of the information, i.e., people are not simply responding to either the verbal or the non-verbal behavior; they are observing both and making a decision about the credibility of the message. Behaviorism is unable to explain how people could make these decisions.

11.29:   Eye contact, body orientation, facial expressions and gestures are easiest to use because they can be implemented anywhere in a classroom. Proximity is more difficult to use since it involves moving to a specific place in the classroom.

11.30:   Caring is typically communicated through eye contact, body orientation (orienting directly toward the receiver), and proximity (moving closer). As we saw in Chapter 10, the best indicator of caring is the willingness to spend time with the student. Firmness is indicated with tone of voice in addition to eye contact, proximity, and direct body orientation.

11.31:   The approaches to intervention take learners' emotional needs into account, for example, both *"I"-messages* and *active listening*. *"I"-messages* include the feelings generated in the sender, and a person who is *actively listening* responds to both the intellectual and emotional content of the message. Humanistic views of motivation take the "whole" person into account, which includes learners' emotions as well as their intellectual needs. The "whole" person is most concretely illustrated in Maslow's hierarchy.

11.32:   The teacher didn't demonstrate the characteristics of active listening. In returning to her work she didn't devote her full attention to the student, nor did she respond to the intellectual and emotional content of the student's message.

11.33: As we saw in 11.21, teaching is very complex, sophisticated, and demanding, and even veteran teachers' working memories can easily become overloaded. When their working memories become overloaded, they have little or no working memory space to monitor learner behavior, therefore lacking withitness.

11.34: According to social cognitive theory, the non-occurrence of an expected punisher acts as a reinforcer. A disruptive student expects to be punished (admonished) for misbehavior, and when this doesn't occur, the disruption is reinforced. In addition, it is vicariously reinforced for the other students; their inhibitions are reduced.

11.35: Shirley demonstrated withitness in at least three places. First, as the students were making the transition from writing to math, she touched Brad on the arm and pointed to his folder, reminding him to return from his window-gazing. She also "caught" Kevin when he tapped Alison, was aware that he, and not Alison, was the cause of the disruption, and she intervened in that instance before she moved over to Sondra, since his disruption was more severe than her note passing. These moves indicated that she knew what was going on in her classroom.

11.36: As the class discussed the information, Karl noticed Barry whispering and saw Kareem poke Katilyna. He asked, "What is the part of the plant that produces fruit?" as he simultaneously moved to Kareem's desk and admonished him. He then watched Kareem as he moved to the front of the room and simultaneously continued his questioning. The ability to perform these actions simultaneously illustrates overlapping.

11.37: A possible I-message might be the following: "Student talking interrupts my teaching, this makes me lose my train of thought and I get annoyed when my train of thought is disrupted."

11.38: Consistency relates to Piaget's concept of *equilibrium*. Consistently enforced rules allow students to predict the consequences of their behaviors, making the environment understandable, which allows students to remain at equilibrium.

11.39: Shirley remained with Sondra until Sondra moved. She stayed and watched to be certain of compliance before she turned her full attention away from Sondra.

11.40: Long interventions interfere with connected discourse. Long interventions are incidental to the topic being discussed, and we saw in the chapter that incidental information interjected without indicating how it relates to the topic can cause the discourse to become "disconnected" or "scrambled." Effective teachers keep their lessons on track and spend less time on matters unrelated to the topic than do their less effective counterparts.

11.41: According to Piaget, children are innately egocentric, meaning they don't consider events from others' points of view. This means that they must learn that their actions affect others.

11.42: Cindy is applying the concepts of *cuing, modeling, positive reinforcement*, and *vicarious reinforcement*. Her comment is a cue for the rest of the class, she is attempting to use Ted as a model for the rest of the students. Ted is being positively reinforced, and the rest of the class is being vicariously reinforced.

11.43: There are at least two possible explanations for teachers' tendency to focus on undesirable behaviors. First, because of the complexity of classroom activities, desirable behavior tends to "melt" into the overall flow of teaching and learning, while misbehavior is simply more noticeable. Second, in most classrooms desirable behaviors considerably outnumber undesirable ones, making it impossible to focus on all of them. Focusing on a few then requires careful judgment--to avoid a perception of favoritism-- which further increases classroom complexity.

11.44: Cognitive perspectives view learners as active, thinking beings. This means that they realize that the behaviors are inappropriate and will accept the responsibility to stop the inappropriate behavior.

From a behaviorist perspective, no reinforcers for the inappropriate behavior are given when the behavior is ignored. According to behaviorism, if a behavior isn't reinforced, it becomes extinct.

11.45: The teacher is trying to use Jimmy as a *model*, i.e., she wants the other students to imitate Jimmy's behavior, and the teacher is trying to *vicariously reinforce* the other students. By directly reinforcing Jimmy--praising him--she is vicariously reinforcing the other students.

11.46: A cognitive view better accounts for this preference. The fact that the students indicate a preference suggests that they're thinking about the process, which is better accounted for by a cognitive view. When the teacher reminds the students of the rule and the consequences, the students process the information and adapt their behavior.

11.47: Many behaviors are learned through modeling. Rough desists can become modeled behaviors which students then imitate. Rough desists increasing undesirable behavior can also be explained from a different cognitive point of view. Learners form a schemata for the environment, and this schemata describes disruptive behavior as acceptable.

11.48: Since ignoring Jason's behavior hasn't produced positive results in the past, ignoring the behavior could now communicate lack of commitment to her policy. At this point she probably needs to apply a consequence. Later, if his behavior improves, and he *briefly* talks to one of his buddies, she may choose to ignore the behavior.

11.49: In dealing with violence and aggression immediate actions are called for. Short-term actions would be at the "applying consequences" end of the continuum. Other interventions are skipped because of the seriousness of the act and the need to immediately stop the problem.

11.50: Research indicates that problem solving simulations can be helpful. In using simulations you might ask the student to recreate the circumstances leading up to the earlier fights. Since the boy has been in several fights, more extensive intervention may be necessary, such as counseling by the school psychologist or counseling outside the school setting.

11.51: Increased parental involvement also helps parents become better informed about school activities and their importance. This information puts them in a better position to help their youngsters with academic tasks and also increases the likelihood that they will offer more encouragement, which can increase student motivation.

11.52: The present school is a stimulus similar to a conditioned stimulus (the parents' own school experiences), so the present school elicits conditioned responses similar to the original conditioned responses (the angers, disappointments, and nervous stomachs Rich identifies in the quote). The parents generalize--emotionally--from their own experiences to the present school.

11.53: Three simple techniques would be to write letters to parents in their native language, learn to verbally greet parents in their native language, and invite students to attend conferences with their parents to help translate information for their parents.

11.54: A basic comprehension-checking strategy is asking questions. This might be done over the phone with the parents, in a face-to-face conference or by sharing the letters with another teacher.

11.55: The letter demonstrates firmness by taking a proactive approach to classroom management, clearly communicating expectations. Caring is communicated through the tone of the letter which is positive and upbeat. Because the letter elicits the cooperation of both students and parents it is also democratic.

11.56: Perhaps the most effective way of communicating caring is calling parents on teachers' personal time, such as in the evening. Even if the call is unproductive, it communicates that teachers care enough to spend their personal time to help students. Teachers can also send notes, letters, and work samples home, and greet students and parents together when parents bring their children to school.

Application Exercises

Exercise 11.1

1. Identify the amount of time allocated for science and social studies in Shirley Barton's class. What does this allocation suggest about her instructional priorities?

2. What percentage of Shirley's allocated time in math was actually devoted to instruction?

3. Consider students' engaged time in Shirley's class. Based on your analysis of the lesson, was it equal to, slightly less than, or significantly less than her instructional time? Provide the basis for your answer with information from the lesson.

4. Using at least one example from the lesson, explain how Shirley maximized her students' academic learning time.

5. Three characteristics of effective organization were described in the chapter (Table 11.2). Identify an example of each in Shirley's lesson.

6. Identify an example in Shirley's lesson where she demonstrated effective communication through clear transition signals.

7. Examine Shirley's questioning behavior. Based on information in the case study, explain how she combined her monitoring and verbal feedback skills to effectively interact with Jon, Tim, Gayle, and Karen.

8. Explain how Shirley's interaction with Emerson was a mechanism for maximizing academic learning time.

Exercise 11.2

Read the following episode, then answer the questions that follow.

> Joe, a fifth-grade teacher, stopped by to pick up Andrea, his fiancee and an eighth-grade science teacher. They fell into a discussion of student discipline and looked at Andrea's rules, which were listed in her classroom:
>   1. Do not speak without permission.
>   2. Do not laugh, snicker, make jokes, or in any way react to another student's answer.
>   3. Do not leave your desk without permission.
>   4. Be prepared and ready when class begins.
> "My list is similar," Joe commented, "except I don't have your second one."
> "I knew I would need it," Andrea responded, "so I laid it on them. And we work on it all the time. Every time it happens, I stop the class for a moment and we discuss it, and they have another example to think about. This is a tough one for junior high students.
> "I originally told them," she explained, "that part of the reason we were in school was to learn to respect each other and treat each other decently, and this rule would help us learn to do that."

1. How do Andrea's comment, "I knew I would need it," in reference to her second rule, and Joe's lack of a similar one relate to our discussion of student characteristics?
2. Using one of the guidelines for forming rules as a basis, critique Andrea's first three rules.

3. Using a different guideline than in Item 2, critique Andrea's fourth rule.

4. Using a third guideline, criticize Andrea's second rule in the context of her remark, "so I laid it on them."

5. How does Andrea's comment, "And we work on it all the time," illustrate our discussion about making rules and procedures work?

6. How does Andrea's comment in the last paragraph illustrate one of the guidelines suggested for forming rules?

Exercise 11.3

1. Look again at the examples with Vicki Williams and Donnell Alexander on page 467 of your text. Identify two important characteristics of effective organization present in Donnell's case that were missing in Vicki's.

2. Look at the case study illustrating Judy Harris's work with her students in the Windows On Classrooms at the end of the chapter. Identify at least three characteristics of a democratic classroom that Judy demonstrated in her teaching.

3. Mr. Adams's class is off-task and disruptive when they are supposed to be doing seatwork. He says, "If you don't do your homework, you'll flunk the test; if you flunk the test, you could flunk the course; if you flunk the course, you'll have to go to summer school. Now none of us wants to go to summer school, do we? So let's get started on our homework."

   What concept from our discussion of essential teaching skills was Mr. Adams demonstrating, and what would have been a more effective approach to getting his students on-task?

4. Look again at Isabelle Rodriguez's work with her ninth graders on page 472 of your text. Analyze the effectiveness of her behavior, using the concepts of withitness and overlapping as the basis for your assessment.

Translate the following into "I-messages" using the guidelines in the last section.

5. "No assignment? We're never going to learn that way!"
6. "Felicia, be quiet! We can't just blurt out the answers."
7. "Sean, turn around. I like the front of your head better."

Exercise 11.4

Alberto Mancini is an eighth-grade math teacher. He has finished an explanation of decimals and percents, and has assigned the students their homework for the next day. He is circulating among the students when Heather gets up, goes to her locker at the back of the room, and noisily shuffles materials in it.

"Heather," Alberto says evenly, "we don't leave our seats without permission."

"I'm just getting some stuff out of my locker," she shoots back.

Alberto walks up to her, looks her in the eye, and says quietly, "I want you to sit down now."

"I need this stuff. You let Karen go to her locker."

"Heather, you know the rules. That's a behavior point lost."

Heather stomps to her desk and loudly slams her books on the floor.

Alberto steps up to her and whispers, "That's a second point, Heather. Please see me after class."

Heather stops after class, and sits down sullenly. Alberto pulls his chair out from behind his desk and sits facing her directly. "Do you have anything you want to say?" he queries.

She sits sullenly, saying nothing.

"If you have anything that you would like to say to me privately, Heather, I'll be happy to listen anytime," he says, leaning toward her. He hesitates a few seconds, then continues, "Now, let me get to the point so we both understand. We must have rules in our classroom, as we discussed at the beginning of the year. I am going to enforce the rules," he continues emphasizing the last sentence and leaning forward again. "It's your choice to break them or not break them, and you know the results.

"I know that you understand what happened today," he continues pleasantly, "but I'll briefly outline it for you to be sure it's clear. . . . Karen asked for permission, and I gave it. She quietly and quickly went to her locker. I believe that you knew you were breaking the rule, and I believe you also know now that you were being disrespectful to your classmates, yourself, and me by slamming your books on the floor. I'll be calling your parents tonight to explain why you'll be serving detention tomorrow. . . . I'll expect to see no more of this in the future," Alberto says pleasantly, getting up. "Here's a tardy slip that will get you into Mrs. Evans's class."

The next morning, Alberto greets the class as he always does and treats Heather as if nothing happened the day before.

1.   Using the guidelines and concepts developed in the section on interventions, write an analysis of Alberto's effectiveness in dealing with Heather. Use illustrations taken directly from the example in your description.

2.   Identify at least three examples of effective preventive management techniques that Alberto employed in dealing with Heather. Use illustrations taken directly from the example in your description.

Feedback for Application Exercises

Exercise 11.1

1. A half hour each was allocated for science and social studies. Compared to the 55 minutes allocated to math and the hour and a half each for reading and language arts, this suggests a lower priority placed on these subjects.

2. Shirley got her math lesson started at 10:01, and she finished at 10:52. As a result, of her allocated time of 55 minutes, 52 minutes were devoted to instruction. She only lost 5% of her allocated time to noninstructional activities. This represents a much more efficient use of allocated time than is typical in most classrooms.

3. While we can't be certain about the attentiveness of each class member based on a written case study, the evidence we have indicates that her engaged time was very high. In any classroom, engaged time will be lower than instructional time.

4. Academic learning time is the combination of success and engagement. As we saw in Item 3, high engagement rates are difficult to infer from a written anecdote, but we can see that Shirley made an attempt to actively involve students in the lesson. Active involvement strongly correlates with high engagement rates. In terms of success rates, most of Shirley's questions led to correct answers, and when they were initially unable to answer, Shirley prompted them, so they were able to give an acceptable response. (As a specific example, Shirley prompted Emerson when he was initially unable to answer.)

5. Shirley demonstrated excellent organizational skills: 1) she started her math lesson within a minute of the time it was scheduled to begin; 2) she prepared her illustrations of equivalent fractions the night before and had them at her fingertips when she needed them; 3) her routines were well established as evidenced by the children passing their papers forward without being told. Her transition from reading to math took only three minutes.

6. Shirley simply signaled a transition by saying, "We're going to shift gears because I've got another, different kind of problem." This communicated to the students that they were on a topic that was new but related.

7. First, Shirley made it a point to call on a variety of students, she called on the students by name, and she asked the question first and identified the student second.

She was also alert and careful to react to individual student's answers in the questioning process. For example she simply said, "Good," to Gayle, "Fine," to Tim, and "Excellent," to Jon in response to each because they answered with confidence. In contrast, when Karen gave an uncertain answer, Shirley responded, "Yes, good, Karen. I saw you actually counting them." Monitoring allowed her to match feedback to students' responses.

8. When Shirley asked Emerson "And what kind of parts?" he was unable to answer. She then asked, "How do these parts compare to each other?" which allowed him to answer, ". . . They're all equal." Shirley supplied enough prompts to be certain that Emerson was successful in answering. He was involved, and the combination of success and involvement is characteristic of academic learning time.

Exercise 11.2

1. Andrea is a junior high teacher, and students at this age tend to pick at each other, making remarks and putting their classmates down. By contrast, Joe's fifth graders are less inclined to demonstrate those behaviors, and as a result, a rule such as Andrea's second one is less necessary for his students.

2. Andrea's first three rules are stated negatively: "Do not . . ."

3. Her fourth rule is not specific. "Be prepared and ready. . ." has an uncertain meaning.

4. "Laying it on them" doesn't allow any student input.

5. "Working on it all the time" is merely another way of indicating that she is carefully monitoring her rules and procedures.

6. This comment indicates that she provided a rationale for the rules that she is using.

Exercise 11.3

1. Donnell had her handouts prepared in advance and had them ready to go when her class started. She then began immediately as the bell rang. Vicki was still organizing her handouts as the students came into the room, and she didn't get started on time.

2. First, Judy's class was extremely orderly, and the limits for behavior were very clearly established. Second, Judy provided leadership in the way she conducted her class. Her goals were clear, she carefully guided the learning, and she accomplished this while maintaining order. Third, her learning activity began when she asked the students to find the longitude and latitude of the cities. As a result, when she went over the answers, each had an investment in them because of already having worked the problems. She also promoted a sense of belonging by calling on individual students to respond, and in this way promoted involvement.

3. Mr. Adams was overdwelling on the students' behavior. As a result his discourse became disconnected or scrambled. The essential teaching skill involved is *connected discourse.*

4. Isabelle demonstrated both withitness and overlapping. At the same time that she was helping Vicki, she was monitoring the rest of the class (overlapping), and she moved immediately to Ken and Lance when they began their horseplay.

In the following responses note how they: 1) address the behavior, 2) describe the behavior in terms of its effect on the teacher, and 3) describe the teacher's feelings generated by the behavior.

5. You must get your assignments in on time. When you don't, I have to give you make-up work, and I get tired and frustrated when I have to spend my time that way.

6. Felicia, blurting out the answers is against the rules. This makes it difficult for me to try to give everyone a chance to answer, and I'm uncomfortable when I can't give everyone an equal chance.

7. Sean, when you're not facing me, I don't know if you're paying attention, so I have to repeat my directions. I get worn out and irritable when I have to repeat directions.

Exercise 11.4

1. Alberto demonstrated several characteristics of effective interventions. First, he kept his encounter with Heather very brief and he didn't get in an argument with her. He followed through by seeing her after class and explaining the consequences. While Heather protested to the contrary, Alberto was consistent in his dealing with her. He didn't force Heather into any admission of guilt, thereby forcing a power struggle. His consequences for misbehavior were clear and he administered them.

2. First, Alberto had clearly stated rules for which rationales were provided. This occurred in the planning phase. Second, he was firm in his dealings with Heather. Third, he communicated clearly, addressed the behavior, and was assertive in his response.

TRUE/FALSE QUESTIONS: Write T in the blank if the statement is true, and write F if the statement is false.

_____ 1. The correlation between instructional time and learning is higher than the correlation between engaged time and learning.

_____ 2. According to research, in question and answer sessions teachers typically direct questions to individual students rather than letting anyone answer who wishes to do so.

_____ 3. The concept classroom management and the concept discipline mean the same thing.

_____ 4. Rules are very important for beginning teachers, but veterans rarely use them.

_____ 5. If rules and procedures are taught well enough at the beginning of the year, monitoring them later on should not be necessary.

MULTIPLE-CHOICE QUESTIONS. Circle the best response in each case.

6. Third period in Bartram Middle School begins at 10:00 a.m. and ends at 10:50. Kristy Williams, one of the teachers, typically starts her math class at 10:02. Her friend, Kevin Anderson, typically gets started about 10:04. Of the following, the best conclusion we can make based on this information is:

    a. Kristy is a more effective teacher than is Kevin.

    b. Kristy's students are on task more than are Kevin's.

    c. Kristy has more allocated time than does Kevin.

    d. Kristy is better organized than is Kevin.

7. Darcia Myers, an eighth grade English teacher, typically spends about 7 minutes after the bell rings taking role, handing out papers, and writing assignments on the board. Bonnie Ossi, who teaches in the room next to Darcia, writes her assignments on the board during the time the students are moving from one class to another. Based on this information, which of the following conclusions is most valid?

    a. Darcia's allocated time is greater than Bonnie's.

    b. Darcia's engaged time will be greater than Bonnie's.

    c. Bonnie's allocated time is greater than Darcia's.

    d. Bonnie's instructional time will be greater than Darcia's.

    e. Bonnie's academic learning time will be greater than Darcia's.

8. Of the following, teachers' understanding of the content they teach is most strongly related to:

    a. high expectations.

    b. organization.

    c. precise language.

    d. academic focus.

9. A teacher in a discussion of the Northern and Southern Colonies prior to the Civil War says, "We've looked at the economic conditions in the North in the middle 1800s. Now we're going to shift and look at the economy in the South during this same period." Of the following, the teacher's comment best illustrates:

    a. effective lesson organization.

    b. ineffective lesson organization.

    c. effective communication.

    d. ineffective communication.

    e. ineffective lesson focus.

10. A teacher displays the following sentence on the board:

Studying is important if you want to be successful.

She then asks, "How is the word 'studying' used in the sentence? Ed?"
". . . It's a verb," Ed answers.
She responds, "Not quite. Help him out, . . . Kathy?"

Of the following, the best assessment of the teacher's response to Ed's answer is:
   a.   effective lesson organization.
   b.   effective communication.
   c.   ineffective communication.
   d.   ineffective sensory focus.
   e.   ineffective feedback.

11. Ms. Jeffreys says to her students, "Let's do this once more. What did Timmy just say about the setting of the story?"
   This question is most closely related to:
   a.   emphasis.
   b.   enthusiasm.
   c.   closure.
   d.   feedback.

12. You are studying direct objects with your students and you display the following sentence on the board.
   Ramon kicked the ball to Jack.
You ask Alice, one of your students, "What is the direct object in the sentence?" Alice sits quietly, saying nothing. According to research, which of the following statements or questions is most effective?
   a.   "Can someone help Alice out here?"
   b.   "Look, Alice, the sentence says 'Ramon kicked the *ball*.' *Ball* is the direct object."
   c.   "The direct object receives the action of the verb. *Ball* is the direct object."
   d.   "What did Ramon kick, Alice?"

Use the following description for Items 13-15.

You are a seventh grade science teacher conducting a lesson on plant parts and the function of each of the parts. You begin the lesson by reaching down behind your desk and picking up a large plant that you bought at a flower shop. You show the students the different plant parts, and as you're explaining the functions of each part, Rodney begins poking Jennifer with a ruler. At the same time Jimmy is whispering to Susan across the aisle.

13. If you are "withit" which of the following best describes how you should respond?
   a.   First stop Jimmy's whispering, since it is least serious, and then concentrate on Rodney.
   b.   First stop Rodney and then stop Jimmy.
   c.   Stop Rodney immediately and ignore Jimmy.
   d.   Stop the lesson and discuss the rule about keeping hands and feet to yourself with the whole class.

14. Which of the following best describes "overlapping?"
    a. Stop the lesson and discuss the rule about keeping hands and feet to yourself with the whole class while making eye contact with Rodney.
    b. While you're explaining the functions of the plant parts move over to Rodney, take his ruler, and continue standing by him for a moment.
    c. Stop the lesson briefly, admonish Rodney, and then continue with the lesson.
    d. Stop the lesson briefly, tell Rodney to put his ruler away, tell Jimmy to stop whispering, and continue with the lesson.

15. Having the plant behind your desk at the beginning of the lesson best illustrates:
    a. lesson organization.
    b. lesson withitness.
    c. lesson momentum.
    d. lesson overlapping.

16. Karen Johnson's tenth graders are working on their next day's English homework as she circulates among them. She is bending over helping Leroy when Jeff and Mike begin whispering loudly behind her.
    "Jeff. Mike. Stop talking and get started on your homework," she says glancing over her shoulder.
    The boys slow their whispering, and Karen turns back to Leroy. Soon they are whispering as loudly as ever.
    "I thought I told you to stop talking," Karen says over her shoulder again, this time with a hint of irritation in her voice.
    The boys glance at her and quickly resume whispering.

Which of the following best describes the above incident?
    a. Karen's intervention is effective, because she attends to a management incident at the same time she conducts instruction.
    b. Karen's intervention is ineffective, since her verbal and nonverbal behavior are incongruent.
    c. Karen's intervention is effective, since most of the students are working diligently.
    d. Karen's intervention is ineffective, since she didn't actively listen to the students.

17. You have a rule that prohibits talking without permission. As your fifth graders are doing seatwork, Sonja briefly whispers something across the aisle and then resumes working. Based on the discussion of the "intervention continuum" in the chapter, which of the following is the best course of action?
    a. Ignore the behavior since it was brief.
    b. "Desist" the behavior immediately, to prevent it from happening again.
    c. Openly praise one of the students who is working conscientiously and diligently.
    d. Remind Sonja of the rule, and suggest that she come to you if she has a question.

18. Mrs. Harkness is teaching the rule, "Bring all needed materials to class each day," to her students. She discusses the rule, provides examples, and then asks the students to describe some of the materials they should bring. She follows up by simulating getting ready for school and gathering the materials she needs. Of the following, the best prediction of the grade level Mrs. Harkness teaches is:
    a. first grade.
    b. fifth grade.
    c. seventh grade.
    d. tenth grade.

19. Based on the criteria for effective rules, which of the following rules is best stated?
    a. Do not speak unless you are called on by the teacher.
    b. Always come to class prepared.
    c. Avoid embarrassing your classmates.
    d. Leave your desk only when given permission.

20. One of your sixth graders has been chronically disruptive. You warn him, he stops briefly, and then becomes disruptive again. You state, "Please go to the timeout area." He looks at you and says, "Do I have to?"
    Based on the suggestions of assertive discipline, of the following, your best course of action is:
    a. Restate your demand, reminding him of the consequences for defiance.
    b. Explain to him the reason for the no-talking rule and leave it at that.
    c. Ask him why he is refusing to comply with your demand.
    d. Send him a non-verbal signal to be quiet.

Jan, a kindergarten teacher, Rod, a fifth grade teacher, an eighth grade physical science teacher named Dawn, and Joe, a tenth grade world history teacher are all at a party and begin talking "shop," specifically how they manage their classrooms.
Assume their students' characteristics are consistent with patterns identified by research.

21. The one for whom establishing explicit boundaries and predictable consequences is most critical is:
    a. Jan.
    b. Rod.
    c. Dawn.
    d. Joe.

22. The one whose students need rules to be explicitly taught, practiced and reinforced is:
    a. Jan.
    b. Rod.
    c. Dawn.
    d. Joe.

23. Students finish a worksheet in Mrs. Wood's class, while she is working with a reading group. When individuals are finished, they get up from their desks and deposit the worksheet in a folder at the front of the room. Mrs. Wood continues working with the reading group without saying anything to the students doing the worksheet. This process best illustrates which of the following?
    a. A classroom procedure
    b. A classroom rule
    c. Teacher withitness
    d. Teacher overlapping

24. As Mrs. Hayes is helping Janet with one of the problems on the seatwork assignment, Rene, who has had her hand up, nearly shouts, "Mrs. Hayes, I can't do this one. I've had my hand up for five minutes."
    "Shouting out is against the rules," Mrs. Hayes responds, as she turns to Rene. "It disrupts my work with other students, and I get irritable when I'm repeatedly disrupted."
    Of the following, Mrs. Hayes behavior best illustrates which of the following?
    a. An "I-message"
    b. A passive response
    c. An assertive response
    d. A hostile response
    e. Active listening

1. f
2. f
3. f
4. f
5. f
6. d   Better organization results in increases in instructional time.
7. d   Minimizing time lost from administrative tasks increases a teacher's instructional time.
8. c   Teacher understanding of content is directly related to the precision of a teacher's language.
9. c   Signalling a transition from one topic to another is one aspect of effective communication.
10. e   Effective feedback provides corrective information. By turning the question to another student, the teacher put Ed in a passive role and gave him no corrective information.
11. a   Asking a student to repeat an answer is repetition, which is a form of emphasis--a part of effective communication. (See page 455 of the text.)
12. d   A prompt is the best response to a student non-answer. It assists the student while still moving the lesson forward.
13. b   Being "withit" also includes differentiating between less and more serious infractions and dealing with the more serious matter first.
14. b   Overlapping involves the ability to do more than one thing at once.
15. a   One part of organization involves having materials prepared in advance and easily accessible.
16. b   Cognitive approaches to intervention suggest that verbal and non-verbal behaviors must be congruent.
17. a   The intervention continuum suggests using the least intrusive or disruptive technique first.
18. a   Younger children need to be taught rules and need to have them demonstrated and explained explicitly and carefully.
19. d   Options a and c are stated negatively; Option b isn't as clear as would be suggested.
20. a   Assertive discipline focuses on consequences for following and breaking rules.
21. c   Junior high or middle school students benefit most from explicit management boundaries.
22. a   Younger children benefit most from rules being explicitly taught and practiced.
23. a   Classroom procedures create routines that help organize classroom life.
24. a   "I" messages identify the behavior, attempt to communicate how the student's behavior affects the teacher and the feelings generated.

CHAPTER 12: TEACHER-CENTERED APPROACHES TO INSTRUCTION

Chapter Outline

 I. Characteristics of teacher-centered instruction
 II. Planning for teacher-centered instruction
  A. Prerequisites to effective planning
   1. Knowledge of content
   2. Pedagogical content knowledge
   3. Knowledge of learners and learning
  B. A teacher-centered planning model
   1. Specifying objectives
    a. Mager's behavioral objectives
    b. Gronlund's instructional objectives
    c. Objectives in the cognitive domain
    d. Objectives in the affective domain
    e. Objectives in the psychomotor domain
   2. Preparing learning activities
   3. Organizing learning activities
    a. Task analysis: A behavioral planning tool
   4. Assessing learner understanding
  C. Instructional Alignment: A key to learning
 III. Direct Instruction
  A. Procedural skills
  B. Models of direct instruction
  C. Steps in direct instruction
   1. Introduction and review
   2. Presentation
   3. Guided practice
   4. Independent practice
   5. Homework
 IV. Lectures and lecture-discussion
  A. Organized bodies of knowledge
  B. Lectures
  C. Lecture-discussions
  D. Lecture-discussion: A theoretical analysis
 V. Accommodating learner diversity: Classroom interaction
  A. Classroom interaction: Research results
  B. Accommodating diversity: Experimental programs
   1. KEEP: The Kamehameha early education program
   2. Wait time: Working with Native American students
  C. Learning about student interaction patterns
 VI. Putting teacher-centered instruction into perspective

Chapter Objectives

- Describe the characteristics of teacher-centered instruction.

- Explain how teacher-centered planning occurs.

- Identify the elements of direct instruction.

- Describe the elements of effective lectures and lecture-discussions.

Chapter Overview

As you have moved through your text, your understanding of learning and the factors that affect it has gradually developed. You examined the characteristics of the learners you will teach in Chapters 2-5 and the nature of learning itself in Chapters 6-9. You then examined learner motivation in Chapter 10, and the interdependence of effective instruction and orderly classrooms in Chapter 11, as you studied productive learning environments.

We now examine instruction, beginning with teacher-centered approaches, and Chapter 13 we turn to learner-centered instruction. As you study this chapter, you will see that the content is closely related to the information you studied in previous chapters that examined student learning. That makes sense; expert teachers consider their students and the process of learning as they design and implement instruction.

When students are learning well-defined content that they all are expected to master, teacher-centered instruction can be effective. Expectations are clear, lessons are highly structured and predictable, and learners practice and receive feedback. Objectives are clear, lessons remain focused on the objectives, and the teacher takes primary responsibility for guiding learning.

When teachers teach procedural skills, such as adding fractions with unlike denominators or writing sentences with appropriate subject-verb agreement, *direct instruction* is a useful approach.

Lecture-recitation, designed to teach organized bodies of knowledge, combines short periods where teachers present information, which are followed by teacher questions that gauge students' understanding. As additional segments of teacher presentation and comprehension checks are added, teachers ask additional questions that encourage students to examine the relationships among the segments.

Feedback for Margin Questions

12.1: Karen Johnson understood that density is a difficult concept for students, and she represented it by compressing cotton in a cup, so the students could *see* that the cotton was more compact (more dense). She also used the wood blocks, the water and vegetable oil, and the screen door to illustrate the concept. Her ability to generate these representations reflect her pedagogical content knowledge.

Shirley Barton's pedagogical content knowledge was reflected in the fact that she had the students fold papers to illustrate equivalent fractions. As with Karen's representations, the students could *see* that 1/3 = 2/6 and 1/2 = 3/6, for example.

12.2: The answer to the first question is yes. Teachers could have thorough knowledge of content and still not be able to represent the content in such a way that it would be understandable to learners. We saw research, cited in Chapter 1, which indicated that math majors were no more able than nonmajors to represent math topics in understandable ways.

The answer to the second question is no. It would be virtually impossible to know how to represent content in understandable ways without understanding the content itself.

12.3: Linear is implied in the fact that the model moves from *specifying objectives*, to *selecting learning activities*, to *organizing learning activities*, to *designing assessments* in essentially a "straight line."

Since it makes sense that *selecting and organizing learning activities* would logically follow *specifying objectives*, and *designing assessments* would complete the cycle, it is a rational process.

12.4: An objective written according to Mager's format might be, "Given a passage students haven't read, they will identify the main idea in each paragraph." *Given the passage students haven't read* is the condition, *identify* is the behavior, and *each* is the criterion.

12.5: Using Gronlund's format the object might appear as follows:
Understands 1. Describes main idea
main idea 2. Identifies main idea in a paragraph
3. Correctly uses main idea in a paragraph

12.6: "Defines adjectives" would be classified as a knowledge-level outcome. "Identifies adjectives in sentences" is a comprehension-level task, and "makes writing attractive by creatively using adjectives" is a synthesis-level outcome (using adjectives creatively requires a synthesis-level outcome).

12.7: This is most likely a "valuing" level goal. However, you could also argue that this suggests an "organization" level goal, where they would act upon their values by taking more science in high school.

12.8: The lower primary grades place more emphasis on psychomotor goals (as well as affective goals), whereas the upper grades tend to focus more on cognitive goals. The emphasis on the psychomotor domain generally decreases as learners move through the K-12 curriculum.

12.9: Mrs. Mahera's work with her first graders on page 269 in Chapter 7 is a good illustration of designing and implementing learning activities to meet this goal.

12.10: A brief task analysis might appear as follows:

Terminal Behavior: Using adverbs in sentences
Prerequisite Skills: 1) Define adverb
2) Locate adverbs in sentences
3) Identify instances when these are used correctly and incorrectly (e.g., He played good. vs. He played well.)
4) Use adverbs correctly in sentences.
Sequence: The objectives listed above should be in proper sequence.
Diagnose: Develop an instrument that has four sections corresponding to the above skills.

12.11: Procedural skills and concepts are similar in two ways. First, they are both illustrated with examples. In some cases the number of examples is essentially unlimited. For instance the number of subtraction problems that learners can practice on is virtually endless, and the number of metaphors that learners can create is also virtually unlimited. Second, learners improve as they practice procedural skills, and learners' understanding of concepts increases the more practice they have working with them. For example, the more metaphors learners see and create, the better their understanding of metaphors becomes.

Procedural skills and concepts differ in one way. There is no set of procedures to follow in learning concepts, whereas there is in learning procedural skills.

12.12: Review is important for activating background knowledge. Activating background knowledge is important, because background knowledge will influence learners' perception of the new information they're studying. Also, encoding involves forming mental representations and linking new to existing understanding.

Introduction and review help attract learners' attention, hopefully arouse curiosity, and satisfy learners' needs to understand what they're studying and why (task comprehension in the Model for Promoting Student Motivation).

12.13: Social interaction is one of the characteristics of constructivism. Discussion capitalizes on social interaction.

12.14: The *presentation* phase is most important to ensuring successful independent practice, and it is in this phase that we see the most difference between effective and ineffective teachers. If the presentation phase is ineffective, both guided practice and independent practice will be confused and difficult. Remember, independent practice strengthens earlier understanding; it does not teach the skill. If teachers have to provide a great deal of explanation during independent practice (seatwork), error rates increase and student achievement decreases (Brophy & Good, 1986).

12.15: If students do their homework, they *expect* to be reinforced for it in some way, such as being given credit toward their final grade. According to social cognitive theory, the nonoccurrence of expected reinforcers can act as punishers and reduce behavior. If students aren't given credit for doing their homework, they are likely to expend less effort on subsequent assignments, which is an intuitively sensible outcome.

12.16: David Shelton in Chapter 7 and Kathy Brewster in Chapter 9 are two teachers that taught organized bodies of knowledge.

12.17: Darren's comment best illustrates *introductory focus*. Darren was trying to attract the students' attention and provide a framework for the lesson.

12.18: Darren's goal in studying the French and Indian War was to help the students understand some of the causes of the American Revolutionary War. She could broaden the integration further by helping the students understand causes of other revolutions, such as the French Revolution and the Russian Revolution. She could also broaden the integration by asking the students to look for patterns in the causes of revolutions.

12.19: First, she did a brief *review* when she asked Adam, "About where are we now in our progress?" and her comprehension monitoring was also a form of review. Second, she demonstrated *introductory focus,* as we saw in 12.17. Third, her map provided a form of *sensory focus.* Fourth, her questioning illustrated *equitable distribution*; for example, in the brief episode Alfredo, Troy, Danielle, Josh, Tenisha, Sarah, Dan, and Bette all responded to questions. Fifth, her communication was effective. She used *precise terms,* and her *discourse* was *connected.* Sixth, she was *well organized.* Her maps were readily available, and she spent little time in displaying them.

12.20: Behaviorism is implied in the quote. The quote states that, "Silence is interpreted as the absence of knowledge." This doesn't account for "knowing" that isn't demonstrated in the form of an observable behavior. "Topics are normally introduced in small and carefully sequenced steps," is instruction based on behaviorist views of learning. Small specific steps allow the teacher to identify what behaviors will be reinforced.

12.21: If low achievers are admonished for calling out when they know an answer--since they don't have established patterns of success--their inclination to try and participate can be reduced. Similarly, students who come from home environments that tolerate (or even promote) interruptions can experience cultural conflict if they are admonished for interrupting, and they may also become less inclined to participate.

12.22: Wait-times of 3-5 seconds were described as desirable in Chapter 11. In the situations described in this section, wait times might be much longer, such as up to 10 or 15 seconds.

12.23: As an example, look again at Sam Barnett's work with his students. He did a good job of making the concept of place value meaningful for his students.

The teacher in the lesson you just read might have the students make four groups of 10 interlocking cubes (or popsickle sticks with beans glued to them) and five loose cubes beside the groups. She could then have them hold up one of the groups of 10 and describe it, being sure that they said something such as, "This is one group of 10 cubes." She could then have them describe how many groups of 10 they had and how many loose ones they had. She could then write the numeral 45 on the chalkboard and have students describe the four, carefully linking it (verbally) to the four groups of 10, and verbally linking the 5 to the five loose cubes. (Another problem with the lesson as described is that merely circling the tally marks isn't concrete enough for the students to conceptualize that they are supposed to represent a group.)

Application Exercises

Exercise 12.1

Laurie Zentz is an elementary teacher studying Native Americans from different regions of the country.

"At the beginning of the school year, I had decided that my students should have a better understanding and appreciation of other cultures. I hope to spark some interest, so maybe they'll read about some other cultures on their own. When I saw a chapter in the social studies book on Native Americans, I decided to focus on their culture and life-style.

"My major goal was to have the students see these different Native American tribes as people.

"When we're finished, they'll be able to identify the tribes when I describe their lifestyle and where they live," Laurie comments in describing her unit. "I show a couple of films that really do a good job of illustrating the characteristics of each tribe, and then we have 'Native American Day' when kids dress up in native costume and explain how the tribe they represent worked and lived,' she went on. "I also give them a solid test on the stuff. I have some drawings and descriptions of hypothetical groups, and they have to identify the tribe based on the information I give.

"It's a lot of work," she comments finally. "We have to find a day when we can invite the other grades in to see our 'village,' and getting all the presentations scheduled is a mess. But it's worth it. They get a lot out of it, and they like it."

1. Identify each of the elements of the Teacher-Centered Planning Model in Laurie's description of her planning.

2. What level of the cognitive taxonomy is best illustrated in Laurie's objective, ". . . they'll be able to identify the tribes when I describe their lifestyle and where they live."

3. What level of the affective taxonomy is best illustrated in Laurie's goal, "I hope to spark some interest, so maybe they'll read about some other cultures on their own."

4. Describe *instructional alignment*. Based on the evidence in the case study, is Laurie's instruction aligned? Explain.

Exercise 12.2

1. Examine the following list of skills and concepts.

    When adding *ing* to a word ending in a consonant, simply add *ing* if the final consonant is preceded by a long vowel sound or another consonant, but double the consonant if it's preceded by a short vowel sound.

    When simplifying an arithmetic expression, first complete the operations in parentheses, then multiply and divide left to right, and finally add and subtract left to right.

    The concept *adverb*.

    The amount of work done on an object is equal to the force exerted on it times the distance it moves.

    Select one of the topics and describe how it would be taught using the basic direct instruction model. Include specific examples and a description of each of the four steps in the model.

Exercise 12.3

Read the following case study illustrating a teacher using the Lecture-Discussion Model (Adapted from Kauchak & Eggen, 1998), and answer the questions that follow:

1.   Velda Houston is a ninth-grade American government teacher continuing a unit on the Constitution including topics such as the electoral college, the branches of government, and the role and function of each branch.

2.   Velda displayed a transparency illustrating the large-state plan and the small-state plan, together with the cases of compromise that resulted in our present legislative and executive branches of the government.

3.   As the bell rang, and Velda began, "Listen everyone. . . . To begin our lesson on the Constitution, I'd like to pose a problem to you. Mrs. Brown [another teacher in the school] has a special project she wants done, and she wants the smartest kid she can find to do it. Tim wants the job and thinks he is qualified. He's a good writer and gets good grades on his essays. However, Jo also wants the job, and she thinks she is better qualified than Tim. She's a whiz in math. What is Mrs. Brown going to do?"

4.   "What are they supposed to do in the project?" Katy wondered.

5.   "Well, a variety of things," Velda responded. "Mrs. Brown will have them doing different things at different times."

6.   "Boy, it's hard to tell," Ken added. "How would you know?"

7.   "Maybe take them both," Sue suggested. "Could she do that?"

8.   "That's an excellent idea, Sue. Think about that everyone." She paused a moment and then went on, "The situation we're going to discuss today is sort of an analogy to Mrs. Brown's problem. The makers of our country's Constitution were in a dilemma when it came to making a decision about how to elect our leaders. The compromises that had to be made are what we're going to discuss today."

9.   Velda then strode across the front of the room gesturing animatedly with her hands, emphasizing key points, and continued by saying, "I know I've said it before, but it's so important I'll have to repeat it again. The Constitution was a series of compromises between people like you and me. Just as Mrs. Brown could compromise and perhaps take both Tim and Jo, the people who developed the Constitution had very different views of where this new country was heading. To arrive at a product they could all agree on, they had to compromise."

10.   "The forms of the compromise are diagrammed on the transparency you see," Velda said, displaying the information she had outlined on the overhead.

11.   She continued, "The nature of this compromise process came out very clearly in the part of the Constitution having to do with the way we elect the members of Congress. Originally, when our forefathers were writing the Constitution, there was a lot of disagreement about how votes in the legislature should be allocated. States like Rhode Island wanted each state to have the same number of votes. Delaware felt the same way. On the other hand, New York and Pennsylvania wanted the votes to be determined by the number of people in the state. . . . Each idea seemed the most fair to the states who proposed them. The small states wanted them allocated by state; the large states wanted the votes to be distributed on the basis of population. Both of the ideas seemed fair, and neither side wanted to give in."

12.   "So, as a compromise, they created a legislature with two bodies. The House of Representatives was based on population and today we have 435 representatives and the more populous states have many more representatives than smaller ones. On the other hand, the Senate has two members from every state. So, now we have fifty states, times two, equal 100 senators.

13.   "Now, let's analyze this process of compromise. How were the states supporting the two proposals different? Miguel?"

14.   ". . . New York was a large state, and Rhode Island was a very small state."

15.   "Yes, good, Miguel," Velda smiled. "And what does that mean? Jamie?"

16.   ". . . Well, it was bigger," Jamie responded hesitantly.

17.   "Bigger land area or bigger population or what?" Velda continued.

18.   ". . . Both, I think," Jamie continued, "But probably the bigger population was the most significant."

19.   "Yes, good, Jamie. Now why would the large states feel the way they did, and also why would the small states feel the way they did? What do you think?. . . Dick?"

20.   ". . . It would relate to power," Dick answered. "If the representation was made on the basis of population, the large states would be much more powerful than the small states."

21.   "On the other hand, what would happen if representation were completely equal among the states?" Velda continued. "Toni?"

22.   ". . . It would sort of throw the balance in the favor of the smaller states. It would mean a state like Wyoming with very little population could maybe stop a proposal from a very populated state like California."

23.   "So as part of the process of compromise what part of the legislature is based on population? . . . Camille?

24.   ". . . Uhh, . . . the . . . House of Representatives?"

25.   "Excellent, Camille. The total number of representatives is 435. The number of representatives from each state is determined by population. That would make populous states happy. And what part of the compromise made the smaller states happy?. . . Kareem?

26.   "The Senate?"

27.   "Why, Kareem?"

28.   ". . . Because, . . . er, . . . every state gets two, regardless, . . . no matter how big or little . . . they are."

29.   "Excellent thinking everyone!" Velda commented energetically.

1. Identify the *comprehension monitoring* phase of the lesson. Include specific dialogue from the lesson that illustrates this phase.

2. Identify the *integration* phase of the lesson. Include specific dialogue from the lesson that illustrates this phase.

3. Look at paragraphs 3-8 in the lesson. What essential teaching skill from Chapter 11 is best illustrated in these paragraphs? Explain.

4. Look at Velda's questioning in 13, 15, 19, 21, 23, and 25. What aspect of effective questioning is best illustrated in these paragraphs.

5. Select a topic of your choice. Then, describe how you would teach the topic using lecture-discussion.

Feedback for Application Exercises

Exercise 12.1

1. Laurie's objective is stated near the beginning of the case study: ". . . they'll be able to identify the tribes when I describe their lifestyle and where they live."

    As an illustration of the second phase of the model Laurie selected the films and designed "Native American Day" which included dressing in native costumes and explaining their tribe to others.

    Her organization of learning activities occurred when she chose to sequence the films first, followed by the presentations to the other students. Her scheduling of presentations was part of the organization process.

    Laurie's assessment was the test she gave.

2. Comprehension level. Their lifestyle and where they live are characteristics, and the students are identifying the tribes based on the characteristics.

3. Valuing. By reading about cultures on their own, they're showing commitment and maintaining involvement without assignments or prompting from the teacher.

4. Her instruction was aligned. Her goal was for the students to understand the lifestyle of Native American tribes and how their lifestyle related to where they lived. Her films illustrated lifestyle and her "Native American Day" was also consistent with the goal. Her test was consistent with her goal. She gave them drawings and descriptions of hypothetical groups and they had to identify the tribes based on the information she provided.

Exercise 12.2

1. In each case the lesson would begin with a review of the previous day's work. In the case of the rule about adding the "ing" suffix, the teacher would review consonants, long vowel sounds, short vowel sounds, single and double consonants, and two different consonants at the end of words.

The math teacher would review each of the operations as well as operations combined with parentheses.

In teaching the concept of adverb, the teacher would review adjectives, nouns, and pronouns including examples of adjectives describing the other two parts of speech.

The teacher would review and illustrate force and movement.

In the second (presentation) phase the language arts teacher might include examples such as:

| run | running | jump | jumping | speed | speeding |
| get | getting | talk | talking | go | going |

(Ideally these examples would be embedded in the context of a written passage.)

An example for the math teacher could be:

$$4+5(2+6)-8/4$$

(As with the language example on suffixes, embedding the skill in the context of a problem would be more meaningful than presenting it in the abstract.)

The English teacher would use examples such as:

The boy quickly ran up the stairs.
The children were talking loudly.

(As in the two previous cases, embedding the examples in context is better than presenting them in isolation.)

The science teacher could use examples such as pulling a student sitting in a chair across the room. This could be contrasted with pushing on the wall showing force without movement.

In each case the teacher would give students an assignment. In the first case, students would have to form words where the suffix was added; in the second students would have to simplify a series of expressions; in the third they would have to identify adverbs in sentences; and in the fourth the students would have to determine if work was being done or not. During the guided practice phase, the teacher would have the students work an example and would then discuss it with the class. She would repeat the process--probably once or twice--until she was satisfied that students could work the rest of the problems on their own.

In the independent practice phase, students would work the remainder of the exercises on their own under the supervision of the teacher.

Exercise 12.3

1. To illustrate the *comprehension-monitoring* phase, let's look at some of the dialogue:

    13.   Velda: Now, let's analyze this process of compromise. How were the states supporting the two proposals different? Miguel?

    14.   Miguel: . . . New York was a large state, and Rhode Island was a very small state.

    15.   Velda: Yes, good, Miguel. And what does that mean? Jamie?

    16.   Jamie: . . . Well, it was bigger.

    17.   Velda: Bigger land area or bigger population or what?

    18.   Jamie: . . . Both, I think. But probably the bigger population was the most significant.

The comprehension-monitoring step of the cycle serves two important functions. First, it makes the lesson interactive and draws students into the process. When they know they will be questioned about the material that was just presented, they are more likely to listen, and they're reinforced for doing so. If teachers expect all students to listen and participate and hold them accountable through questioning, they are more likely to remain involved with the lesson. On the other hand, if teachers talk for extended periods, or ask questions that are answered by only a few, the rest of the students are likely to "tune out."

The second function of comprehension monitoring is to obtain feedback--for both the teacher and the students. The quality of student responses helps teachers determine the extent to which they understand the material, and teachers can then adjust the presentation accordingly. If students are not understanding, there is no point in proceeding; teachers need to reteach the misunderstood or confusing material.

2. To illustrate the *integration* phase of the cycle, let's look again at some of the dialogue.

    19.   Velda: Yes, good, Jamie. Now why would the large states feel the way they did, and also why would the small states feel the way they did? What do you think?. . . Dick?

    20.   Dick: . . . It would relate to power. If the representation was made on the basis of population, the large states would be much more powerful than the small states.

    21.   Velda: On the other hand, what would happen if representation were completely equal among the states? Toni?

    22.   Toni: . . . It would sort of throw the balance in the favor of the smaller states. It would mean a state like Wyoming with very little population could maybe stop a proposal from a very populated state like California.

In this short excerpt we see that Dick offered a cause and effect relationship between the population of states and power, and Toni hypothesized another relationship based on equal representation. Understanding these perspectives was essential to understanding the need for compromise, the central focus of this cycle. Combining integration with comprehension monitoring can result in a thorough understanding of the relationships in an organized body of knowledge.

Integration is the natural extension of comprehension monitoring. The difference between the two is in the type of questions teachers ask. In the integration step, students are asked to establish cause-and-effect relationships, make predictions and hypothesize. The exact question depends on the content being taught; the essential characteristic is that the questions cause students to search for links with other ideas in the lesson.

3. These paragraphs illustrate *introductory focus*. In them, Velda attempted to attract the students' attention and provided a framework for the rest of the lesson.

4. In these paragraphs, Velda illustrates *equitable distribution*. She called on a variety of students, and she called on the students by name.

5. The responses to this item will vary. Check with your instructor to get feedback about this assignment.

TRUE/FALSE QUESTIONS: Write T in the blank if the statement is true, and write F if it is false.

_____ 1. According to research, a thorough understanding of content is adequate to allow teachers to plan effectively

_____ 2. According to Mager, a behavioral objective should state an observable behavior, the conditions under which the behavior will occur, and the materials necessary to perform the behavior.

_____ 3. Gronlund feels that stating conditions and criteria in an objective is essential for regular classroom instruction.

_____ 4. Application, analysis, synthesis and evaluation level cognitive objectives and activities make up the major part of classroom questions, exercises, and tests.

_____ 5. Teacher-centered instruction is most effective for teaching well-defined content that all students are expected to master.

MULTIPLE-CHOICE QUESTIONS: Circle the best response in each case.

6. Which of the following best illustrates pedagogical content knowledge?
   a. Mr. Duckworth describes the events leading up to the Spanish-American War. In the process he outlines events, such as the sinking of the battleship Maine, in Havana harbor.
   b. Mrs. Ramos writes short case studies about the students' loyalty to their school, their language, and their favorite music and social events to be used as analogies for the concept *nationalism* as she begins a unit on the events leading up to World War I.
   c. Mr. Helmsley explains that the ocean currents run from south to north along the coast of Europe, so the climate is more moderate than would be expected for the latitude of the countries.
   d. Mrs. Armstrong shows the students a map of the United States that illustrates land forms. She then explains the agricultural areas of the country based on the information in the map.

7. Which of the following is **NOT** a step in a task analysis?
   a. Ms. Gardner determines that her biology students need to be able to dissect a worm during a 45 minute lab class well enough to identify major organs and systems.
   b. She lists the materials she will need: worms, dissecting instruments, disinfectant, labels, charts, and lab coats for day of the dissection.
   c. She knows from a previous quiz that some of her students will need to learn to identify some of the organs while others will need help with the fine motor skills required in the actual dissection process.
   d. Ms. Gardner makes a list of all the things that her students will need to know before the lab class in order to succeed at the activity planned.

8. Which phase of the Teacher-Centered Planning Model is being planned when Ms. Gardner (in Item 7) decides to ask her students to draw from memory a labelled diagram of their dissections the day following the lab class?
   a. Specifying objectives
   b. Preparing learning activities
   c. Organizing learning activities
   d. Designing assessment procedures

9. At which level of the cognitive taxonomy would the following activity be classified?

After the teacher demonstrates the use of the formula for finding the area of a circle, $A = \pi r^2$, students are given new examples of circles for which they're asked to find the area on their own.

   a. Knowledge
   b. Comprehension
   c. Application
   d. Analysis
   e. Synthesis

10. If students in Item 9 were asked to draw and measure their own circles using compasses and rulers in addition to calculating the areas, in which domains of instruction would they be operating?

   a. Cognitive and affective
   b. Cognitive and psychomotor
   c. Affective and psychomotor
   d. Cognitive, affective, and psychomotor

11. Jeanna Evans wants her students to write persuasive essays using correct punctuation and grammar. She presents the students with a list of sentences that use incorrect grammar and punctuation, and she has the students rewrite the sentences using correct grammar and punctuation. The next day she gave them a test in which they had to write a persuasive essay using correct grammar and punctuation.

Of the following, which is the most valid conclusion?

   a. Jeanna's instruction is aligned, because the goal was for the students to write using correct grammar and punctuation, and she had them practice writing using correct grammar and punctuation.
   b. Jeanna's instruction is not aligned, because she didn't appear to explain the rules before she gave the assignment.
   c. Jeanna's instruction is aligned, because her test was similar to her goal.
   d. Jeanna's instruction is not aligned, because she had the students write isolated sentences during her learning activity.

12. Direct instruction is based primarily on:
   a. behaviorism.
   b. social cognitive theory.
   c. information processing.
   d. constructivism.

13. The step of direct instruction that most applies *scaffolding* is:
   a. introduction and review.
   b. presentation.
   c. guided practice.
   d. independent practice.

14. Of the following, the best example of a procedural skill is:
   a. Solving an algebraic equation for the value of x.
   b. Understanding the concept of equivalent fractions.
   c. Knowing that in the number 236, the 2 represents 2 hundreds, the 3 represents 3 tens, and the 6 represents 5 ones.
   d. Identifying adjectives and adverbs in sentences.

15. For which of the following goals is direct instruction most effective?
   a.   For students to be able to find the percent decrease of retail items that are placed on sale
   b.   For students to understand why the Spanish influence in the Americas decrease in the 17th and 18th centuries
   c.   For students to understand the formation of genetic hybrids
   d.   For students to relate the personal backgrounds to the writings of 20th century American authors

Meg Ryan wants her students to solve problems such as, "You have 50 milliliters of a 25% alcohol solution. How much water must you add to make a 10% solution?" She shows the students a graduated cylinder with the alcohol solution in it. She asks the students to identify cases where they might want to dilute solutions or increase the strength of solutions. She also has them offer some estimates of how much water they should add. She then models a solution, and assigns them problems to work as she walks among them to see how they're progressing. Periodically, she will make comments and offer brief suggestions. She then gives them ten problems to solve as homework.

16. Is Meg's goal appropriate for the direct instruction model?
   a.   Yes, because her instruction was aligned.
   b.   No, because her students were solving algebra problems, and algebra problems are not appropriate for direct instruction.
   c.   Yes, because her problems involved learning procedural skills, and procedural skills are effectively taught with the direct instruction model.
   d.   No, because direct instruction doesn't involve using physical demonstrations, such as her graduated cylinder and the alcohol solution in it.

17. Of the following, the step in the direct instruction model that was best illustrated when Meg had the students estimate how much water they should add to dilute the solution is:
   a.   introduction and review.
   b.   presentation.
   c.   guided practice.
   d.   independent practice.

18. Of the following, the part of Meg's lesson that is intended most to help the students reach *automaticity* is:
   a.   showing them the graduated cylinder and asking them to identify cases where they might want to dilute solutions.
   b.   modeling a solution to the problem.
   c.   having them work problems while she walked among them and made comments.
   d.   doing the homework assignment.

19. Of the following, which is related most closely to the popularity of lectures as a teaching method?
   a.   The difficulty of many of the topics teachers teach
   b.   The limitations of our working memories
   c.   The preference of students for lecture compared to other forms of instruction
   d.   The general effectiveness of lecture for most content areas

20. Of the following, what is the most important weakness of lectures as a teaching method?
   a.   Lectures are inappropriate for many content areas.
   b.   Lectures put students in a passive mode.
   c.   Lectures require high levels of teaching expertise.
   d.   Lectures are complex; they quickly overload teachers' working memories.

21. Which of the following is the best description of an organized body of knowledge?
    a. A definition that includes the name of a concept, a superordinate concept, and the characteristics of the concept.
    b. Two parts of a rule, such as adding apostrophe s for forming a singular possessive as one part of the rule, and adding an apostrophe to nouns ending in s for plural possessives as the other part of the rule.
    c. The relationship between two concepts that is stated in a principle.
    d. Combinations of concepts, principles, and generalizations and the relationships among them.

22. Which of the following goals is most appropriately taught with the lecture-discussion model?
    a. Finding equivalent fractions
    b. Applying Newton's Law of Inertia to everyday examples
    c. Using figurative language to make writing more attractive
    d. Explaining the impact of Columbus's discovery of the New World

Bill Englehart wants his students to understand similarities between the heavy influx of immigrants to the United States in the early 20th century compared to another heavy influx during the 1980s. He describes conditions in Europe in the early part of the century and he also notes that the Vietnam War that ended in the 1970s resulted in many Southeast Asians coming to this country. After a few minutes he asks Felicia to summarize what has been discussed to this point. After Felicia and three other students offer comments, he adds some information about an influx of Russian immigrants after the collapse of Communism, Cambodians after the Pol Pot purges, and several other groups. He then asks Jennifer to identify similarities in some of the reasons for immigration during the two time periods, and after Jennifer responds he asks Don to identify two reasons why people immigrate.

23. Is Bill's topic appropriate for the lecture-discussion model?
    a. Yes, because he is teaching an organized body of knowledge
    b. No, because he is comparing two different time periods on history, which is inappropriate for lecture-discussion
    c. Yes, because he interspersed his presentations with questioning that put the students in an active role
    d. No, because some of his students may be immigrants or the children of immigrants, so he should have used a more learner-centered approach in his instruction

24. When Bill had Felicia summarize what had been discussed to that point in the lesson, the phase of lecture-discussion best illustrated was:
    a. introduction and review.
    b. presenting information.
    c. monitoring comprehension.
    d. integration.

25. Of the following, which is the best assessment of teacher-centered instruction?
    a. Teacher-centered instruction focuses on lower-level objectives and breaks content into small pieces.
    b. The quality of teacher-centered instruction depends on the expertise of the teacher implementing it.
    c. Teacher-centered instruction emphasizes performance instead of understanding.
    d. Teacher-centered instruction is based on behaviorist views of learning.

Self-Help Quiz Answers

1. f
2. f
3. f

4. f

5. t

6. b   Pedagogical content knowledge includes the ability to represent topics in ways that are meaningful to students (as well as an understanding of what makes topics difficult to learn). Mrs. Ramos is the only teacher who actually *represented* the topics. The other teachers merely described or explained the topics.

7. b   Task analysis involves breaking a skill down into its component parts, and it involves identifying the prerequisite skills. It doesn't include materials.

8. d   ". . . draw from memory a labelled diagram of their dissections the day following the lab class," is a form of assessment.

9. b   This activity may appear to be application. However, the students aren't asked to make a decision about what formula to use. They merely "plug" the numbers for each circle into the formula and get the answer.

10. b   ". . . draw and measure their own circles using compasses and rulers," is a psychomotor task, and calculating the areas is a cognitive task.

11. d   Jeanna's goal was for the students to be able to write persuasive essays using correct grammar and punctuation. During her learning activity, her students had no opportunity to practice this skill and receive feedback. Because her test was congruent with her goal doesn't make her instruction aligned.

12. c   Direct instruction is based primarily on information processing. (Table 12.7 on page 512 of your text relates the steps in direct instruction to their corresponding information processing elements.)

13. c   During the guided practice phase of direct instruction, the students perform the skill under the teacher's watchful eye. She provides only enough help to be certain that they are making progress. Providing this support is *scaffolding*.

14. a   Solving an algebraic equation involves implementing a skill; all the other choices involve declarative knowledge.

15. a   Finding percent decrease is a procedural skill. The other goals involve an organized body of knowledge. Direct instruction is most effective when teaching procedural skills.

16. c   Solving percent mixture problems is a procedural skill, and procedural skills are effectively taught with the direct instruction model.

17. b   The teacher tries to help the students understand the skill during the presentation phase of the lesson. Estimating is designed to increase learner understanding.

18. d   Homework is independent practice. Independent practice is designed to promote automaticity.

19. b   Lectures are relatively simple, so they are less likely to overload teachers' working memories than are other methods.

20. b   A basic principle of learning is that learners are active. Lectures tend to put learners in a passive mode.

21. d   An organized body of knowledge is a combination of facts, concepts, principles, and generalizations and the relationships among them.

22. d   Explaining the impact of Columbus's discovery is an example of an organized body of knowledge, which can be taught through lecture-discussion.

23. a   Bill's topic involves an organized body of knowledge.

24. c   Summarizing is a powerful comprehension monitoring strategy.

25. b   No strategy is any better or worse than the teacher implementing it.

CHAPTER 13: LEARNER-CENTERED APPROACHES TO INSTRUCTION

Chapter Outline

I. Characteristics of learner-centered instruction
   A. Learners at the center of the learning process
      1. Learner-centered psychological principles
      2. Implications of student-centered learning for teachers
   B. Teaching for understanding
   C. Misconceptions about learner-centered instruction
II. Planning for learner-centered instruction
   A. Identifying goals and outcomes
   B. Designing and organizing learning activities
      1. Authentic tasks
      2. Multiple representations of content
   C. Assessing current understanding
   D. Planning for social interaction
   E. Creating productive learning environments
   F. Planning for assessment
III. Types of learner-centered instruction
   A. Discovery learning
      1. Types of discovery
      2. Research on discovery learning
      3. Guided discovery: An application
   B. Inquiry
   C. Discussions
      1. Characteristics of effective discussions
         a. Focus
         b. Student background knowledge
         c. Emphasis on understanding
         d. Student-student interaction
      2. Obstacles to effective discussions
   D. Cooperative Learning
      1. Introducing cooperative learning
      2. Specific approaches to cooperative learning
         a. Student teams achievement divisions (STAD)
         b. Jigsaw II
      3. Cooperative learning: Theory and research
      4. Cooperative learning: A tool for capitalizing on diversity
         a. Grouping
         b. Learning tasks
         c. Training
         d. Monitoring
   E. Individualized instruction
      1. Varying time available for learning
      2. Varying learning activities
      3. Varying instructional materials
      4. Research on individualized instruction

     F.   Learner-centered instruction: Utilizing technology
        1.   Good and bad reasons for using technology
        2.   Using technology to improve learning
            a.   Representing difficult-to-teach topics
            b.   Creating and using databases
            c.   Facilitating interaction
            d.   Developing problem solving skills
            e.   Drill and practice
IV.   Putting learner-centered instruction into perspective

Chapter Objectives

- Identify differences between teacher-centered and learner-centered approaches to planning.

- Identify characteristics of learner-centered instruction.

- Describe the elements of learner-centered planning.

- Discuss the relationship between cognitive views of learning and learner-centered instruction.

- Describe features of different learner-centered approaches to instruction.

Chapter Overview

Learner-centered approaches to instruction are based on the belief that learners construct their own understanding rather than recording it as it is delivered to them "prepackaged" by the teacher. Learner-centered approaches to instruction emphasize the learner being at the center of instruction, promote teaching for understanding and utilize multiple representations of content.

Planning for learner-centered instruction involves processes similar to planning for teacher-centered instruction, such as setting goals, designing learning activities, and preparing assessments, but the planning focuses on guiding learners as they construct understanding instead of merely presenting information.

A variety of learner-centered approaches exist, such as guided discovery, inquiry, discussions, cooperative learning, and individualized instruction. Technology can often be used to enhance learner-centered instruction.

Guided discovery occurs when the teacher identifies a content goal, arranges the information so patterns can be found, and uses questioning to guide students to the goal. Inquiry involves learners in data gathering designed to test hypotheses that have been offered as answers to problems or questions. Discussions are designed to stimulate thinking, challenge attitudes, and develop interpersonal skills. Cooperative learning has been found to be effective in developing interpersonal skills and in promoting friendships and positive attitudes among students who differ in achievement, cultural backgrounds, gender and ability. Varying time, materials, and learning activities are ways of capitalizing on individualization. Technology is effective for representing topics difficult to represent in other ways, preparing databases, promoting interaction among learners, developing problem-solving ability, and drill and practice.

Feedback for Margin Questions

13.1:   Cognitive and humanistic theories of motivation are reflected in the learner-centered psychological principles. Principle 8 refers to learners' "natural curiosity," "optimal novelty," and "difficulty." These are consistent with cognitive views of motivation.

Principle 7 refers to learners' "emotional states." Humanistic views of motivation consider learners' emotions. (Recall that humanistic views of motivation consider the "whole person.")

Behaviorism is not reflected in the *Principles*. We see no reference to reinforcers or changes in behavior as the result of reinforcers.

13.2: The limitations of our working memories is what makes learner-centered approaches to instruction difficult. Learner-centered instruction is much more sophisticated and demanding for teachers than is a simple teacher-centered approach, such as lecture.

Developing skills, such as questioning, to the point of automaticity is one way of overcoming the limitations of working memory.

13.3: "Assessing conclusions based on observation" and "confirming conclusions with facts," are demonstrated when students "justify their thinking."

13.4: Placing students into groups allow them to capitalize on the benefits of social interaction in promoting learning. (As you recall, the influence of social interaction on learning is one of the characteristics of constructivism.) The disadvantage is that classroom management is more difficult, and unless students have well-defined tasks, they may waste time.

13.5: As Scott said to himself, "I explained it so carefully. . . Why are they still having trouble?" If simply explaining was effective, the students wouldn't be still having trouble.

13.6: This refers to metacognition. Note also that behaviorist approaches don't consider learner metacognition.

13.7: Not necessarily. In Chapter 7, David Shelton, for example, didn't have authentic tasks, but his instruction was effective, and his goals were appropriate.

13.8: Multiple representations of content refer to *variety* in examples. (As you recall, *variety, quality*, and *context* were three important factors that influence transfer.)

13.9: The teacher will be unlikely to get comments from all students, the ones who do comment are likely to be the highest achievers, so the teacher might conclude that current understanding is more thorough than it actually is.

13.10: "Clear" and "meaningful" means that all the information the students need to understand the topic being taught is in the example. In the case study at the end of Chapter 2, for instance, Jenny Newhall's demonstration showed that air was in the glass when the glass was inverted in the fishbowl. When she tipped the glass over, the children could see air bubbles come out. Kathy Brewster's analogy about the students being on a "crusade" was also a meaningful example. The students could imagine the idea of a crusade based on the analogy. Other teachers, such as Diane Smith, David Shelton, Sue Brush, and Shirley Barton also used meaningful knowledge representations.

13.11: Behaviorist approaches would only require that the teacher identify the specific behaviors that the learners will demonstrate. Then the teacher would reinforce them for demonstrating these behaviors. This is a simpler process than considering all the other factors discussed in the contextual planning model.

13.12: Students are typically in a more *active* role during guided-discovery activities than they are during direct instruction activities. Typically, spend more time asking questions during guided discovery lessons and also that students are more involved in guided discovery than in direct instruction.

13.13: This statement best illustrates *introductory focus*. She referred back to it in the end when the lesson came to closure.

13.14: The characteristic is *multiple representations of content*. Each illustrates guided discovery in a different way. You construct your understanding of using guided discovery based on your study of them.

13.15: Guided discovery and inquiry are similar in that both involve students examining data from which conclusions are made. For instance, Scott's students had their observations of the frequency of the pendulum compared to the length, weight, and angle. Judy's students had their observations of the latitude lines and the longitude lines, from which they constructed the concepts of *longitude* and *latitude*.

They are different in that the data the students use in inquiry are designed to test an hypothesis, and the hypothesis is a suggested answer to a problem or question. The data in a guided-discovery lesson lead to a concept, generalization or rule (the concepts *longitude* and *latitude* in Judy Nelson's case). The data aren't used to test an hypothesis.

To make his lesson guided discovery, Scott would simply have had the students measure different lengths of pendulums, different angles, and different weights, and observe the change (if any) in frequency. His goal would have been for the students to understand the relationships between frequency, length, weight, and angle. For students to be able to design experiments wouldn't have been a goal.

It would have been difficult for Judy Nelson to conduct her lesson in an inquiry format because it would have been difficult for her to design a cause-effect problem that incorporated the concepts *longitude* and *latitude*, since her students didn't understand the concept before she did the lesson. (Her goal was for them to understand the concepts.)

13.16: If properly done, learners are active in each case. Also, in each case information is organized to be meaningful. One problem can be that direct instruction sometimes deteriorates into a simple performance-oriented lesson as we saw in the lesson on place value, and lecture-discussion can deteriorate into pure lecture.

13:17: Scott's lesson had some of the characteristics of a discussion. For example, the lesson was focused (on designing and conducting the experiment), it emphasized understanding, and there was a great deal of student-student interaction. However, the students lacked background knowledge, and discussions more commonly focus on broader topics than we saw in Scott's lesson, such as we saw in Darren Anderson's lesson. Also, discussions are designed to promote goals, such as learning democratic processes, developing tolerance for dissenting views, and critically examining attitudes and values. Critically examining attitudes and values wasn't a part of Scott's lesson.

13.18: She introduced cooperative learning quite effectively. Her task was short and simple, it was clear and specific (write observations on paper), the written observations provided a product, and she monitored the students' work. We have no evidence about them moving into and out of the groups, nor the amount of time they had to work.

13.19: Positive interdependence is accomplished with STAD by having each student's improvement points contribute to group awards. If a student's quiz score is higher than his or her average, they are awarded improvement points. The team is then given awards based on the average number of improvement points they earn.

Positive interdependence is accomplished with Jigsaw II by having each student be accountable for a portion of the content and teaching that content to their teammates.

13.20: Individual accountability will be accomplished most commonly with tests and quizzes. Unless carefully planned and organized, group grades are often ineffective.

13.21: The primary reason is probably the fact that they are in direct contact with each other. As they interact, they find that they probably have much in common with each other. In whole-group activities, they rarely have opportunities to interact directly with each other.

13.22: Responses to this question will vary. You might want to share your idea with your instructor and have him or her give you some feedback on your problem.

13.23: Choice would be desirable for areas, such as project work in social studies, science, literature, or art. It would be less effective in basic skill areas.

13.24: Social interaction is one of the characteristics of constructivism, and social interaction is particularly important when working on higher-level outcomes, such as problem solving. Individualization doesn't promote social interaction.

13.25: The first thing teachers should consider are their goals. If their goals can be better reached with than without technology, using technology is appropriate. However, using technology merely for the sake of using technology is not appropriate.

13.26: *Curiosity* and *challenge* are two characteristics of intrinsically motivating activities. Technology can be designed to capitalize on both by presenting intriguing problems. A problem such as the one that appears on page 568 of your text is an example.

13.27: Making simulations "interactive" relates to the concept of *activity* in Chapter 7. The more active learners are, the more likely it is that the information learners are studying will be meaningfully encoded into long-term memory.

13.28: Data bases will most commonly include organized bodies of knowledge (which are combinations of facts, concepts, generalizations, and principles). Databases can be organized to illustrate connections in the information in the database, which makes it more meaningful.

13.29: A spreadsheet would be best compared to a calculator.

13.30: Automaticity is important to prevent overloading learners' working memories.

Application Exercises_____

Exercise 13.1

Look again at Shirley Barton's lesson that introduced Chapter 11 (beginning on page 447 of your text). Assess the extent to which her lesson was student centered. Cite specific information from the case study for your answer.

Exercise 13.2

1. Look at the second general statement related to the *learner-centered psychological principles* in Figure 13.2 on page 538 of your text. To what theory of learning does this general statement most closely relate? Explain.

2. Look at *Principle 9* in Table 13.1 on page 537 of your text. What theory of learning is most reflected in the *description* of this principle? Explain.

3. Identify the *Principle* in Table 13.1 that most uniquely reflects humanistic views of learners. Explain.

Exercise 13.3

Look again at the case study involving Diane Smith and her students (beginning on page 144 of your text). What strategy (such as lecture-discussion, direct instruction, guided discovery, cooperative learning, or individualization) was Diane primarily implementing in her lesson. Cite specific evidence from the case study indicating that the lesson used that strategy.

Exercise 13.4

Of Diane Smith's lesson (beginning on page 144 of your text), David Shelton's (beginning on page 239), or Shirley Barton's (on page 447), which would be most likely to benefit from the use of technology? Explain how technology might enhance the lesson.

Feedback for Application Exercises_____

Exercise 13.1

1. Shirley's overall orientation toward her lesson was student-centered. After she conducted her initial review, she began her lesson with the problem of adding 1/2 of one cake to 1/3 of another, and she guided the students as they developed their own understanding of equivalent fractions rather than merely presenting them with an algorithm. This process reflected her emphasis on *teaching for understanding*.

The most specific example of student-centered instruction occurred when she asked the class to prove that adding the top numbers was the way to add fractions, which was followed by Natasha's explanation and the discussion between Natasha and Adam. Let's look again at some of the dialogue.

Shirley: How might we prove that adding them up is the thing to do? . . . Anyone?
Natasha: We have three pieces there (pointing to the first drawing), and if we had two more pieces, we would have five altogether, so it would be 3/8 and 2/8, which would be 5/8 altogether.
Shirley: What do the rest of you think about that?
Adam: I don't think so. It looks like 5/16 to me.
Natasha: No, look. We have only eight pieces altogether.
Adam: What about the other drawing?
Natasha: We're not on the other drawing. We're on this one. I said put two more pieces on this one.

216

This teacher-student, and student-student interaction captures the idea of learners at the center of the learning process.

Exercise 13.2

1. This statement most closely relates to information processing. *Strategic processing and control* refer to metacognition, which is an important component of information processing. No other theory of learning emphasizes metacognition.

2. This statement also reflects information processing. Guided practice is noted in the description of the principle. Guided practice is a feature of direct instruction, and direct instruction (when done effectively) is grounded in information processing. Guided practice is designed to help learners encode information into long-term memory.

3. Principle 7 most uniquely reflects humanistic views of learners. This is the only principle that refers specifically to learners' emotional states, and humanistic views most strongly reflect learners' emotions, such as feelings of safety, belonging, and self-esteem.

Exercise 13.3

Diane was using *guided discovery* in her lesson. She provided data--the length of the students' pencils, the color of the students' hair, together with the sentences that she wrote on the board--and based on the information together with her questioning, the students constructed an understanding of the concepts *comparative adjectives* and *superlative adjectives*.

Exercise 13.4

Of the three lessons, David Shelton's would be the one most likely to benefit from using technology. Technology could offer little to Diane's lesson. Her representations were quite effective as she used them. The same thing is true in Shirley's case. In David's case, however, a videotape or videodisc that illustrated "globs" coming off the sun would have been a better representation than his transparency. Technology might also be used to illustrate other characteristics of the solar system better than David was able to without technology.

TRUE/FALSE QUESTIONS: Write T in the blank if the statement is true, and write F if it is false.

_____ 1. Assessment isn't a part of learner-centered instruction, since learner-centered instruction is intended to guide learners' evolving understanding of the topics they study.

_____ 2. Since learner-centered instruction focuses on learners, it is less demanding for teachers than is teacher-centered instruction.

_____ 3. Clear goals are more important for teacher-centered instruction than they are for learner-centered instruction.

_____ 4. Planning for learner-centered instruction is similar to planning for teacher-centered instruction in that goals, learning activities, and assessments are considered in both approaches to planning.

_____ 5. Assessing learners' current understanding is emphasized to a greater extent in planning for learner-centered instruction than it is in planning for teacher-centered instruction.

MULTIPLE-CHOICE QUESTIONS: Circle the best response in each case.

6. Which of the following is one of the learner-centered psychological principles?
   a. Learners' intrinsic motivation to learn
   b. Learners' expectation of positive reinforcers
   c. Providing appropriate modeling of procedural skills
   d. Providing opportunities to facilitate existing behaviors

7. Which of the following best illustrates *teaching for understanding*?
   a. Asking students to recall a definition of a concept
   b. Requiring that students remember important factual information
   c. Asking students to cite evidence for a conclusion
   d. Asking students to know important rules and procedures

8. Mrs. Laureano is teaching the concept *insect* to her students. She displays the definition, "Insects are cold-blooded animals with an exoskeleton, three body parts, and six legs." She then shows students pictures of an ant, a beetle, a butterfly, and a mosquito, telling the students that they're insects.

   As an application of learner-centered approaches to instruction, of the following, the best assessment of the implementation of her lesson is:
   a. it is inconsistent with learner-centered instruction, since she merely told the students that the examples were insects, and there was no evidence of discussion in the lesson.
   b. it is inconsistent with learner-centered instruction, since she provided the examples instead of having the students find the examples for themselves.
   c. it is inconsistent with learner-centered instruction, since understanding the concept *insect* isn't an authentic task and therefore shouldn't be taught.
   d. it is consistent with learner-centered instruction, since she used multiple representations of content (her pictures of the insects.)

   Phenix, a science teacher wants her students to understand the characteristics of the solar system. She prepares a model showing the planets in their relative distances from the sun. She explains the model, pointing out that the first four planets are called the inner planets and the other five are called the outer planets.

   Loretta, a social studies teacher wants her students to understand how geography, economy, and recreational patterns are interrelated. She shows the students a map that illustrates different geographic regions, such as mountains and plains, a matrix comparing the economies of the regions and pictures illustrating the recreational patterns of different regions.

Jonah, a math teacher wants his students to be able to simplify arithmetic expressions and has his students simplify a series of expressions such as 3 + 5(8 -2) - 7.

Ruben, a fourth grade teacher, wants his students to identify the correct verb in sentences, such as "Andrea and Jose (is, are) the fastest runners on the girls' and boys' track teams." He has the students complete a series of exercises in which they have to identify the correct verb.

9. The teacher that is *most* consistent with the concept of *multiple representations of content* is:
    a. Phenix.
    b. Loretta.
    c. Jonah.
    d. Ruben.

10. The teacher that is *least* consistent with the concept of *multiple representations of content* is:
    a. Phenix.
    b. Loretta.
    c. Jonah.
    d. Ruben.

11. The teacher whose instruction was *least* well aligned was:
    a. Phenix.
    b. Loretta.
    c. Jonah.
    d. Ruben.

Use the following information for Items 12-14.

Consider the following list of goals.
    1. You want your students to acquire interpersonal skills and to learn to take turns in expressing their opinions as they design a procedure to investigate the effect of density on the evaporation of liquids (such as how fast does alcohol evaporate compared to water, since alcohol is less dense than water).

    2. You want your students to understand that parenthetical expressions are set off by commas, and you want the students to be as involved as possible in the activity.

    3. Your students have been reading *The Grapes of Wrath* and you want them to consider the characters in the book in the context of the book's setting. You want to be as certain as possible that each student in the class has the opportunity to express his or her view.

12. Of the following, the learner-centered strategy that is likely to be most successful for reaching the *first* goal is:
    a. unstructured discovery.
    b. guided discovery.
    c. a discussion.
    d. cooperative learning.
    e. individualized instruction.

13. Of the following, the learner-centered strategy that is likely to be most successful for reaching the *second* goal is:
    a. unstructured discovery.
    b. guided discovery.
    c. inquiry.
    d. cooperative learning.

14. Of the following, the learner-centered strategy that is likely to be most successful for reaching the *third* goal is:

    a.   unstructured discovery.

    b.   guided discovery.

    c.   a discussion.

    d.   individualized instruction.

15. Effective discussions strongly emphasize the development of critical thinking in students. Of the following, the factor that most impacts the students' ability to think critically is:

    a.   a lesson that remains focused on the question or problem being discussed.

    b.   students' extensive knowledge base.

    c.   high levels of interaction among the students.

    d.   a facilitative teacher.

Use the following information for Items 16-21.

Mrs. Carlsen wants her students to understand that when we exert a force on an object, it will go faster and faster, i.e, it *accelerates*. Mrs. Carlsen explains acceleration, such as an object speeding up as it drops, but the students continue to have difficulty with the concept of *acceleration*. So, Mrs. Carlsen shows a computer simulation that illustrates acceleration of a dropped ball in slow motion. The students work in groups to discuss what they've seen, and Mrs. Carlsen scaffolds them until they understand that when they see the distance between the images of the ball get greater and greater, the ball is accelerating. Gradually, they begin to understand the idea of *acceleration*.

Mrs. Hall wants her students to learn to work with each other to gather information and solve problems. She has different students study the geography of a region, others study the climate, still others the economy, and still others the government and educational systems. The students compile their information, sharing what they've found with their peers. After the unit is complete all students individually are given a test that covers the content.

Mrs. Williams wants her students to understand the concept *hyperbole*. She shows the students a series of sentences, such as "I had a million pages of homework to do last night," and "His descriptions were the most beautiful prose I've ever read ." Mrs. Williams has the students work in groups of three to identify what the sentences have in common, and as Mrs. Williams and the class discuss their findings, they gradually conclude that an unrealistic exaggeration is involved, and they reach the concept *hyperbole*. When they're finished, all students use the classroom computers to write paragraphs in which statements of hyperbole are embedded.

Mrs. Price wants her students to know what kinds of materials conduct electricity. She gives the students batteries, wire, bulbs, and packets of materials including paper clips, popsickle sticks, rubber bands, aluminum foil, brass buttons, bolts and nuts. She directs them to work with the batteries, bulbs, wire, and materials and see what kinds of conclusions they can make.

Mr. Polanski wants his students to be able to consider what might affect how fast water evaporates. They offer different possibilities, such as the temperature of the water (for example, being placed in a sunny window versus the refrigerator) and the size of the opening of the container (such as the water being in a cake pan versus a small-mouthed jar). They work in groups to put water in different locations in the room and in large-mouthed and small-mouthed jars and see how much the water level has gone down each day. They conclude that both the temperature and the size of the opening affect the rate of evaporation. They use their classroom computers to graph the relationship between the temperature and the rates of evaporation.

16. Based on the goal and learning activity, the teacher who was attempting most to implement *unstructured discovery* as a strategy was:

    a.   Mrs. Carlsen.

    b.   Mrs. Williams.

    c.   Mrs. Price.

    d.   Mr. Polanski.

    e.   None of the teachers attempted to implement *unstructured discovery* as his/her primary strategy.

17. Based on the goal and learning activity, the teacher who was attempting most to implement *guided discovery* as a strategy was:

    a.   Mrs. Carlsen.

    b.   Mrs. Williams.

    c.   Mrs. Price.

    d.   Mr. Polanski.

    e.   None of the teachers attempted to implement guided *discovery* as his/her primary strategy.

18. Based on the goal and learning activity, the teacher who was attempting most to implement *inquiry* as a strategy was:

    a.   Mrs. Carlsen.

    b.   Mrs. Hall.

    c.   Mrs. Price.

    d.   Mr. Polanski.

    e.   None of the teachers attempted to implement *inquiry* as his/her primary strategy.

19. Based on the goal and learning activity, the teacher who was attempting most to implement *cooperative learning* as a strategy was:

    a.   Mrs. Carlsen.

    b.   Mrs. Hall.

    c.   Mrs. Williams.

    d.   Mr. Polanski.

    e.   None of the teachers attempted to implement *cooperative learning* as his/her primary strategy.

20. Based on the goal and learning activity, the teacher who was attempting most to *utilize technology* to reach the goal was:

    a.   Mrs. Carlsen.

    c.   Mrs. Williams.

    d.   Mrs. Price.

    e.   Mr. Polanski.

    e.   *Utilizing technology* was not an integral part of reaching the goal for any of the teachers.

21. Based on the goal and learning activity, the teacher who was attempting most to implement *individualized instruction* as a strategy was:

    a.   Mr. Hall.

    b.   Ms. Williams.

    c.   Mrs. Price.

    d.   Mr. Polanski.

    e.   None of the teachers attempted to implement *individualized instruction* as his/her primary strategy.

22. Of the following, which is emphasized most in learner-centered instruction?
    a.   Effective reinforcers
    b.   Learner self-esteem
    c.   Humanistic views of learning
    d.   Deep understanding of content

23. Which of the following views of learning is most consistent with learner-centered instruction?
    a.   Behaviorist views of learning
    b.   Humanistic views of learning
    c.   Psychoanalytic views of learning
    d.   Cognitive views of learning

24. Temma and John are a bit behind their classmates academically, so while the rest of the students work on their language arts assignment for the next day, Mrs. DeLeon quietly moves to the back of the room with them. They work on some additional exercises while Mrs. DeLeon gives them enough help to be certain that they're making progress. Temma and John then complete the assignment at home.

Of the following, the best description of the strategy Mrs. DeLeon is using to help Temma and John is:
    a.   Inquiry, because Mrs. DeLeon inquires with Temma and John about their difficulties.
    b.   Cooperative learning, because Mrs. DeLeon, Temma, and John are cooperating in the efforts to complete the assignment.
    c.   Guided discovery, because Mrs. DeLeon is providing scaffolding for Temma and John.
    d.   Individualized instruction, because Mrs. DeLeon is providing for additional learning time for Temma and John.

Self-Help Quiz Answers_____

1.   f
2.   f
3.   f
4.   t
5.   t
6.   a   Learners' intrinsic motivation to learn is emphasized in Principle 8. None of the other choices is suggested in the *Principles*.
7.   c   Providing evidence is a thought-demanding process, as is explaining, justifying thinking, providing additional examples, generalizing, and relating parts to wholes. None of the other choices require these thought-demanding processes.
8.   a   Learner-centered instruction emphasizes that teachers guide learning rather than merely explain content, and discussion (social interaction) is an important part of the process. Multiple representations of content, alone, don't make instruction learner centered (Choice d). Learner-centered instruction doesn't require that students find their own examples (Choice b), and teaching the concept *insect* is an appropriate goal (Choice c). (The "authenticity" of the concept *insect* can be argued both ways.)
9.   b   The map, the matrix, and pictures are three different ways of representing aspects of the topic. In each of the other cases, the forms of the representations remained the same.
10.   a   Phenix showed only the model of the solar system, and she then verbally explained the inner and outer planets. While the form of the examples is the same for Jonah and Ruben, at least they had a series of examples.
11.   a   Phenix's goal was for the students to understand the characteristics of the solar system, but all she did was identify the inner and outer planets. The model and this explanation only help the students understand one characteristic of the solar system.

12. d   The students are collaborating on a problem, and part of the goal is for the students to learn interpersonal skills and learn to take turns. These are goals best reached with *cooperative learning*.

13. b   Wanting students to reach a content goal with high levels of involvement is reached best with guided discovery. Guided discovery is generally more effective than unstructured discovery (Choice a), no problem is involved (Choice c), and the goal doesn't emphasize cooperation (Choice d).

14. c   Since the students have read the book, their background knowledge about the characters should be adequate, considering the characters in the context of the book's setting requires higher-order thinking, and giving as many students as possible a chance to be heard are consistent with goals best reached in a discussion.

15. b   While each of the choices are important for effective discussions, learners' background knowledge is the most important factor in their ability to think critically.

16. c   Mrs. Price is providing the students with materials and asking them to make any conclusions they can. There is no evidence in the description that she is providing any guidance, there is no inquiry problem or question involved in the activity. There is also no evidence of goals related to cooperation.

17. b   Mrs. Williams's goal is for the students to understand the concept *hyperbole*. The description says that she and the students discuss their findings, suggesting that she is providing some guidance. While they work in pairs, their collaboration isn't related to the goal.

18. d   Wanting the students to investigate how fast water evaporates is an inquiry problem.

19. b   Mrs. Hall was implementing Jigsaw II, which is a form of cooperative learning.

20. a   Mrs. Carlsen is capitalizing on the use of technology to illustrate topics that are hard to otherwise illustrate.

21. e   None of the teachers was attempting to individualize instruction.

22. d   The two characteristics of learner-centered instruction are *learners at the center of the teaching-learning process* and *teaching for understanding*. While aspects of humanistic views of students (Choice c) and learner self-esteem are important (Choice b), they are not at the core of learner-centered instruction.

23. d   Learner-centered instruction emphasizes that learners are active, that they think strategically, and that they construct their own understanding. These are characteristic of cognitive views of learning.

24. d   By working with the students and having them complete the assignment at home--when the rest of the students complete it in class--the teacher is increasing the time for learning. Modifying time is one form of individualized instruction.

CHAPTER 14: ASSESSING CLASSROOM LEARNING

Chapter Outline_____

I.   Classroom assessment
    A.   Functions of classroom assessment
    B.   Measurement and evaluation
        1.   Formal and informal measurement
        2.   The need for systematic assessment
    C.   Validity: Making appropriate evaluation decisions
    D.   Reliability: Consistency in measurement

II. Traditional assessment
    A.   Teachers' assessment patterns
    B.   Designing valid test items
        1.   Multiple choice items
            a.   The stem
            b.   Distracters
            c.   Measuring higher-level learning
        2.   True-false items
        3.   Matching items
        4.   Completion items
        5.   Essay items: Measuring complex outcomes
    C.   Using commercially prepared test items

III. Authentic assessment
    A.   Performance assessments
        1.   Designing performance assessments
            a.   Specifying desired outcomes
            b.   Selecting the focus of evaluation
            c.   Determining the appropriate degree of realism
            d.   Selecting evaluation procedures
        2. Evaluation methods with performance assessments
    B.   Portfolio assessment: Involving students in authentic assessment

IV. Effective assessment practices
    A.   Designing assessments
        1.   Tables of specifications: Increasing validity through planning
    B.   Preparing students for assessments
        1.   Teaching test-taking strategies
        2.   Reducing test anxiety
        3.   Specific test-preparation procedures
            a. Preparing students for alternative assessments
    C.   Administering assessments
    D.   Analyzing results
    E.   Accommodating diversity in classrooms: Reducing bias in assessment
        1.   Being careful with wording in assessment items
        2.   Making provisions for non-native English speakers
        3.   Accommodating diversity in scoring

V.   Grading and reporting: The total assessment system
    A.   Designing a grading system
        1.   Formative and summative evaluation
        2.   Norm and criterion-referenced evaluation
        3.   Tests and quizzes

4. Alternative assessments
5. Homework
B. Assigning grades: Increasing learning and motivation
   1. Raw points or percentages?

Chapter Objectives

- Describe and explain basic assessment concepts.

- Describe classroom teachers' assessment patterns.

- Identify characteristics in specific assessment items that detract from their validity.

- Construct alternative assessments in your content area or grade level.

- Apply effective assessment procedures in classrooms.

Chapter Overview

Your study of this text is nearing completion. To this point you have examined the nature of learning and the influence that student characteristics, motivation, classroom management, and effective instruction all have on the amount students achieve. We now turn to the process of assessment, which is an effort to answer the question, "How much have students learned?"

Assessment involves all the processes and tools teachers use to make decisions about their students' progress. These decisions are evaluations, and the information they're based on are called measurements.

Valid measurements are consistent with stated goals. Reliable measurements are consistent; unreliable measurements cannot be valid. One of the strengths of objective test formats, such as multiple-choice, is their high reliability. Essay tests tend to be unreliable.

Teachers in the elementary grades use performance measures, they rely more on informal measures and commercially prepared tests to a greater extent than do teachers of older students, and they also place a greater emphasis on affective goals. The tests middle and secondary school teachers prepare most commonly use completion and matching formats, and they are composed of mostly knowledge/recall items.

Alternative assessments ask students to demonstrate skills similar to those required in the real-world. Systematic observations, checklists, and rating scales can all be used to increase the validity and reliability of alternative assessments. Portfolios involve students in the design, collection and evaluation of their own work.

Effective teachers prepare their students for tests by specifying precisely what will be on the tests, giving students a chance to practice responding to items under testlike conditions, and establishing positive expectations for student performance.

Effective teachers are sensitive to the possibility of bias as they design and implement their assessment systems. Bias can result from students' lack of experience with evaluation procedures, unequal access to irrelevant content knowledge and problems with language.

Decisions about the relative weight of tests, quizzes, homework, and performance measures are left up to individual teachers. These factors together with the processes of preparing students for tests and administering them make up the teacher's total assessment system.

14.1:   Both frequently and infrequently announced quizzes use a fixed-interval reinforcement schedule, which produces "scallops" where behaviors increase just before reinforcement and decrease after reinforcement. Frequent quizzes produce smaller "scallops" (students study every day for daily quizzes rather than only once a week for weekly quizzes, for example).

14.2:   Teachers should describe in general terms what the test will cover, the format for testing, and the kinds of responses that will be expected. However, if the exact content is specified, students limit their study to that content, and overall learning is reduced. Frequently missed items should be discussed in class, and students should have the opportunity to discuss all the items they missed in private if they choose to do so. Not all test items can be discussed in class because the process is time consuming, and it is not a good use of time for students who answer most of the items correctly.

14.3:   Both types of formats are similar in their goals--to gather information to make instructional and evaluative decisions. They differ in the ways that they gather data. Traditional formats employ paper and pencil measures and ask students to work alone; alternative formats ask students to perform in different ways and often require student cooperation or collaboration. Advantages of traditional formats are ease of administration and familiarity; a major disadvantage is validity-they are poor at measuring important outcomes like higher-order thinking and problem-solving. This is a major advantage of alternate formats; disadvantages for these include time, energy and familiarity.

14.4:   The best example of an informal measurement was Kathy's checking students' seatwork as she circulated around the class. (Kathy giving two problems every day at the beginning of class appears to be quite systematic, and if it is, it is more a formal than an informal measurement.)

14.5:   An example of a systematic assessment would be a test or quiz, for which the teacher planned and prepared students. Unsystematic assessments would be responses from students in question and answer sessions or observations of students' nonverbal behaviors.

14.6:   An example would be a measurement written in English for a student whose English is limited. Another example would be a test item that assumes common cultural background (e.g. knowledge of Christianity or baseball), which some students may not have.

14.7:   Based only on the information we have in the directions, the first grader has questionable validity, since the teacher didn't specify that one of his/her grades depended on creativity. Grading for punctuation and grammar is valid if it is reliable.

14.8:   The most workable option is short, frequent quizzes. The frequency will have the effect of increasing overall reliability.

14.9:   Elementary classrooms tend to be skill-oriented, focusing on math, reading, and writing skills. It's easier to assess skills using performance assessments than other types of items. Performance assessment also increases validity, as we'll see in a later section. Also, it's hard to assess many of the things taught in the secondary schools with performance measures.

14.10: More of the content in math and science lends itself to problem solving--a common task that goes beyond the knowledge level--than does the content in other areas, so it is easier for teachers to write application items involving problem solving in these areas. Creating test items involving problem solving in American History, for example, is demanding and time consuming for teachers.

14.11: The item is invalid, because the students got the incorrect answer because of ambiguity and not because they didn't understand the content. The item can still be reliable, however, because the scoring on the item is consistent. At the very least you should rewrite the item before using it again. On the present test, you could "throw the item out" for purposes of evaluation.

14.12: If they are written clearly and require an *exactly worded* answer, they are objective. However, as soon as answers are allowed to vary and teacher judgment is involved in assessing the quality of the answer, the item becomes more subjective.

14.13: The simplest way to fix the item is to rewrite the stem so it reflects one question, such as "Which of the following is part of the circulatory system?" A question about the function of the circulatory system should be a separate item.

14.14: The following represent one way to "fix" these problems:

1. Which of the following is a function of the circulatory system?
    a. To support the vital organs of the body
*   b. To transport the blood throughout the body
    c. To transfer nerve impulses from the brain to the muscles
    d. To provide for the movement of the body's large muscles

2. Of the following, the definition of population density is:
    a. the number of people that live in your city or town.
    b. the number of people that voted in the last presidential election.
*   c. the number of people that live on a certain area of land.
    d. the number of people in cities compared to small towns.

3. Of the following, the most significant cause of World War II was:
    a. American aid to Great Britain.
    b. Italy's conquering of Ethiopia.
    c. Japan's war on China.
*   d. the devastation of the German economy.

4. Which of the following is the best description of an insect?
    a. They have one pair of antennae on their head.
*   b. They have three body parts.
    c. They live in water.
    d. They breathe through lungs.

5. The one of the following that is <u>not</u> a reptile is a(n):
    a. alligator
    b. lizard
*   c. frog
    d. turtle

6. Which of the following illustrates a verb form used as a participle?
    a. He ran quickly to the door.
*   b. I saw a jumping frog contest on TV yesterday.
    c. Thinking is hard for many of us.
    d. To forgive is an admirable trait.

14.15: All of these items are at the knowledge/recall level, a typical problem for true-false items.

14.16: Some examples of content that lends itself to the matching format include: 1) animals and plants and their classification, 2) countries/states and capitals 3) chemical elements and symbols, and 4) historical figures and their contributions.

14.17: Possible items might include:
   a)   What is the term used to describe a belief, view, or judgment formed about a particular matter?
   b)   What is the present day capital of the country of Canada?

14.18: If spelling and grammar were specified in your instructor's criteria, taking off points is valid. If not, taking off points is not valid.

14.19: These are primarily problems with validity. The items are often reliable, but invalid because they are incongruent with goals.

14.20: An example of an authentic assessment would be for Shirley to present a problem such as the following:

   We're having a pizza party. One pizza is cut into 12 pieces, another into 6 pieces, and a third into 4 pieces. Elroy ate one piece from each pizza. How much pizza did he eat altogether?

   (Even more authentic would be for the students to actually have a pizza party where pizzas cut into different numbers of slices were served, and having the students determine how much one person or a group of people ate.)

14.21: Essay items can be performance assessments to the extent that they tap higher-level thinking in real life situations. For example, asking students to write an essay on a topic of their choice, using available resources, would be closer to the idea of a performance assessment than a closed book, timed test, with the teacher specifying the topic.

14.22: Realism influences validity by matching the evaluation more closely with our ultimate goal--driving in a variety of traffic settings. Less realistic evaluation settings can be more reliable because they are easier to score consistently, but this increased reliability comes at a price (decreased validity).

14.23: A rating scale might appear as follows:

DIRECTIONS: Assess each of the test items using the following dimensions. For each dimension circle a 5 for an excellent performance, 4 for a very good performance, 3 for a good performance, 2 for fair, and 1 for poor.

5 4 3 2 1   States one clear problem in the stem.
5 4 3 2 1   Each distracter is plausible.
5 4 3 2 1   Wording in the stem and correct choice are dissimilar.
5 4 3 2 1   Phrasing in the correct choice and distracters are similar.
5 4 3 2 1   The correct choice and distracters are similar in length.
5 4 3 2 1   Negative wording is appropriately emphasized.
5 4 3 2 1   All distracters have different meanings.

14.24: Each of these methods of evaluating performance can increase validity by encouraging the teacher to systematically link evaluation to important goals. They can increase reliability by increasing evaluation consistency.

14.25: Some products that the portfolio could include might be student responses to math facts, responses to word problems based on the book used in the class, responses to "real world" problems generated either by the teacher or the students, as well some record of the thought processes that went into the solution. In addition, students might be asked to comment on their growth in math over time, evaluating strengths and weaknesses.

14.26: Constructing a table of specifications before instruction has the advantage of helping to focus instruction. The disadvantage is that instructional adaptations would not be reflected in the table of specifications, so students' understanding of the content covered in the changes would probably not be measured. A table constructed after instruction would likely reflect adaptations, but it wouldn't help the teacher in making decisions about goals and emphasis.

14.27: She is partially consistent. Her procedure ensures that every objective is measured, but a table of specifications also specifies the number of items or emphasis given to each topic as well as the level of the item. Based on the evidence we have, she is giving all objectives equal emphasis, and we know nothing about the levels of her items.

14.28: As Tanya discussed the upcoming test she: 1) reminded students to read directions, 2) encouraged students to go on if they got stuck, and 3) reminded them to go back to reconsider the ones they skipped.

14.29: The testing situation is a conditioned stimulus, which elicits the feelings of dread as conditioned responses. The testing situation *is associated with* some previous experience, such as failure, which was an unconditioned stimulus. This failure produced embarrassment, or some other emotion, as an unconditioned response, and this unconditioned response is *similar* to the conditioned response--dread.

Thoughts, such as concerns about failure, having to retake the course, or disappointing parents can occupy working memory space leaving less space that can be devoted to the problem.

14.30: In addition to the specific suggestions in the text you might: 1) put three or four questions/problems at the beginning of your tests that all the students are virtually guaranteed to answer correctly; 2) have the test-anxious student come in after school and then give her some practice problems/questions that use the same format as you will use on the actual test. As she works on the practice items, make encouraging statements to her; 3) talk to her parents or other caregivers and strongly encourage them to take performance pressure off her; and 4) carefully monitor her work (without making it obvious) and drop a gentle hint if you see her beginning to panic. If you believe her anxiety is a danger to her emotional health, you should contact the school counselor and seek his or her advice about the problem.

14.31: First, the teacher should schedule ample time for the students to complete the test. Then, one reminder about 15 or 20 minutes before the time expires would be appropriate. Continuous reminders will likely have the effect of increasing test anxiety, particularly if students are having difficulty finishing in the allotted time.

14.32: From a behaviorist point of view, positive results serve as reinforcers; from a humanist perspective, knowledge of positive results are indicators of personal growth; knowledge of results--either positive or negative--allow learners to understand how they did and why they performed the way they did, which according to cognitive theorists is an important intellectual need. (It is on this need that the variable "task comprehension" in the Model For Promoting Learner Motivation is based.)

14.33: Content bias endangers validity because students can potentially miss questions for reasons other than not understanding the content.

14.34: Typically, formative evaluation is most valuable for young, at-risk and low-ability students because research indicates that these students' metacognition is less well developed than their counterparts, and they have problems monitoring and regulating their own learning progress. Formative evaluation provides them with valuable information to monitor their learning progress.

14.35: If the assessment system is based on a scale, such as 90-100 for an A, 80-89 for a B, etc., it is criterion referenced. If the teacher used a distribution and assigns As, Bs, Cs, etc., on the basis of the distribution, it is a norm-referenced system. The former assigns grades on the basis of preset criteria, the latter based on comparisons of students to each other.

14.36: According to social cognitive theory, the nonoccurrence of expected reinforcers can serve as punishers, and the nonoccurrences of expected punishers can serve as reinforcers. When learners complete homework, they expect some form of reinforcement, such as a homework grade or credit for having done it. If they get no grade or credit, the expected reinforcement doesn't occur, which serves as a punisher making it less likely that they will work conscientiously on the assignment in the future.

With respect to copying, you might first talk to the students, reminding them that copying will result in less learning and lower test scores. Then, base at least some portion of your tests on the homework, and in discussing tests point out these links.

14.37: The answers to this question will vary. If the situation you're in is typical, it will involve a point system. Most university faculty are quite clear about their grading systems.

Exercise 14.1

Answer Items 1–4 on the basis of the following case study.

Ginger Kelly's second graders have finished subtraction of one-digit from two-digit numbers without regrouping and are now working on subtraction of one-digit from two-digit numbers with regrouping. Her goal is for them to be skilled at identifying and solving problems that both do and do not require regrouping. She has four students working problems at the board while the others do the same problems at their seats.

"Now let's try one more," she directs, seeing that the four students have gotten the problem right. She then gives the class another problem.

As they work, she notices Erin gazing out the window instead of working. She goes to Erin's desk and, to her delight, finds that Erin has already correctly finished the problem.

"Good work, Erin!" she exclaims after seeing Erin's paper.

"They've got it," she says to herself, seeing that the students at the board have again done the problem correctly.

Ginger then tells her students they will have a quiz the next day on problems similar to these.

The next day, Ginger gives her students a 10-problem quiz involving subtraction of one-digit from two-digit numbers, 7 of which require regrouping. The students are told to show all their work on the work sheet.

1. Identify at least two examples of informal measurement and at least one example of formal measurement in the case study.

2. Ginger concluded, "They've got it," as she watched the students work. Based on the information in the case study, assess the extent to which the conclusion was valid at that point in her instruction. Give reasons for your assessment.

3. Based on the information in the case study, assess the extent to which Ginger's quiz was valid and how likely it was to be reliable. Give reasons for your answer.

4. What is the primary advantage of informal measurement? What is the primary danger in using informal measurements?

5. What is the primary function of formal measurement?

Exercise 14.2

Examine each of the following items and analyze them according to the criteria specified in Table 14.3 on page 586 of your text. An item may be effective according to the criteria, or it may be inconsistent with *one* or *more than one* of the guidelines.

1. Of the following, the best explanation for why the South lost the Civil War is:
    a.   the North had better military leadership.
    b.   there were more big cities in the North.
    *   c.   the North had more industry that could support an army, whereas the South was mostly agricultural.
    d.   it was too hot in the South.

2. Which of the following is a characteristic of young, rugged mountains?
   a.   They always have U-shaped valleys.
   b.   They have gently flowing streams.
* c.   They have rugged, rocky peaks that extend above the tree line.
   d.   All of the above.

3. Which of the following best illustrates an omnivore?
* a.   Ben is an animal of the forest. He spends most of his time in the winter in a long sleep. He roams around searching for the berries he loves to eat. When he is near a stream, he will also sometimes catch fish.
   b.   Billy is a high mountain animal. He has a thick coat to protect him from the cold. He has to scrape and scratch through the snow to get to the tender mosses that make up most of his diet.
   c.   Sylvia lives in a nest near the top of a huge tree. She spends much of her time soaring through the air searching with her keen eyes for the rabbits and rodents that she brings back for her young.
   d.   Sally spends most of her time in the water in the far north. On warm days, she lies near the water to sun herself before diving for the fish that make up her diet.

Look at the following sample items taken from a commercially prepared test and analyze them according to the criteria specified in this section of the chapter. In cases of inconsistency, describe specifically how the items fail to meet the criterion.

A.   Complete each sentence below by filling in the blanks.
     1.   About _____ percent of the earth's surface is covered by water.
     2.   The strength of earthquakes is measured on the _____ scale.
     3.   Very dry regions of the earth are called _____.

B.   Underline the word or group of words that will make each sentence read correctly.
     1.   A landmass almost entirely surrounded by water is called a(an) (isthmus, peninsula).
     2.   Mountains are areas of (high, low) relief.
     3.   The outer layer of the earth is called the (crust, mantle).
                World Neighbors: Teacher's Resource Book (1985), p. 147 & 148.

4. The completion items

5. The alternative response items

Exercise 14.3

Abdul Kalif was attempting to teach his middle school students to write persuasive essays. To motivate his students he focused their essays on the new school's search for a school mascot. As he planned for his instruction he decided to provide several models and use students to give feedback about first drafts. To assist the students in their evaluation of each others' essays he developed a scoring rubric that had written descriptions of key elements (e.g., "Explicitly stated position at beginning of essay."). When the projects were done he presented them to a panel of experts (other teachers) who decided which ones would appear in the school newspaper. In addition, he encouraged students to include these in their growing collection of personal writing samples.

1. What efforts did Abdul make to increase the authenticity of his measurement efforts?

2. What forms of authentic assessment did Abdul use to measure his students' writing ability?

3. What steps did Abdul take during planning to increase the validity and reliability of his measurements?

4. What evidence is there that Abdul utilized portfolio assessment?

Exercise 14.4

1. Your students are taking a test, and the intercom breaks in saying, "Ms. . . . , a parent, is on the phone. She needs to talk to you. She says it's important. Can you come to the office for a moment?" Using the information in this section as a basis, describe the most appropriate response to the request.

2. You have worked harder than you thought possible to get your students ready for an important test. "They have to be ready," you say to yourself. "Nobody could do a better job of teaching than I did here." To your chagrin, most of the class do very poorly on the test, and many of the responses seem to indicate a lack of effort on the part of the students. Based on the information in this section, which of the following is the best response to the students? (Provide a rationale for your decision.)
   - a. We did a good job on the test. Now let's try and keep it up.
   - b. Here are your test results. I believe if we work a little harder we can probably improve on the next test.
   - c. We didn't do as well as I had hoped considering that we prepared so much. Let's try and redouble our efforts for the next test.
   - d. I'm quite disappointed in the test results. Considering how hard I worked to get you ready, it doesn't look like some of you studied as much as you could have.

Exercise 14.5

1. Look again at Ginger Kelly's work with her second graders in Exercise 13.1. Suppose that in Ginger's grading system 94% to 100% was an A, and 86% to 93% was a B. Suppose further that six students got an A on the quiz because they got all the problems right, and eight more got a B because they missed only one problem. Is Ginger's system norm-referenced or criterion-referenced? Explain why.

Feedback for Application Exercises

Exercise 14.1

1. Ginger was making informal measurements when she watched the students doing the practice problems at the board. While they might appear to be formal measurements, she wasn't getting the same information from all the students under the same conditions, so they were informal. She was also making an informal measurement when she noticed that Erin was gazing out the window rather than working. The quiz was an example of a formal measurement.

2. At that point in the lesson, Ginger's conclusion was not valid. Her conclusion was based only on the performance of the four students at the board (and Erin). She didn't have any information about the performance of the other students.

3. Ginger's quiz was both valid and reliable. Her goal was for the students to identify and solve problems that require regrouping, and 7 of the problems she gave required regrouping while 3 did not. (The only uncertainty in the relationship between the goal and assessment is that technically the students are not solving problems; they're merely applying an algorithm.) Reliability would be dependent upon scoring consistency as well as the length and the appropriate difficulty of the quiz.

4. Informal measurements are valuable in making routine decisions, such as whom to call on and when, how long to conduct an activity, how much review is needed, and when to intervene if students are off-task. Since informal measurements are not always reliable, grading decisions based on them may not be valid, and teachers must be careful to include measurements for grading purposes that are formal and systematic.

5. Formal measurements are used for important decisions, such as when to move on to a new topic or assigning grades.

Exercise 14.2

1. Item 1 can be criticized on the basis of the following criteria:

a)   Choice D is implausible, and putting an implausible distracter at choice D is particularly unwise since test-wise students are unlikely to choose it anyway.
b)   Choice C is the answer. Having some of the answers as choice C is appropriate, of course, but it is often overused.
c)   The correct answer is longer than the other distracters.

2. Item 2 can be criticized on the basis of the following criteria:
a)   It uses "all of the above" as a distracter.
b)   The absolute term "always" appears in choice A.
c)   The right answer is again choice C.
d)   The right answer is longer than the other distracters.
e)   The term "rugged" appears in both the stem and the right answer.

3. Other than the fact that each distracter is lengthy and requires that students are capable readers, Item 3 meets the criteria. It is particularly effective in that the characteristics of omnivore are illustrated rather than merely giving the names of animals. For instance, suppose the item were written as follows:

Which of the following best illustrates an omnivore?
   a. Bear
   b. Mountain goat
   c. Eagle
   d. Seal

As written, it requires students to know the diet of each animal. They could understand the concept of omnivore but not know that a bear is one, and miss the item for that reason. That would make the item invalid.

4. The Completion Items: While the blanks are of equal length, two of the three items have the blank in the body of the sentence. Items 2 and 3 are not clearly phrased so that only one possible answer is correct.

5. Alternative Response Items: Numbers 2 and 3 are "give aways" for a test-wise student. Students with only a vague understanding of mountains would likely choose "high" over "low," even if they had no idea of what "relief" meant. The notion of "crust" being the outer layer can be determined from experiences, such as the "crust" of a piece of bread.

Exercise 14.3

1. Abdul did several things to try to make his assessment task more authentic. First, he focused on an issue that was important to students. Second, he used a panel of experts to judge the essays. Finally, he had students submit their essays to the school paper.

2. Basically Abdul used a performance assessment. At the end he encouraged students to include their essays in their portfolios.

3. During planning Abdul used a scoring rubric that he developed into a rating scale for students to use.

4. Portfolios have two essential characteristics: 1) they collect and display samples of students' work and, 2) they involve students in the planning. Both aspects were present in Abdul's lesson.

Exercise 14.4

1. While there is no single "correct" response, teachers should make every effort to remain in the classroom and carefully monitor their tests. On this basis an appropriate response would be, "My students are taking a test and I can't leave them. Please take a message, and I'll call Ms. _____ as soon as I can." In the case of an extreme emergency, either the principal should handle it, or s(he) should come down to your classroom to monitor your students while you go to the front office.

2. As with Item 1, there is no absolute right or wrong answer. However, based on the background material and the information in the item, choice B is preferred.

The rationale is as follows:

Choice A is misleading and could even be called dishonest. In order to maintain credibility the teacher must remain "real."

Choice C is not a "bad" response. The only advantage in choice B by comparison is that it is stated in positive terms.

Choice D is undesirable. The implication is that "I" worked hard, but "you" didn't come through. Even if this is true, it doesn't help student performance, and may even detract from effort on subsequent tests.

Exercise 14.5

1. Ginger's system is criterion-referenced. Getting all the problems right is a 100%, and missing one is a 90% (9 out of 10 correct). The students are evaluated according to a pre-set standard and are not compared to each other.

TRUE/FALSE QUESTIONS: Write T in the blank if the statement is true, and write F if it is false.

_____ 1. A test item could be invalid and still be reliable.

_____ 2. A test item could be unreliable and still be valid.

_____ 3. According to research examining the effects of assessment on learning, teachers should give fewer tests in low achieving classes than in higher achieving classes.

_____ 4. Formal measurements are usually less reliable than are informal measurements.

_____ 5. If students understand a topic, and they respond incorrectly to a test item measuring the topic, the test item is invalid.

MULTIPLE-CHOICE QUESTIONS: Circle the best response in each case.

Look at the following four descriptions, and use the information for Items 6, 7, and 8.

1. A teacher gives a 20 item quiz on flower plants.
2. A teacher sees a student squint as she looks at the chalkboard.
3. A teacher calls on a student.
4. A teacher marks B+ on a student's essay.

6. The evaluation(s) is/are:
 a. 1,3,4.
 b. 1,4.
 c. 3,4.
 d. 3.
 e. 4.

7. The formal measurement(s) is/are:
 a. 1,4.
 b. 2,3.
 c. 1,2,3.
 d. 1.
 e. 4.

8. The informal measurement(s) is/are:
 a. 1,2,3.
 b. 2,3.
 c. 1,3.
 d. 2.
 e. 3.

Use the following information for items 9-12.

A goal for the tenth grade English department at Geneva Lakes High School is for all the students in the tenth grade to be able to write essays in which they make and defend an argument. Different teachers approach measurement of the goal differently.

After discussing arguments, supporting evidence, and giving a series of examples, Mrs. Baldwin gives the students in her class five written essays and asks the students to decide which essay best makes and defends an argument and which essay makes and defends an argument least well.

Mr. Brannan has all the students in his class write essays in which they make and defend an argument.

Mrs. Duncan has a class discussion in which individual students take a position. Some of the other students defend the position, while others take issue with the position. In all cases the individuals must provide evidence when they defend or take issue with the position. Mrs. Duncan then evaluates the students based on their responses in the discussion.

Mr. Combs describes the process of making and defending an argument. He then gives some examples of arguments and asks the students to write a series of statements that supports the argument.

9. The teacher whose measurements are most likely to be valid is:
    a. Mrs. Baldwin.
    b. Mr. Brannan.
    c. Mrs. Duncan.
    d. Mr. Combs.

10. The teacher whose measurements are least likely to be valid is:
    a. Mrs. Baldwin.
    b. Mr. Brannan.
    c. Mrs. Duncan.
    d. Mr. Combs.

11. The teacher whose measurements are most likely to be reliable is:
    a. Mrs. Baldwin.
    b. Mr. Brannan.
    c. Mrs. Duncan.
    d. Mr. Combs.

12. The teacher whose measurements are least likely to be reliable is:
    a. Mrs. Baldwin.
    b. Mr. Brannan.
    c. Mrs. Duncan.
    d. Mr. Combs.

Use the following information for Items 13-15.

You are conducting a question and answer activity to review the parts of the cell with your class of 27 students. In your review you call on about two-thirds of the students, and most of them answer the questions correctly. You conclude that the class understands the material.

13. Of the following, noticing that the students answer most of the questions correctly best illustrates:
    a. a formal measurement.
    b. an informal measurement.
    c. an evaluation.
    d. an assessment system.

14. Of the following, concluding that the class understands the material best illustrates:
    a. a formal measurement.
    b. an informal measurement.
    c. an evaluation.
    d. an assessment system.

15. Which of the following best describes your conclusion?
    a. It is reliable but not valid.
    b. It is both reliable and valid.
    c. It is unreliable and therefore invalid.
    d. It is invalid and therefore unreliable.

16. Joe Williams and David Negge both have "the students' ability to assess a conclusion" as a goal for their students. They both assign an essay where the students assess the conclusion that Spain's, Britain's, and France's goal in exploring the New World in the 16th and 17th centuries was primarily economic. Joe constructs a set of criteria to be used in scoring the essay. David does not. They both score the essays and assign students' grades. Of the following, which is the most accurate statement?
    a. David's assessment is likely to be less reliable than Joe's and therefore less valid as well.
    b. David's assessment is likely to be less reliable than Joe's but they are equally valid.
    c. Both teachers' assessments are likely to be invalid, since they are essays.
    d. Both teachers' assessments are valid and reliable since the assessments are consistent with their goals.

Four teachers were discussing their test-anxious students.

Mrs. Rowe commented, "I have them practice on items that are similar to those that will be on the test. Then I try to motivate them by mentioning in passing that some of the items on the test will challenge them, and they're going to have to do some thinking."

"I do the same thing, meaning I have them practice," Mr. Potter comments, "but I don't say anything one way or the other about how difficult the test will be."

"I do stress reduction activities with my class," Mrs. Richards adds. "Just before we begin the test, I have them close their eyes, visualize themselves doing well on the test, and take a few deep breaths. Then we start."

"I do something a little different," Mr. Lareau adds. "I tell them that I know they will do well, and I tell them to be ready for a test every day, because I'm not going to tell them when we're having it, except that it will be sometime during the week. It keeps them on their toes."

17. Based on research, the teacher *most* effective in *reducing* test anxiety in his/her students is likely to be:
    a. Mrs. Rowe.
    b. Mr. Potter.
    c. Mrs. Richards.
    d. Mr. Lareau.

18. Based on research, the teacher *least* effective in *reducing* test anxiety in his/her students is likely to be:
    a. Mrs. Rowe.
    b. Mr. Potter.
    c. Mrs. Richards.
    d. Mr. Lareau.

Use the following information for Items 19-20.

Gigi Parker is emphasizing grammatically correct writing and expression of thought in writing with his/her students. She has begun using *portfolios*, where systematic collections of her students are placed for review and evaluation. She puts work samples in the portfolio at least three days a week, and she is careful to date the samples to help in assessing her students' progress. In examining her students' work, she checks for grammar, punctuation, spelling, and clear expression of thought, and she assigns grades on that basis.

19. If Gigi is consistent with patterns identified by research, which of the following is most likely?
    a.   Gigi is an elementary teacher.
    b.   Gigi is a middle school teacher.
    c.   Gigi is a high school teacher.

20. Based on the information about Gigi's assessments, which of the following is the most accurate statement?
    a.   They are likely to be both reliable and valid.
    b.   They are likely to be reliable but not valid.
    c.   They are likely to be valid but not reliable.
    d.   They are likely to be both _invalid_ and _unreliable_.

Look at the four following goals and assessments.

Mrs. Andrews, a seventh-grade teacher wants her students to be able to solve problems involving percentages. She gives her students several problems such as:
John had $45 and he spent $35 on a new shirt. What percentage of his money did he spend on the shirt?
Mr. Bowden, a fourth-grade teacher, wants his students to write paragraphs that accurately obey grammar and punctuation rules. He gives his students several exercises in which they have to put in correct verb forms to maintain subject-verb agreement and other exercises that they punctuate properly.
Mrs. Fisher, a third-grade teacher, wants her students to understand the concept _insect_. She brings in several "bugs" and has them identify those that are insects (versus spiders and other animals).
Mr. Morgan, a fifth-grade teacher, wants his students to understand the function of maps. He has his students design and draw a map of their school to a scale that they choose.

21. The teacher whose assessment is most nearly authentic is:
    a.   Mrs. Andrews.
    b.   Mr. Bowden.
    c.   Mrs. Fisher.
    d.   Mr. Morgan.

22. The teacher whose assessment is least authentic is:
    a.   Mrs. Andrews.
    b.   Mr. Bowden.
    c.   Mrs. Fisher.
    d.   Mr. Morgan.

Four teachers are discussing their assessment procedures.
Mr. Ganyo comments, "I give the tests back, we go over them, and then I tell the kids to put them in their notebooks."
Mrs. Anderson responds, "I give them their scores and tell them that they can come in and discuss the tests in detail with me in one-on-one sessions before or after school if they want to."
Mr. Wilson adds, "I give the tests back, but we don't discuss them. I've gotten tired of putting up with the students' arguments about the way they've been scored."
Mrs. Mashima nods, "I give them back and we go over them. Then I collect them, because I revise and use the items again. I tell them they can come in and discuss them with me one-on-one if they are confused."

23. The teacher whose assessment procedure is _most_ effective based on research is:
    a.   Mr. Ganyo.
    b.   Mrs. Anderson.
    c.   Mr. Wilson.
    d.   Mrs. Mashima.

24. The teacher whose assessment procedure is *least* effective based on research is:
    a. Mr. Ganyo.
    b. Mrs. Anderson.
    c. Mr. Wilson.
    d. Mrs. Mashima.

25. Look at the following test item.

Which of the following is a function of the digestive system?
    a. To circulate the blood
    b. To protect vital body organs
* c. To digest the food we eat and turn it into usable fuel for our bodies
    d. To transfer nerve impulses

There are at least three problems with this item. Identify the problems. Then rewrite the item to make it more effective.

Self-Help Quiz Answers

1. t
2. f
3. f
4. f
5. t
6. c   Decisions teachers make on the basis of their measurements are evaluations. Assigning a grade obviously involves a decision, but so does calling on a student. Measurements teachers use in making a decision about whom to call on might include one or more of the following: the student's hand is raised, the student appears inattentive, the student has not been called on for several minutes, the student has been unable to answer correctly, and this is a question he or she is likely to be able to answer.
7. d   Formal measurements systematically gather information.
8. d   Informal measurements are gathered in an incidental way during the course of a lesson or day.
9. b   Having each student make and defend an argument in an essay is most consistent with the objective.
10. a   Judging others' arguments is not the same as making and defending your own argument. In each of the other cases the students were involved to a certain extent in defending an argument. Providing essays and having the students judge the extent to which the essay effectively makes and defends an argument, as Mrs. Baldwin did, would be an excellent *learning activity* that would be designed to help the students reach the goal.
11. a   Evaluating the five essays is a convergent task and could be scored reliably.
12. c   Evaluating oral discussions would be highly unreliable.
13. b   An informal measurement gathers information incidentally during the course of the lesson.
14. c   An evaluation is a decision based on measurement.
15. c   Since you didn't ask the same information from all students and didn't systematically tap their knowledge, your conclusion would be unreliable and therefore invalid.
16. a   Essays are notoriously unreliable. The absence of scoring criteria suggests unreliability leading to lack of validity.
17. b   Providing them with practice will help reduce test anxiety. Practice together with suggesting that some of the items will be challenging, as Mrs. Rowe did, can be effective in increasing motivation and self-efficacy, but it can increase anxiety for highly test-anxious students. Stress reduction, in and of itself, is generally ineffective.
18. d   Surprise or pop quizzes tend to increase rather than decrease anxiety.

19. a   Elementary teachers tend to use more work samples than do teachers at higher levels.

20. a   They are consistent with her goals, she collects them systematically and she makes evaluation decisions based on pre-established criteria.

21. d   Drawing their own map of a school would be the most authentic.

22. b   Artificial exercises taken out of context are least authentic.

23. d   Going over items, collecting and revising them for re-use and allowing students to come in again are all effective practices.

24. c   Lack of feedback on specific items greatly decreases the instructional value of tests and quizzes. While Mrs. Anderson's procedure isn't particularly effective, the option of going over the test in detail remains open to the students who will take the initiative to do so.

25. Potential problems include: 1) the correct answer is c (this is appropriate if choice c isn't overused); 2) the correct answer contains the word "digest," and the word "digest" is also in the stem; and 3) the correct choice is significantly longer than the distracters.

An improved item might appear as follows:

Which of the following best describes the function of the digestive system?
    a.   To circulate the blood
*   b.   To turn food into usable fuel
    c.   To protect vital body organs
    d.   To transfer nerve impulses to various parts of the body

APPENDIX: STANDARDIZED TESTING

Appendix Outline

I.   Standardized tests
     A.   Functions of standardized tests
          1.   Student assessment
          2.   Diagnosis
          3.   Placement and selection
          4.   Program evaluation and improvement
          5.   Accountability
     B.   Types of standardized tests
          1.   Achievement tests
          2.   Diagnostic tests
          3.   Intelligence tests
               a.   A short history of intelligence tests
               b.   The Stanford-Binet
               c.   The Wechsler Scales
               d.   Individual versus group intelligence tests
          4.   Aptitude tests
     C.   Evaluating standardized tests: Validity revisited
          1.   Content validity
          2.   Predictive validity
          3.   Construct validity
II. Understanding and interpreting standardized test scores
     A.   Descriptive statistics
          1.   Frequency distributions
          2.   Measures of central tendency

241

3. Measures of variability
4. Normal distribution
B. Interpreting standardized test results
1. Raw scores
2. Percentiles
3. Stanines
4. Grade equivalents
5. Standard scores
6. Standard error of measurement
III. Issues in standardized testing
A. The accountability movement: Holding teachers and students responsible for learning
1. Minimum competency testing
B. Standardized testing with alternative formats
IV. Student diversity and standardized testing
A. Bias in measurement
1. Bias in content
2. Bias in testing procedures
3. Bias in test result use
B. Alternative Tests
1. System of Multicultural Assessment (SOMPA)
2. Kaufman Assessment Battery for Children (KABC)
C. Clinical Approaches

Appendix Overview

Standardized tests are given to large groups under uniform conditions, and they are scored with uniform procedures. An individual's performance is then compared to a norming group, consisting of comparable people who have taken the test under similar testing conditions. Standardized testing is extremely important and somewhat controversial. The calls for national reforms in education are virtually all based on the fact that American students perform less well on standardized tests than do their counterparts in other industrialized countries.

Achievement tests measure student learning in different content areas; diagnostic tests give detailed descriptions of students' strengths and weaknesses in particular skill areas; intelligence tests attempt to measure an individual's ability to think in the abstract, solve problems, and the capacity to acquire knowledge. Aptitude tests are designed to predict a student's potential for future learning, and they measure general abilities developed over long periods of time. The high school SAT and ACT are two examples of aptitude tests.

Validity is a central concern in evaluating and selecting standardized tests. Content validity represents the overlap or match between what is taught and what is tested. Predictive validity is an indicator of a test's ability to gauge future performance. Construct validity examines the extent to which a test actually measures what it is designed to measure.

Teachers use statistical methods to understand and interpret the vast amount of information gathered on standardized tests. Measures of central tendency--the mean, median, and mode--describe a group's performance as a whole, and the range and standard deviation give an indication of the variability in the scores.

For large samples, standardized test scores tend to approximate a normal distribution. In normal distributions, the mean, median, and mode are the same score, about 68% of all scores are within one standard deviation from the mean, and about 98% of the scores lie within two standard deviations from the mean.

Students' performances on standardized tests are commonly reported in several ways: percentiles, a ranking compared to all others who have taken the test; stanines, which describe scores in bands distributed from the mean; grade equivalents, that compare students to average scores for a particular age group; or standard scores, that describe scores in standardized deviation units from the mean. The standard error of measurement on a test gives a range of scores into which a student's true score is likely to fall.

As our student populations become more diverse, the issue of bias in testing has become increasingly controversial. Critics believe that many standardized tests reflect white, middle-class values, and discriminate against other cultures and socioeconomic groups. Three common forms of bias existing in standardized tests include content bias, bias in testing procedures, and bias in test use.

Application Exercises

Exercise A.1

Analyze the following to determine whether an achievement, aptitude, diagnostic, or intelligence test is being considered. In addition decide whether content, predictive, or construct validity is involved.

1. Teachers at Jefferson Elementary School were trying to decide whether Ken Bradbury needed supplemental resource help. To gather information to be used in making this decision a standardized test was administered to determine his overall potential for learning. One of the teachers objected to the use of the test, questioning whether test content accurately matched the school's curriculum.

2. Teachers at Westlake Middle School were trying to decide which of their students should be recommended for an accelerated science program. One of the counselors mentioned the Science Process Test and said that it had been successfully used at other schools in the district. One of the teachers asked if the items on the test would be worth the trouble and really tell them anything that grades wouldn't.

3. Second-grade teachers were attempting to ascertain their students' strengths and weaknesses so that they could do a better job of steering students to the appropriate learning centers designed to augment different areas of the curriculum. One of the teachers mentioned a detailed district-wide assessment instrument that measured literacy and math skills. Another teacher questioned whether the test matched the specific things they were doing at their school.

4. Controversy raged at Lincoln Elementary School. The school had moved to a whole language approach to language arts that stressed writing and novels. Some parents wondered if their children were still learning "basics" like grammar and punctuation. The ad hoc committee decided to use a standardized test to compare Lincoln students' performance in these areas with other schools, but one teacher objected, stating that the curriculum wasn't designed to teach isolated skills.

Exercise A.2

Students are given a standardized test, and the results indicated that Tamara scored in the 50th percentile, Joey scored in the 70th, and Helen in the 90th.

1. Identify the stanine for each student.

2. Identify the approximate z-score and T-score for each student.

3. What is each student's IQ according to the Wechsler scales?

4. Maria takes the Scholastic Aptitude Test and finds that she scored an 1100, 600 in math and 500 in English. What is her approximate percentile rank in math and English?

5. Rhonda scores a 62 on a test with a mean of 50 and a standard deviation of 8. If the test results approximate a normal distribution, what is Rhonda's:
    a. Approximate percentile rank?
    b. Stanine?
    c. z-score?

6. A test is given with a mean of 60, a median of 60, a mode of 60 and a standard deviation of 5. Approximately half the group of students who took the test scored from 55 to 65 on the test. Of the following, which is the best conclusion?
    a. The scores fit a normal distribution.
    b. The scores do not fit a normal distribution.
    c. We don't have enough information to determine whether or not the scores fit a normal distribution.

Explain your answer.

7. Joanne scores a 45, Franklin scores a 40, and Monica scores a 35 on a test with a standard error of 3. Which of the following statements are true? (More than one answer may be true.)
    a. Joanne's true score *is* higher than both Franklin's and Monica's.
    b. Franklin's true score *is* higher than both Joanne's and Monica's.
    c. Franklin's true score *might be* higher than both Joanne's and Monica's.
    d. Monica's true score *might be* higher than both Joanne's and Franklin's.
    e. Joanne's true score *is* higher than Monica's and *might be* higher than Franklin's.

Explain your answer in each case.

Exercise A.3

You carefully followed the procedures suggested for preparing your students for tests, which were outlined in your text. You then give your class the test and you find that Jaramillo, one of your students of Hispanic descent, missed over half of the items on a 20-item test, while only one of your white students missed more than five items. Jaramillo is a recent immigrant to the United States, but his background in English is good. Which of the following is the most accurate statement?
    a. The test is biased against students of Hispanic background.
    b. The test is not biased against students of Hispanic background.
    c. We don't have enough information to evaluate the test for bias.

Explain your choice.

Feedback for Application Exercises

Exercise A.1

1. Overall potential for learning is one characteristic of an intelligence test. The match with the school's curriculum suggests a concern with content validity.

2. The teachers at Westlake were interested in a content-specific aptitude test. The teacher's concern centered around predictive validity.

3. A detailed assessment aimed at content is characteristic of a diagnostic test. The teacher questioned whether the test had content validity and whether it matched the content of the curriculum at that school.

4. The test could be either a standardized achievement or diagnostic test, depending upon the degree of detail and specificity. The teacher was questioning its content validity, or the match with their curriculum.

Exercise A.2

1. Tamara is in stanine 5, Joey in stanine 6, and Helen in stanine 8.

2. Tamara has a z-score of 0 and a T-score of 50, Joey a z-score of approximately .5 and a T-score of 55, and Helen a z-score of approximately 1.4 and a T-score of 64.

3. Tamara's IQ is 100, Joey's is approximately 107, and Helen's approximately 120.

4. Maria's approximate percentile rank in math is 84, and her approximate percentile rank in English is 50.

5. Rhonda's score indicates that she is 1.5 standard deviations above the mean. On this basis: a) her approximate percentile rank would be 92, b) she would be in stanine 8, and c) her z-score would be 1.5.

6b. The best conclusion is that the scores do not approximate a normal distribution. While the mean, median, and mode are all the same, a normal distribution has approximately 68% of all scores falling from one standard deviation below the mean to one standard deviation above the mean. This distribution has half the scores falling from one standard deviation below to one standard deviation above the mean.

7c,e. Because the standard error is 3, Joanne's true score is probably between 42 and 48, Franklin's is between 37 and 43, and Monica's is between 32 and 38.

This means choices c and e are true.

Exercise A.3

(C) We don't have enough information to make a conclusion about test bias. First, we don't know why Jaramillo missed the items. Second, we don't know about the performance of other students of Hispanic descent. We can't make any conclusions about test bias until we have more information about the test content.

Self-Help Quiz

TRUE/FALSE QUESTIONS: Write T in the blank if the statement is true, and F if it is false.

_____ 1. Standardized tests tend to be less reliable than are teacher-made tests.
_____ 2. Grade equivalents indicate the grade in which a learner should be placed.
_____ 3. Standardized tests typically are not used as a basis for assigning grades to students.
_____ 4. Aptitude and intelligence are synonymous terms.
_____ 5. The mean of a distribution of scores is more strongly influenced by extremely high or extremely low scores than is the median in a distribution of scores.

MULTIPLE-CHOICE QUESTIONS: Circle the best response in each case.

6. Your school has implemented a new math curriculum in the fourth grade that emphasizes the National Council of Teachers of Mathematics *Curriculum and Evaluation Standards*. The four fourth-grade teachers are somewhat uneasy about some of the emphasis in the curriculum and are concerned about whether or not the students are "getting" what they need to be getting at the fourth-grade level. Of the following, to answer their question, which of the following would be the school's most valid decision?
   a. Have the four math teachers create a series of exercises that are consistent with the curriculum objectives, administer the exercises, and compare the four grades.
   b. Select a standardized achievement test in math, administer the test to the four classes and analyze the results.
   c. Select a standardized diagnostic test in math, administer the test to the four classes and analyze the results.
   d. Combine the results of the teacher-made exercises and the diagnostic test and analyze both.

7. You are on a team that is making decisions about placing students in a program for the gifted. Of the following, which measure would you be *least* likely to consider in this process?
   a. Teacher recommendations
   b. Achievement test results
   c. Aptitude test results
   d. Diagnostic test results

8. Of the following, the two that are most closely related are:
   a. aptitude and achievement tests.
   b. aptitude and diagnostic tests.
   c. intelligence and diagnostic tests.
   d. achievement and diagnostic tests.
   e. achievement and intelligence tests.

9. Your school has been focusing on higher-order and critical thinking in your students, and you have measured your students abilities in that area. To see how much progress you've made in that area you want to give another standardized test that measures the students' present critical-thinking abilities. In selecting the test, which of the following is your school's primary concern?
   a. Content validity
   b. Construct validity
   c. Predictive validity
   d. Face validity

10. The horizontal axis of a normal distribution at any particular point best represents which of the following?
   a. The raw score on a test.
   b. The number of people who attained a particular score on a test.
   c. The mean score of the people who took the test.
   d. The standard deviation of the scores on the test.

A student takes a 60-item subtest of a standardized test. The subtest has a mean of 48 with a standard deviation of 6. The student gets a 54 on the subtest.

11. The 54 on the subtest is best described as the:
    a.   raw score.
    b.   standard error.
    c.   standard score.
    d.   stanine score.

12. Of the following, the best estimate of the student's percentile ranking is:
    a.   96.
    b.   90.
    c.   84.
    d.   50.

13. Of the following, the best estimate of the student's stanine ranking is:
    a.   5.
    b.   6.
    c.   7.
    d.   8.
    e.   9.

A subtest of a standardized test has a mean of 40 with a standard deviation of 4. (Assume a very large sample so the test results nearly fit a normal distribution.) George scores a 46 on the subtest.

14. Based on this information, the best approximation of the following of George's percentile rank is:
    a.   40.
    b.   44.
    c.   84.
    d.   90.
    e.   98.

15. Cory scores a 44 on the same subtest. Of the following the best description of Cory's stanine is:
    a.   5.
    b.   6.
    c.   7.
    d.   8.
    e.   9.

16. On this test George's T-score would be:
    a.   45.
    b.   46.
    c.   55.
    d.   60.
    e.   65.
    f.   75.

17. On this test George's z-score would be:
    a.   -1.0.
    b.   -1.5.
    c.   1.0.
    d.   1.5.
    e.   4.6.

18. Ellen scores a 77 on a standardized test that has a *standard error* of 4. Of the following, which is the most valid conclusion?
    a.   Ellen's true score is likely to be somewhere between 77 and 81.
    b.   Ellen's true score is likely to be somewhere between 73 and 77.
    c.   Ellen's true score is likely to be somewhere between 73 and 81.
    d.   Ellen's true score is likely to be somewhere between 75 and 79.

19. Diane is in the 55th percentile, Jerome is in the 65th percentile, and Juanita is in the 75th percentile of a standardized test. Of the following, which is the most valid conclusion?
    a.   The difference between Diane's and Jerome's raw scores is greater than the difference between Juanita's and Jerome's raw scores.
    b.   The difference between Jerome's and Juanita's raw scores is greater than the difference between Jerome's and Diane's raw scores.
    c.   The difference between Diane's and Jerome's raw scores is equal to the difference between Juanita's and Jerome's raw scores.
    d.   We can't make a conclusion about differences in raw scores when we only have access to information about percentiles.

20. Deanna, a beginning third grader, has a grade equivalent score of 5.5 on a standardized reading achievement test. Of the following, which is the most valid conclusion?
    a.   Deanna is an advanced reader.
    b.   If one exists, Deanna should be placed in a reading program for gifted students.
    c.   Deanna should be placed in fifth grade reading.
    d.   Deanna's parents should be advised to consider having Deanna skip the third grade and move into the fourth grade.

21. On a subtest of a standardized test Warren scores at the 88th percentile. The year before he had scored at the 80th percentile on the same test. Of the following, which is the most valid conclusion?
    a.   Warren scored as high or higher than 88 percent of the people who took the test during this year's administration of the test.
    b.   Warren answered *exactly* 88 percent of the items on the test correctly during this year's administration of the test.
    c.   Warren answered *approximately* 88 percent of the items on the subtest correctly during this year's administration of the test.
    d.   Warren answered 8 percent more of the items correctly on this year's administration of the test than he answered correctly on last year's administration of the test.

22. You have two sets of scores, which are as follows:

    Set A: Mean--40 Median--40   Standard deviation--4
    Set B: Mean--40 Median--41   Standard deviation--6

Of the following, which is the most accurate statement?
    a.   The students' performance for both sets was equal since the means are the same.
    b.   The scores in Set B tend to be spread out more than the scores in Set A.
    c.   The students in Set B actually performed better, according to the test, than those in Set A since the standard deviation is higher than in Set A.
    d.   The students in Set B actually performed better, according to the test, than those in Set A since both the median and standard deviation are higher than they are in Set A.

23. Kathy, one of Mrs. Mahoney's students in tenth grade honors English, got a high B the first grading period and an A- the second grading period. Mrs. Mahoney commented periodically on Kathy's good work on her essays. However, Kathy didn't score particularly highly on the PSAT (Preliminary Scholastic Aptitude Test), scoring in the 48th percentile on the verbal section. By comparison, most of the rest of the class scored in the 80th percentile or higher. The results were sent to Mrs. Mahoney, who then passed them along to Kathy.

Kathy's father proofread her essays as he had done the first two grading periods, but Kathy got a C the third grading period. "I'll bring it back up, Dad," she vowed. However, she got another C the fourth grading period and also got a C for the year.

Based on the information in the case study, which of the following is the most likely explanation for the decline in Kathy's grades?
   a. Her motivation declined, and with it, the quality of her work.
   b. Kathy's self-esteem was lowered as a result of her modest performance on the PSAT and as a result her performance suffered.
   c. Having scored lower than her peers, Kathy no longer felt capable of competing with them and her efforts were reduced.
   d. Mrs. Mahoney's perception of Kathy's ability was adversely affected by Kathy's PSAT results.

24. An item from the WISC-III shows students pictures with a missing element in each, such as a scissors with the bolt that holds the two parts of the scissors together missing. Suppose some of the students taking the test have virtually no experience with scissors. Which of the following is the most valid conclusion?
   a. Since the ability to acquire experience is a characteristic of intelligence, the item is valid for all students.
   b. For students lacking experience, content bias exists in the item.
   c. For students lacking experience, bias in testing procedures is likely to exist.
   d. The ability to identify missing elements of pictures is unrelated to intelligence, so the item is invalid for all students.

25. Identify three important differences between standardized and teacher-made tests.

Self-Help Quiz Answers

1. f
2. f
3. t
4. f
5. t
6. d By comparing the results of the teacher-made exercises and the diagnostic test the teachers would have two different perspectives on the question of what students were learning.
7. d Diagnostic tests are useful for identifying specific deficiencies and strengths in a content area.
8. d Achievement and diagnostic tests both measure mastery of content; diagnostic tests are more detailed and specific in their focus.
9. a Content validity refers to the relationship between what is taught and what is tested. Since the school's goal is to ". . . see how much progress you've made in that area . . . " you're concerned about that relationship. (If you were concerned about whether or not the items on the test actually measured higher-order and critical thinking, you would be concerned with construct validity.)
10. a The horizontal axis represents the raw score; the vertical axis represents the number of people attaining a score.
11. a The raw score on a test is the number of items answered correctly.
12. c The student is one standard deviation above the mean, which corresponds to the 84th percentile.
13. c One standard deviation above the mean corresponds to stanine 7.
14. d George's score of 46 is one and one half standard deviation units above the mean; this would translate into a percentile of about 90.

15. c One standard deviation above the mean corresponds to a stanine of 7.

16. e One standard deviation above the mean corresponds to a T-score of 60, and two standard deviations above the mean corresponds to a T-score of 70, so George's T-score would be 65.

17. d A z-score is nothing more than the standard deviation.

18. c A standard error of 4 suggests a band of possible scores of 4 above and below the raw score.

19. b Differences between raw scores result in greater differences in percentiles at the ends of the continuum.

20. a The score indicates that Deanna is an advanced reader; the remaining options are quite speculative.

21. a Percentile scores describe a person's relative position in a group compared to others taking the exam.

22. b A greater standard deviation suggests a greater distribution of scores. The fact that the median is one point higher for the second distribution tells us very little about the differences in overall achievement, particularly when the means are equal.

23. d One of the negative side effects of standardized scores is their potential adverse affects on teacher expectations. All the other options were quite similar, focusing on adverse affects to Kathy's perceptions of herself.

24. b The item unduly penalizes students for their lack of experience with scissors.

25. Some differences include: purposes, number of items, how they are developed, and how scores are reported.